*Write It
When I'm Gone*

ALSO BY THOMAS M. DEFRANK

WITH ED ROLLINS

*Bare Knuckles and Back Rooms:*
*My Life in American Politics*

WITH JAMES A. BAKER, III

*The Politics of Diplomacy: Revolution,*
*War & Peace, 1989–1992*

WITH PETER GOLDMAN, MARK MILLER,
ANDREW MURR, AND TOM MATHEWS

*Quest for the Presidency 1992*

# Write It When I'm Gone

## REMARKABLE OFF-THE-RECORD CONVERSATIONS WITH GERALD R. FORD

### THOMAS M. DeFRANK

G. P. PUTNAM'S SONS

*New York*

‖P

G. P. PUTNAM'S SONS
*Publishers Since 1838*
Published by the Penguin Group
Penguin Group (USA) Inc., 375 Hudson Street, New York, New York 10014, USA
• Penguin Group (Canada), 90 Eglinton Avenue East, Suite 700, Toronto, Ontario
M4P 2Y3, Canada (a division of Pearson Penguin Canada Inc.) • Penguin Books Ltd,
80 Strand, London WC2R 0RL, England • Penguin Ireland, 25 St Stephen's
Green, Dublin 2, Ireland (a division of Penguin Books Ltd) • Penguin Group
(Australia), 250 Camberwell Road, Camberwell, Victoria 3124, Australia (a division
of Pearson Australia Group Pty Ltd) • Penguin Books India Pvt Ltd,
11 Community Centre, Panchsheel Park, New Delhi–110 017, India • Penguin
Group (NZ), 67 Apollo Drive, Rosedale, North Shore 0632, New Zealand
(a division of Pearson New Zealand Ltd) • Penguin Books (South Africa) (Pty) Ltd,
24 Sturdee Avenue, Rosebank, Johannesburg 2196, South Africa

Penguin Books Ltd, Registered Offices:
80 Strand, London WC2R 0RL, England

Library of Congress Cataloging-in-Publication Data

DeFrank, Thomas M.
Write it when I'm gone : remarkable off-the-record conversations with
Gerald R. Ford / Thomas M. DeFrank.
p.      cm.
Includes index.
ISBN 978-0-399-15450-8
1. Ford, Gerald R., 1913–2006.   2. Ford, Gerald R., 1913–2006—Interviews.
3. Presidents—United States—Biography.   4. Presidents—United States—
Interviews.   5. United States—Politics and government—1974–1977.   6. United
States—Politics and government—1977–1981.   7. United States—Politics and
government—1981–1989.   8. United States—Politics and government—1989– .
9. DeFrank, Thomas M.   I. Ford, Gerald R., 1913–2006.   II. Title.
E866.D43      2007                    2007032750
973.925092—dc22
[B]

Printed in the United States of America
1   3   5   7   9   10   8   6   4   2

BOOK DESIGN BY AMANDA DEWEY

*To my parents, Pete and Lillian,*
*and to Melanie and Andrew*

# CONTENTS

F ROM TIME TO TIME I'd covered a few of Gerald R. Ford's press conferences when he was House minority leader, but our first genuine encounter was in the fall of 1973, not long after Richard Nixon introduced him to the nation as the 40th vice president.

It wasn't an auspicious beginning, that first interview. Actually, it was a conspicuous disaster.

After a 1968 summer internship at *Newsweek* and two years as an Army public affairs officer at the Pentagon, I'd rejoined *Newsweek*'s Washington bureau in the fall of 1970. For most of 1973, I'd been covering the American prisoners of war from Vietnam; I was sent to Clark Air Base in the Philippines in February to cover their dramatic return from Hanoi, and was tracking their remarkable resilience as they coped with the reimmersion challenges of a normal existence after many years of brutal deprivation by their North Vietnamese captors.

I'd just returned from a fall vacation in Texas when my bureau chief, the legendary Mel Elfin, informed me I was being assigned to cover

Ford. He'd never amounted to much as a backbench House leader, I was told, but Mel and *Newsweek's* editors had concluded Nixon was finished and that Ford, sooner or later, probably sooner, would be the 38th president. The magazine wanted to have a leg up with the new guy when Nixon resigned or was impeached. "I want somebody who knows him and his people," Elfin said. "Your job is to live with him until he's president." As a twenty-eight-year-old journeyman, I was ecstatic at my sudden good fortune.

On the surface, the assignment seemed promising. Most political correspondents thought Ford a bit of a dullard, but he also had a reputation for being generous with reporters. Columnist Martin Schram, then a rookie from *Newsday* assigned to Sunday duty, once asked him for the name of an aide he could bother at home on the weekends. Ford gave him his own home phone number in Alexandria and encouraged him to call anytime. Unlike some of his predecessors, not to mention successors, he liked reporters and was always a grown-up about their often irksome questioning.

This day, however, I promptly landed myself squarely on Ford's enemies list.

It was Media Day for the vice president designate. He'd been scheduled for wall-to-wall interviews. Reporters were being shuffled rapid-fire through his congressional office like visiting constituents. I'd drawn an afternoon slot. Several down, several more to go.

Ford was wearing a frumpy brown business suit, the sort that reminded me of those Grand Rapids jokes about old Dutch guys wearing wooden shoes. Although he greeted me cordially enough, it was obvious he had more pressing items on his mind. He didn't like my questions, which were about Nixon and Watergate. He kept puffing on his pipe and avoiding eye contact as he delivered a string of canned or monosyllabic answers. Plainly, he wasn't enjoying himself, or my company. After each question, he'd glance at his wristwatch.

The vibes were horrible. Mercifully for both of us, after fifteen minutes of nonanswers I was given the bum's rush out the door. For my taste, Ford had just validated H. L. Mencken's celebrated advice: the only way to look on a politician is down.

I walked out of his office in a huge funk. It wasn't just that as a citizen I had come away monumentally unimpressed with the guy my bosses were certain would be in the Oval Office before long. My angst was way more selfish than that. Jerry Ford was going to be the next president of the free world, and he and I had bombed with each other. That would be my problem, of course, certainly not his. I'd just been handed a plum assignment with a guaranteed ticket to a prized White House posting, and after fifteen minutes on the beat I was already in the Dumpster.

Improbably, our relationship gradually mellowed, helped along by endless journeys together in a tiny twin-engine propjet that in a pre-imperial era seemed like a pretty adequate *Air Force Two.* There were only seven press regulars on the plane, and before long, Ford was routinely topping off those impossibly long days on the road with martinis and chitchat in the press cabin. Eventually, some personal bonding developed.

For whatever reason, he seemed to like us, and even his political adversaries would readily concede it had always been hard work to dislike Jerry Ford.

Who couldn't like a guy, for instance, who seldom passed up a chance to poke fun at himself? One late night, heading back to Washington after eighteen grueling hours on the road, Ford wandered up to the press section to rehash the day's events.

"Say, what did you think of my speech?" he wanted to know.

Usually, there was not a polite answer for that query; with rare exceptions, Ford was a dreadful orator. So none of us ventured an opinion.

"Not worth a damn, was it?" he answered himself, unleashing that signature raucous Midwestern laugh that was so infectious.

More to the point, Ford was a shrewd judge of character. He hadn't survived Washington's cutthroat political combat without being able to figure out who could be trusted and who couldn't. Unless burned, he always gave associates and acquaintances the benefit of the doubt. Our tiny band of reporters never violated his many late-night confidences. Somewhere along the line, we all passed his trust test.

In my case, I'll always believe our professional relationship was cemented in the spring of 1974 during a short chat in Palm Springs, in a hotel not far from where he died. Infuriated by a disparaging remark from a Nixon loyalist and goaded by me, Ford blurted out an amazing political indiscretion, then asked me not to print it. I was literally petrified, especially after the vice president of the United States grabbed my tie and rather forcefully informed me I wasn't leaving until I agreed to forget what I'd just heard. After what seemed like an eternity of gut-churning negotiation, we reached an understanding, and shook hands. I've kept my word to him.

The genesis for this book—even its very title—traces to that brief, powerful Easter encounter. In 1991, after he'd been out of office for fourteen years, I asked him to let me begin a series of regular "obit interviews" that could be published only after his death. In my proposal, passed through Bob Barrett, his first retirement chief of staff, I argued that he could be far more candid with this sort of arrangement, which would be better for history (and for me, of course, which I didn't point out). A few days later, Barrett called back and said we had a deal.

My inspiration for the idea was our April 1974 encounter, although I didn't mention it when making my pitch. I'll never know if that epic exchange was also on his mind when he agreed to this arrangement; regardless, I'll always be grateful he trusted me enough to make this book happen.

Some skeptics have already concluded that Ford saw this arrangement as a way to spin his legacy or settle scores from the grave. I doubt it. He was the most remarkably guileless political figure I've ever known. He had a modest Machiavellian side, but it surfaced only occasionally— like at the 1980 Republican convention in Detroit, when he consciously maneuvered the silly notion of making him the running mate of a guy he didn't like into well-deserved oblivion.

As for our embargoed interviews, I believe the only calculation at play was the impulse, hardwired into his DNA like nothing else, to be a nice guy.

This is not a conventional biography, or a biography at all; several good ones are already in print. Nor does it pretend to be a policy tome. I offer instead what might be called "Conversations with Jerry": an anecdotal memoir of his vice presidential and presidential career, which I covered, anchored by hours of off-the-record reminiscences and remembrances of his twenty-eight years of government service.

The Jerry Ford who emerged from our conversations was profoundly different from his steady if colorless stereotype: funny, reflective, chatty, gossipy—and unusually candid. I'm content to leave the heavy lifting to historians; this book simply attempts to present the human side of an everyday guy, talking—and occasionally dishing—as other former presidents have never done.

Over the years, Ford talked about what he *really* thought of Richard Nixon, his contempt for Nixon's palace guard, and why he never socialized with Spiro Agnew in retirement although they lived a few miles apart in the desert; his experiences on the Warren Commission; how his disdain for Jimmy Carter finally ended, while his profound bitterness toward Ronald Reagan was papered over at best; his never-before-revealed relationship with Bill Clinton, including the astonishing conversation they had during Clinton's impeachment proceedings; why he's been predicting for years that Hillary Clinton could be America's first female president; and why he thought his protégé Dick Cheney was the right running mate for George W. Bush in 2000 but the wrong one in 2004.

I've endeavored to produce a conversational narrative, leavened with numerous anecdotes, illuminations, and reflections on the news, history, and culture of the times in which Ford lived. His commentary is entertaining, surprising, heartwarming, and in some cases historic.

Thirty-two years and 260 days after that 1974 epiphany in the desert, my wife, Melanie (who, like our son, Andrew, has also experienced Ford's generosity of spirit), and I joined thousands of mourners in the Washington National Cathedral to bid farewell to one of the capital's most revered adopted sons.

It was a sunny but bitterly cold Tuesday morning, with swirling gusts driving the wind-chill index into the teens.

Listening to the tributes beneath the massive Gothic arches, I knew Ford would have been embarrassed by the hoopla; in life, he was always politely urging his audiences to sit down and stop applauding, as if he didn't rate a standing ovation.

If ever a piece of music fit a funeral, it was Aaron Copland's aptly titled "Fanfare for the Common Man," performed by the United States Marine Band.

Of course, Ford had nobody else to blame for the pageantry; he'd planned it all himself. The military, which by law runs every ex-president's state funeral, pulls together an off-the-shelf operations plan, then requires the eventual deceased to fill in the blanks during his life. The title of Ford's ops plan was as plain-vanilla as he was: Scenario 38.

As the eulogists celebrated an ordinary man who steered the country through extraordinary times, I remembered a conversation we'd had several years earlier, during a visit to his Rancho Mirage, California, home.

As he walked me to the door of his office after one of our interviews, Ford matter-of-factly volunteered that he'd put me on the guest list for his funeral.

"And I'm going to be damned sore if you don't show up," he said, totally serious.

"Mr. President, I've been saying for years that you're going to outlive us all," I replied, "but in the unfortunate event that I'm wrong about that, I'd be honored to attend."

"Good," he said. "I want you there."

As promises go, it may have been the easiest one I've ever had to keep.

# ONE

# *April 1974*

IRONICALLY, the interview that triggered a relationship with Gerald Ford lasting a third of a century, as well as a unique journalistic arrangement, wasn't even supposed to be an interview. I was just being neurotic.

In today's unappetizing environment of message discipline, control freaks, and endless political spin by phalanxes of cynical, robotic handlers, it's hard to imagine there was ever a time when a reporter could ask to see the vice president of the United States without it being a major production.

But it was a different age, and a different vice president.

Ford had set off on an uncharacteristically long nine-day trip in April 1974 that included a few days of Easter R&R in Palm Springs, sandwiched between political events in Missouri and California. But my first son had just been born, and since I'd missed most of the pregnancy barnstorming with Ford, I pulled myself off the trail to be with mother and child for a couple of weeks.

By the time I was able to catch up with the entourage, I would have missed the first five days of the trip. That was a long time to be out of the Ford loop, so before leaving for the coast I asked Paul Miltich, his press secretary, for some time with the veep once I arrived in the desert. He ran it by Ford, who agreed readily, which was his usual reaction when dealing with his media regulars. Since he and we were flying to Monterey for a full day of events early on the morning of April 18, Ford penciled me in for face time in the late afternoon of Wednesday, April 17, not long after my flight arrived in Palm Springs.

I didn't have much of a reporting agenda in mind; it was little more than a courtesy call, a routine catch-up after being away from the cocoon. I simply wanted to see what I'd missed and to get a fix on what was on his mind. I told Miltich I wasn't looking for a story, just some background.

En route to Palm Springs via Chicago, I leafed through a reading file of Ford clips I'd missed during my paternity leave. One was an April 10 column by William Safire in the *New York Times* headlined "Et Tu, Gerry?" (That was a common error when writing about Ford; it was Gerald with a G, but Jerry with a J.)

A former Nixon speechwriter and lifelong loyalist, Safire had taken Ford to task for perhaps the most boneheaded move of his vice presidency: in a late-night, highball-lubricated *Air Force Two* interview with *The New Republic*'s courtly John Osborne, Ford had openly speculated about which Nixon cabinet members and White House staffers he'd keep (like Henry Kissinger), and which he'd cashier (like Secretary of Defense James Schlesinger and White House press secretary Ron Ziegler), if by chance he became president.

"A few diehards might consider it unseemly for the vice president to be confiding his plans for the assumption of power while the body of the sitting president is still warm," Safire drily observed.

Osborne hadn't written that Ford was his source, but it was so transparently obvious that Ford telephoned Safire to admit his culpability and try, unsuccessfully, to explain away his lapse in judgment.

"Mr. Ford betrays a lack of understanding of the uniqueness of his role," Safire lectured. "He is the first vice president in American history whose own actions could help make him president. He must be at once loyal and independent; both his own man and the president's man; a defender uncorrupted by the defense. This duality requires more political skill than we have recently seen in Mr. Ford; he will miss the brass ring if he grabs at it."

The other item that caught my attention was the transcript of a mid-March public television interview with Bill Moyers by Patrick Buchanan, another rabid Nixon partisan.

In a passage clearly trying to shore up Nixon's shaky political standing by touting his geopolitical strengths, Buchanan had damned Ford with faint praise: "I think Gerald Ford would make a conscientious effort to continue the policies of the President. I like the Vice President. I admire him . . . but I do not think he has the knowledge or range or capacity that the President currently has to conduct American foreign policy."

In other words, the veep was indeed a Ford, not a Lincoln, as he himself regularly observed—and certainly not a Nixon.

His aides liked to stress that as a Yale Law School graduate, Ford knew he had above-average intelligence, so he didn't bristle when detractors poked fun at his candlepower. Maybe so, maybe not; these days we'd call that political spin. But by then I'd been around him enough to know that questioning his loyalty to Nixon was an enormous hot button for him. I already knew he'd been furious after hearing about Buchanan's shot. I had no idea he might still be simmering about those barbs a month later.

Ford was staying at Sunnylands, the lush, secluded private estate of Walter Annenberg, the megamillionaire communications magnate. But because Annenberg didn't want Ford aides and particularly reporters trampling around his home and private nine-hole golf course, Ford also had an office at the low-rise International House Hotel in Palm Springs, where his staff and traveling press were headquartered. That's where I caught up with him an hour or so after arriving in the desert.

The vice president had just come in from the golf links, where, he forlornly admitted, "My handicap took a beating." He was wearing a sky-blue Munsingwear golf shirt with the ubiquitous penguin insignia, khaki slacks, and tan Hush Puppies with white socks.

He greeted me warmly and immediately asked about my family, wanting to know all about the new arrival and saying he and the rest of the traveling crew had missed me and were glad I was back on the tour.

He knew all about the difficult delivery but wanted more details. "I worried about them," he said.

I hadn't planned it to be an interview, but as we got to talking, it inevitably developed into one.

Alternating between puffing on his pipe (Edgeworth was his brand) and sipping ice water from a plastic cup, Ford fretted that nobody believed him when he said he absolutely wasn't running for president in 1976.

"I understand why they don't believe me," he remarked. "They've seen so many alleged noncandidates become candidates that they just don't think anybody is sincere in not wanting to be president.

"I just don't have that terrible drive to be president. And besides, I've taken the blood oath for Betty." He'd promised his spouse he was retiring to Grand Rapids in January 1977, and that was that.

Curiously, however, Ford stuck by his refusal in our February interview to make a Shermanesque statement unequivocally taking himself out of a 1976 run.

"I just don't think a person ought to tie himself down too much," he said. "Circumstances beyond my control could always have some impact."

Like being a sitting president by 1976, I thought to myself. Ford didn't like contemplating that doomsday scenario and hated having the subject brought up, and reporters did bring it up constantly. He claimed he hadn't done any contingency planning, even in his head, and was annoyed about press reports to the contrary.

Even so, he admitted, "You have to be pragmatic even about things you don't want to happen, and the truth is I don't want it to happen. But I don't think about what I might do as president, because it only leads to difficulties. The truth is, I don't sit around making plans, because I don't want it to happen and *I don't think it is going to happen*" (emphasis added).

If it did, though, Ford was absolutely confident he could handle the rigors of the Oval Office.

"I think I've always been qualified for any job I've undertaken, and everything I've done in government over twenty-five years would certainly give me the background, the knowledge, and the friends to do a good job. If lightning should strike, I certainly wouldn't sit there fearful of being incapable of handling the situation."

I reminded him that not all Americans, much less his Democratic critics, agreed with his rosy self-assessment of his talents. Contrary to his staff's disclaimers, talk like that always irked him, and he especially seethed at the notion he was a foreign policy lightweight.

"Most of the people who say that don't know the opportunities I had in the Congress to be fully exposed to international matters," he argued, citing his dozen years on the Defense and Foreign Aid Appropriations subcommittees. He also reminded me that he was one of only five House members on a secret CIA subcommittee that received highly classified intelligence briefings.

"Most of those people who make that comment," he added, "weren't around when I was going through this educational process, and they've become instant foreign policy experts."

He also made clear his annoyance at the frequent political shorthand that he was a low-voltage plodder.

"In my growth in government, I never planned on moving from one spot to another, but I always felt what I was doing would prepare me for the next opportunity. You have to have the confidence that you're available and competent if lightning strikes, and if that's plodding, it seems to have worked. What counts in this world is what works, not what some outsider thinks is a better way."

This zigzag dissertation was very familiar to that tiny band of media regulars who traveled with him. On any given day, Ford could either be Nixon's staunchest defender, or say something that suggested growing distance between the two. Sometimes it was just his sloppy rhetoric, and sometimes it was deliberate. Usually, we never knew which.

Even so, his "if lightning should strike" remark struck me at the time as more than a little pregnant.

I stood to leave, and so did he. But he wasn't finished. He asked me to put away my notebook.

"Before you go, I want to show you something. What do you make of this?"

Under ordinary circumstances, this unscheduled postscript to our conversation would never have happened. But about ten minutes earlier, Miltich had gone into another room to take a phone call, then fallen asleep on a sofa. So it was just the two of us. A reporter's dream, a flack's nightmare: no minders.

Ford handed me a copy of Bill Safire's withering appraisal of his behavior, the very same damning column I'd read on the plane only a couple of hours before.

His tone was more perplexed than angry, but there was no doubt he was annoyed with the pounding he'd been getting from Nixon's men. Clearly, he'd been doing a slow burn for weeks.

"Why would Bill say something like that?" Ford wanted to know. "He knows I've been damn loyal to Dick Nixon. Dick Nixon knows I've been loyal. Why do they do this?"

If this conversation were occurring today, I doubt I'd say what I said then. Chalk my answer up to the impetuosity of youth.

I told him that Safire, Buchanan, press secretary Ron Ziegler, and their fellow White House partisans were kicking the dog because despite their fierce loyalty to Nixon, most of them were pragmatic enough to realize where this Greek tragedy was heading.

"They're angry and they're bitter because they know Nixon is finished," I replied. "It's over. He can't survive, and you're gonna be president."

Before I had time to reflect on my own audacity, Ford floored me with his totally unanticipated answer.

"You're right," he said. "But when the pages of history are written, nobody can say I contributed to it."

I was thunderstruck: Moments before, he'd assured me Nixon would ride out the firestorm. Now, impulsively, he'd blurted out the truth. Four months before it actually happened, three months before the Supreme Court ordered Nixon to turn over the tape recordings that would doom him, Ford had just admitted he knew in his gut that Nixon was a goner and he would soon become America's 38th, and first unelected, president.

Ford was thunderstruck as well—at himself. In a millisecond, he realized the enormity of his mistake, and like many a politician before and since burned by his own loose tongue, he tried to take it back.

"You didn't hear that," he said in an even but urgent tone.

"But I did," I stupidly replied, without thinking.

"Tom, you did *not* hear that."

I was speechless—literally. That wasn't what he wanted to hear.

Ford walked around his desk and confronted me directly, face-to-face. I got an unobstructed view of his blue eyes; they weren't friendly.

Towering above his quarry, he gently grabbed my tie and said in a firm tone of voice, "Tom, you are not leaving this room until we have an understanding."

I said nothing. I couldn't; I was utterly petrified, literally scared beyond words. I was twenty-eight years old, having the time of my life, and the vice president had just dropped a giant Hobson's Choice on my head: agree to forget what I'd just heard and give up an unbelievable scoop, or risk terminally alienating the next leader of the free world, whom I'd been cultivating for the last four months.

We stood there for perhaps fifteen seconds, but the old cliché about something seeming like an eternity is the only accurate way to describe the moment. Out of sheer panic, I was unable to speak.

Then he said, "Write it when I'm dead."

I was too frightened and witless to negotiate, and surrendered my journalistic sword with enormous relief.

"Okay."

Ford let loose of my tie and stuck out his hand; I took it. Our deal was struck.

In an instant, the conversation was expunged from the record. "Nice to see you, Tom," he boomed. He asked me to tell my wife hello, and walked me to the door. "See you tomorrow," he chirped, as if Armageddon hadn't just been averted.

The next morning, the travel corps assembled at the Palm Springs airport for his one-day trip up to Monterey. He greeted me warmly, asked about my wife and son, and said once again he'd worried about them. It was as though our relationship-altering exchange the previous day had never occurred.

It would be seventeen years before we spoke about that seminal moment again.

I never told my superiors at *Newsweek* what I'd heard. But part of me felt unbelievably guilty about that. So after he became president, I tried to salve my conscience somewhat by filing the second clause of what he'd said in April for the issue of the magazine published the Monday after he was sworn in: "When the pages of history are written," *Newsweek* reported him privately saying months earlier, "nobody can say I contributed to it."

As I'd promised him, however, I kept Ford's operative first two words to myself (and my wife, Melanie)—until now.

Admittedly, this astounding display of indiscretion will be seen by most experts and historians as totally out of character for Jerry Ford. For the most part, that's true. Not always, however. He was an extraordinarily nice guy, but the truth is that Ford had one hell of a temper. He usually kept it in check, but every once in a while, he could suddenly erupt with incendiary force—and sometimes blurt out an ill-advised remark before recapturing his composure.

Such an outburst occurred, in remarkably similar circumstances, a couple of weeks after our fateful encounter in Palm Springs, while Ford was on a two-day swing through the South.

Inside the White House, it was common knowledge in the spring of 1974 that the Air Force chief of staff, General George Brown, was about to be elevated to chairman of the Joint Chiefs of Staff. Several senior Air Force officers were being considered to succeed Brown. Ford had his own candidate: General John C. Meyer, the commander in chief of the Strategic Air Command. They were old friends, dating from the days when Meyer was an Air Force liaison officer on Capitol Hill. In fact, the Brooklyn-born officer had been posted as head of the Air Force lobbying operation for the House of Representatives in 1948, the same year Ford was elected to Congress.

Meyer had invited the new vice president to visit SAC headquarters at Offutt Air Force Base, Nebraska, in February, and Ford eagerly accepted. It was a twofer for the veep: a chance to see a friend, and also visit the site of the Woolworth Avenue home in Omaha where he'd been born in 1913.

In early May, Ford knew the White House was close to a decision on the chief of staff job, so he pressed his Air Force aide, Lieutenant Colonel Bob Blake, for a status report.

On May 3, Ford began a two-day swing that included stops in Columbia and Myrtle Beach, South Carolina. Afterward he flew to Hilton Head for a round of golf, memorable only because his tee shot on the first hole beaned a woman spectator.

Shortly after *Air Force Two* landed, Ford's naval aide, Commander Howard Kerr, called Washington and was informed by Blake that Meyer had lost out to General David Jones. The announcement would be made public in about ten days.

After his golf round, Ford was sorting through some paperwork at a desk in his hotel suite when Kerr knocked on the door, walked in, and delivered a message he knew the boss wouldn't like.

That was an understatement. Ford was so enraged that he leaped to his feet and blurted out, "Goddammit, Howard, when *I'm* president this—"

Abruptly, he caught himself in mid-sentence.

"You didn't hear me say that," he barked at his nonplussed naval assistant, who, like me, just had. Unlike me, however, Kerr had the presence of mind and common sense to salute smartly, and excuse himself. Ford sat back down and resumed his reading, still boiling.

He was his usual jovial self by dinnertime. But Ford had been so furious, so momentarily out of control, that Kerr assumed there must have been more to the story. Thirty-three years later, he speculated that Ford may have been led to believe that Meyer would get the job and felt double-crossed by his enemies in the White House. That's a plausible theory; there are always winners and losers in the appointment sweepstakes, and Ford was a big boy about that. It's not likely he would have reacted so viscerally unless there was some perfidy involved in the selection. But Ford never mentioned the matter again to Kerr, and Jones's new job was announced a few days later, on May 14.

In subsequent years, I had several dozen interviews with Ford, including at least thirty during his retirement. But I didn't resurrect our 1974 conversation for seventeen years, and even then it was by accident.

In August 1991, during the first of our write-it-when-I'm-gone interviews, I'd asked him to reminisce about Watergate. At one point in the conversation, he repeated his standard refrain about not really knowing he'd be president until Nixon chief of staff Major General Alexander Haig came to his office in early August to alert him that Nixon's position was imploding rapidly and Ford should prepare for the worst—or best, I suppose, depending on one's view of Nixon and Ford.

"After that meeting, the odds were overwhelming that I would be president," he said. "Of course, even then, Haig was saying, 'One minute he's going to resign, the next minute he's going to fight it through.'"

I felt I had to challenge that sanitized version of history, so I reminded him of our Easter 1974 exchange, when he'd asked me why Nixon's men were trashing him, and I'd replied it was because they knew Nixon was toast and Ford would soon be president. I resurrected our conversation essentially verbatim, ending with his insistence to me that history would conclude he'd never greased the skids for Nixon.

"Well, I felt very strongly about that," he ducked, pointedly not challenging my reminder that he had agreed with me that he'd be president before long.

I tried again by raising a heavily camouflaged version of his Hilton Head exchange with Howard Kerr, whom I didn't name. But I repeated what I'd been told Ford said then: Goddammit, when *I'm* president . . .

He paused for a moment before answering.

"If it happened," he said, "I don't recall it. I can honestly say it *might* have happened, but I don't recall it. And it would be out of character [from] the role I was playing." That was certainly true.

It was significant, of course, that Ford didn't deny our encounter had happened. He couldn't, because it had.

# TWO

# *Air Force Two*

O N JULY 30, 1976, as we flew down to Jackson, Mississippi, where Ford would woo that state's thirty critical swing delegates to the Republican national convention, I interviewed him on *Air Force One*. A couple of weeks later, a photograph of our session arrived with this handwritten inscription: "Sure does beat Air Force #2. Best wishes, Jerry Ford."

Maybe for him, I've said hundreds of times since that brutally hot summer day, but never for me. Covering Ford's presidency was memorable enough, but always a lot less fun than those heady days from December 6, 1973, to August 9, 1974, when Ford was the first unelected vice president in American history. Most of my happiest professional memories are anchored in those eight memorable months traveling at a madcap pace with the man who would be president.

It was a miserable time for the country. The Watergate scandal was in full frenzy, building to what even then seemed like an inevitable outcome. Richard Nixon's foreign policy accomplishments couldn't trump the criminal behavior of his senior lieutenants and mounting evidence of his own complicity in covering up their misdeeds. A Texas lawyer, Leon Jaworski, had been appointed as a special prosecutor. The House Judiciary Committee had launched an impeachment inquiry. The White House was refusing to turn over transcripts of Nixon's secret tape-recorded conversations to Jaworski, and the Supreme Court would have to resolve the impasse.

Protests against Nixon multiplied with each new revelation by the *Washington Post*'s Bob Woodward and Carl Bernstein. One of my enduring images of those days is the autos passing by the White House—Pennsylvania Avenue wasn't closed to traffic then because of security fears like today—incessantly sitting on their horns. (Protesters in Lafayette Park were brandishing signs urging motorists to "honk if you think he's guilty.")

Yet it was a supremely exhilarating time for an apprentice reporter from Arlington, Texas, hurtling around the country amidst a bona fide constitutional crisis and a riveting news story.

Mostly that was because of an ordinary man, who also happened to like reporters, unexpectedly thrust into the crucible of extraordinary times. But improbable as it may seem now, what also made it a magical, mystical experience for many of us was what Ford would laughingly call, in a 1991 interview with me, "that awful plane."

Five years ago, I was at Andrews Air Force Base in the Maryland suburbs, preparing to board *Air Force Two* for a trip with Vice President Dick Cheney. I saw Cheney's sleek Boeing 757 jumbo jet and couldn't help smiling. An Air Force sergeant politely wondered what was so funny.

I told him that my mind's eye had just flashed back to the first *Air Force Two* I'd ever seen, twenty-nine years earlier, on the very same tarmac.

The only resemblance of Jerry Ford's *Air Force Two* to Cheney's upscale version was that they both had a white-and-blue color scheme.

Ford's plane was a tiny VC-131H Samaritan, the military version of the Convair 580 twin-engined propjet.

It was so slow that cross-country trips were interminable, especially when we had to refuel en route. Its 330-mile-per-hour top airspeed was so glacial that on one early flight, as the pilot started the engines, Secret Service agent Jim Huse yelled, "Quiet, please. Prepare to activate slingshot."

Forevermore, we dubbed the aircraft Slingshot Airlines.

As second in line to the presidency, Ford by protocol rated a ritzier plane. But Henry Kissinger had more grandiose tastes than the vice president, so Ford had allowed the secretary of state to have first choice. Henry and his oversized ego made the most of the veep's generosity. Occasionally Ford's military aides would commandeer a larger four-engine jet for him, but it wasn't much to crow about either: a converted C-135 tanker without any windows. We called that one the Flying Sausage. At least it was faster.

As it turned out, that little plane was a godsend for reporters. Unlike today's executive military jets, where the dignitaries sit up front and reporters are relegated to the back of the bus, we sat in the front and Ford's cabin was aft. That meant that on every trip he had to walk past the media gauntlet. It was constant engagement with the press, whether he liked it or not. Much to our satisfaction, we'd soon learn that for the most part, he liked it.

"You're looking bright-eyed and bushy-tailed this morning" was his standard line as he breezed past us, which was seldom the case because we were all usually exhausted by his frenzied pace.

Even Bill Clinton at his most peripatetic was no match for Jerry Ford in traversing America's skies. He was constantly on the go, cramming multiple events into his already-jammed travel schedule.

On July 6, 140 miles out of Dallas en route to a political event, he came up to the press cabin to announce he'd just reached the 100,000-mile mark.

By the time he became president, Ford had logged 130,000 miles visiting forty-one states, averaging nearly a coast-to-coast trip every week for eight months.

How crazed were his itineraries? Only Jerry Ford would begin a two-day vacation to Hawaii with a fourteen-hour Friday in Honolulu with eleven events, the last an evening speech to a Boy Scout convention.

Such scheduling overkill was vintage Ford: he didn't want it to seem he was gouging taxpayers for a very brief downtime weekend at the posh Mauna Kea Beach Hotel on the Big Island of Hawaii.

That sort of forced-march regimen wasn't an aberration; he did it all the time, wearing out aides, Secret Service agents, and reporters half his age.

A one-day trip to Wichita Falls and Tulsa was a typical death-march bruiser: nineteen hours, ending at 2:00 A.M., after five receptions, three speeches, and two press conferences.

Here's a sample of one twelve-day schedule I filed with my editors:

*Monday, May 20*—leave early ayem for Seattle; return Washington two ayem Tuesday.

*Wednesday, May 22*—leave ayem for New York and Delaware, return midnight.

*Thursday, May 23*—leave early evening for New York, return midnight.

*Friday, May 24*—leave ayem for Lansing, Michigan, return midafternoon.

*Saturday, May 25*—leave midafternoon for Boston, return midnight.

*Sunday, May 26*—leave noon for New York and Connecticut, return midnight.

*Tuesday, May 28*—leave midmorning for Charlotte, return one ayem.

*Wednesday, May 29*—leave midday for Birmingham, return one ayem.

*Friday, May 31*—leave midafternoon for New Hampshire, return midnight.

In other words: nine states, nine out-and-back day trips in twelve days.

Like George W. Bush today, Ford liked to sleep in his own bed, so
most of his trips were these marathon one-day stands that had him
arriving home well past midnight. Then he'd turn around and crank it
up again the next morning, usually with only five hours of sleep. And
he loved red-eye flights like no politician I've ever covered.

As vice president, Ford was faced with one of the more daunting as-
signments any American politician has ever confronted. He was
determined to remain loyal to his president, the old friend and former
congressional colleague who'd made him VP. He was also intent on
staying true to his conscience, and much of what he saw unfolding at
the White House troubled him. More than anything else, he was also
desperate to do everything in his power to hold his beloved Republican
Party together amid the wreckage of Watergate.

Every vice president struggles under the yoke of playing second fid-
dle, but Watergate made the part far trickier for Ford. Even in the beginning, when he still believed Nixon was innocent, Ford was smart
enough to realize there was a reasonable chance he might become president anyway. If it happened, he'd need to come before a wounded and
troubled nation as the Great Healer. By defending Nixon too forcefully,
he risked being tarred as an Agnewesque polarizer, diminishing his capacity to reunite the nation.

In retrospect, I believe that's why he left himself some safety valves,
such as saying he believed Nixon was clean "based on the current evidence" or the assurances of others.

He also proved he wasn't a total lapdog one day in Johnstown,
Pennsylvania, when a hotshot local TV anchor prefaced a question with

a reference to "this media-manufactured Watergate crisis." When asked if he agreed, Ford firmly rejected the notion that Watergate was the creation of the Nixon-loathing press.

Juggling multiple obligations and masters was fundamentally impossible, but Ford gave it his best, rhetorically hooking and slicing with maddening regularity. As with sausage-making, legislation, and reporting, Ford's attempts to negotiate that tightrope weren't always a pretty sight.

But it was an intriguing exercise in political Kremlinology, not to mention one helluva lot of fun, for the small band of reporters along for the ride.

Many of our colleagues cycled in and out on Ford trips, but there were seven of us in the core group. Marjorie Hunter of the *New York Times,* who'd covered Ford for years on Capitol Hill, was the senior member. The network reps were Phil Jones of CBS, Ron Nessen of NBC, and Bill Zimmerman of ABC. Bob Leonard of the Voice of America was always urging Ford to speak in Special English, a simpler version of English that the VOA still uses on many of its international broadcasts. David Kennerly, the wisecracking *Time* magazine shooter who later became President Ford's personal photographer, rounded out the group.

As Ford began more or less nonstop travel, a couple of realities quickly became apparent: he was far more popular than Richard Nixon, and he was also a dull, uninspiring speaker. But nobody seemed to care, because he was such a decent soul, the quintessential un-Nixon.

Despite his sometimes reflexive support for Nixon, Ford's popular appeal was undeniable. In February, a Gallup poll showed that if he were running for president against Nixon, he'd beat his boss by a 14 percent margin.

Judged against Ford's abundant list of oratorical defects, those numbers were even more remarkable. After two months of traveling with him, I'd reached the conclusion that the advance book on Ford was true to form. On February 13, I summarized him this way in a file to my editors in New York:

He is basically the poor man's Dwight D. Eisenhower, an earnest plodder whose intellect will never be described as scintillating. He exudes about as much flair and charisma as Calvin Coolidge. He is a terrible orator, one of the worst in recent memory. Although his newly hired ghosters can be expected to improve upon an erratic prose style in which major chunks of his speeches fail to hang together and trail off into dead ends, they probably won't be able to do much for a soporific delivery so deadly it could put an insomniac to sleep, and probably has. What other GOP pol would be injudicious enough, e.g., to claim in public [last week] that "we have a President who has selected the finest people to serve" when most of Nixon's first team have been disgraced by Watergate?

Why, then, all the popular adulation? The answer is deceptively simple: Jerry Ford is a human being cum laude, a down-to-earth, earnest, genuinely likable guy with an infectious laugh and not the slightest hint of pretentiousness. He is a politician of great and genuine sincerity who feels far more comfortable with "Jerry" than "Mr. Vice President." And in a time when virtuous pols seem as scarce as gasoline, Jerry Ford sticks out as a man of abundant decency.

Ford's humanity was demonstrated in all sorts of ways. When Spiro Agnew was vice president, an Air Force JetStar and its crew were kept on call for Agnew's exclusive use. Ford ordered the plane returned to the VIP motor pool. One of the reasons he liked his little Convair turboprop was that it burned less fuel than pure jets. When the Secret Service made him take a Boeing 707 military jet to Vail for Christmas 1973, he made sure that the ten extra seats went to soldiers trying to make it home for the holidays.

When he and Dick Cavett prepared to enter Ford's Alexandria, Virginia, home for a TV taping, the protocol-conscious Cavett inquired,

"Does one precede the vice president?" Ford answered, "In my house you do," holding the door open for his guest.

And when an ice storm delayed *Time* magazine reporter David Beckwith from getting to Baltimore/Washington International Airport in time to make that Christmas holiday flight to Vail, a bone-weary Ford, exhausted from a trip to Madrid for the funeral of an assassinated Spanish official, graciously ordered his jet held on the runway for half an hour until the offending reporter sheepishly arrived from New York. Agnew would never have done that; Nixon would probably have had Beckwith shot on the tarmac.

Neither would Nixon have ever allowed himself to be photographed amid the mellowness of a two-martini evening. That happened one night as we returned to Washington from Florida during the height of the streaking craze, where young men and women would strip naked and run through public places, including that year's Academy Awards show. After Ford pronounced the practice "silly," Maggie Hunter had T-shirts made up that said "Keep on Streaking" and gave him one. After takeoff from Tampa, he put it on and literally sprinted up to the press cabin, gleefully cackling in full frat-boy mode.

As for the bigger Ford picture, we all more or less figured Ford would be president before long, and further suspected that he knew as well.

In most speeches he told a joke about how whenever his motorcade drove past the White House he'd say to himself, "If you worked here, you'd be home already." It infuriated Nixon's courtiers, but was ostensibly designed to reinforce Ford's self-deprecating sense of self. Or was there another message to his one-liner?

Ours was an endless cat-and-mouse game of trying to draw him out on the Watergate issue of the moment, then parsing his language to determine whether he was being imprecise or verbally clumsy, or whether he'd consciously created new distance between himself and Nixon. It was rigorous work: Ford zigged and zagged more than a Singer sewing machine.

(We caught him only once. Leaving Palm Springs for Washington at Easter, Ford shot the breeze on the tarmac with Phil Jones and me while waiting for Betty, who was hobbled by a bone spur operation and having trouble negotiating the *Air Force Two* ramp. Jones chided Ford for his spiffy new glen plaid suit with deep side vents and angled pocket flaps. Ford responded in kind about Jones's bush suit, the sort favored by reporters who'd spent time in Vietnam.

"Are you going to wear that over to the White House?" Ford asked. In an instant he caught himself. "And up to the Hill?" We both knew exactly what he was saying.)

After returning from his Christmas skiing holiday in Vail, Ford began 1974 in unadulterated Nixon waterboy mode. In a January 15 speech to the American Farm Bureau convention in Atlantic City, he declared the impeachment effort the handiwork of "a few extreme partisans" bent on destroying not only the president but the American system.

He was deeply embarrassed, and his credibility wounded, when it became known that the speech had been drafted by the White House. He quickly hired his own ghostwriters to establish some autonomy, but the incident undercut his insistence that he intended to be his own man despite his friendship with Nixon.

On January 21, a Monday, Ford spent an hour and 45 minutes with Nixon and came away convinced his boss was totally clean. The next morning he asserted at a press conference, "The president had no prior knowledge of Watergate, had no part in the cover-up, and has not been party of any of these allegations made by some."

He repeated the same defense to me in an interview the next day, predicting that the House Judiciary Committee would never impeach Nixon and extolling his strength under duress.

"If anyone thinks he is not strong mentally and physically," he con-fided, "they don't know what the facts are. If anybody doubts his desire to move ahead—domestically, internationally, and politically—they haven't seen him lately.

"The president isn't sitting there huddled up, scared to speak out. He's in charge."

In full cheerleader mode, he also predicted that in the unlikely event the committee impeached Nixon, impeachment would lose in the full House by at least 100 votes—probably more when all the good things Nixon was doing in the Middle East came to fruition.

"You're going to see the embargo lifted on Middle East oil," he pre-dicted, "which will have a tremendous psychological attitude on the eco-nomic condition and the public attitude. If a real shot in the arm comes like that, is the House, in that improving atmosphere, going to attack the guy that made it possible? I don't think so."

By the middle of February, he was spending more time on the road than at his desk in Room 275 of the Executive Office Building. Passkey, his Secret Service radio call sign, was the hottest political commodity in the country. (His code name was later changed to Pontiac, legendary chief of the Ottawa Indian tribe and a fellow Michigander.)

More than five thousand speaking invitations had poured into his office from supplicants as diverse as other countries to Girl Scout troops, and one hundred new requests piled up each day.

"All the attention embarrasses me," he told me one day. "It's just not my style. I've always been a self-sufficient individual."

Ford was particularly sought-after by fellow Republicans, who rated Richard Nixon somewhere below the plague as the midterm elec-tions approached.

He left standing orders with his schedulers to say yes to any mem-ber of Congress who needed him to campaign; throughout his vice presidency, half his travel was devoted to Republican Party events.

"Watergate has disastrously damaged our party," he was overheard telling a seatmate on *Air Force Two* in the spring of 1974.

That was an understatement. On February 18, the Democrats won the special election in his old congressional district. It was the first time in sixty-four years that Ford's home turf wouldn't be represented by a Republican, and he was shaken when he heard the news in a phone call from a former aide aboard *Air Force Two* returning from Chattanooga. He was staggered. "It's a beating," he disconsolately muttered over his shoulder to a reporter's question.

By March, Ford's rhetoric was becoming far more cautious. In campaigning for Republicans, he began praising Nixon's policies without managing to use his name. Privately, he advised nervous former congressional colleagues to put similar distance between themselves and Nixon.

About the same time, Ford's aides began whispering to the *Air Force Two* press regulars that in private he was sharply critical of Nixon's handling of his Watergate defense and was urging the beleaguered president to be more forthcoming, with investigators and the country.

On March 2 in Phoenix, without checking with a subsequently enraged White House, Ford told reporters that a federal grand jury's report on Nixon's alleged Watergate involvement should be made available to the House Judiciary Committee.

Why the sea change? Simple: Ford, the consummate party man, was furious with Nixon's statement at a February 25 press conference that he wouldn't resign even if the Republican Party was eviscerated in the process. Ford read that as a to-hell-with-the-party kiss-off, and bitterly resented it.

Around this time, I asked him why he was traveling so much. He didn't mention any obligation to defend Nixon.

"Our party needs some help," he said, "and at the moment I'm the one person who can go to Arizona and Boston and get the party together."

He wouldn't let me use it at the time, but he also said this: "Somebody has to keep this party from falling apart."

There was more to it than that. Desperate to save his party from ruination, Ford also understood what Watergate had done to the fabric of the nation and its confidence in government. Over time, Ford had essentially become America's de facto president.

So while Nixon became a virtual hostage of the scandal, Ford quietly but consciously stepped into the void, assuming much of the show-the-flag function normally the preserve of a president.

Wherever he went, Ford reminded his audiences that this was still a great country, respected throughout the globe, the last best hope for mankind, the arbiter of choice in the Middle East.

"I've been telling as many members of the Class of 1974 as I can reach that the government in Washington isn't about to sink," he said at a Texas college commencement in May. "That it is and will continue to be about as good as concerned and conscientious citizens make it, that the constitutional processes are working as the Founding Fathers intended, without riot or repression and most importantly, without as yet seriously weakening our strength at home and abroad."

It wasn't just political imperative or his reputation as a soft touch that explained why Ford could be found stoically puffing on his pipe at head tables in such backroads locales as Great Bend, Kansas; London, Kentucky; and Charleston, Illinois. Or why he spoke to such normally non–vice presidential groups as the Mobile Home Manufacturers Association, the Tinley Park [Illinois] High School Titans, or the New York Masonic Lodge. Or why he addressed a North Carolina graduating class of sixty-seven.

As one of his closest friends explained, "Jerry understands that he's one of the few people in a position to keep this country from falling apart."

Meanwhile, Nixon was cratering, and Ford knew it. Suddenly, he was far more his own man. At a March 11 fundraiser in Boston, he praised Francis Sargent as one of America's finest governors—just five days after Sargent had suggested America would be better off if Nixon resigned.

Earlier that day, he damned Nixon with faint praise with some Harvard kids. While insisting he hewed to a "high degree of loyalty" to Nixon, he also said, "I don't happen to believe on the basis of evidence that I am familiar with . . . that the president was in any way connected with Watergate per se, and I don't believe that he had any part in the cover-up—*but time will tell*" (emphasis added).

On March 30 in Chicago, he denounced Nixon's reelection committee, familiarly known as CREEP (Committee to Re-elect the President), for caring more about its candidate than about the Republican Party. He dismissed the committee as "an arrogant, elite guard of political adolescents" and recommended that all future national campaigns be run by the Republican and Democratic National Committees.

That night I cabled this assessment to my editors after checking with two of Ford's closest aides: "Ford's paramount responsibility (in his view) is to save the Republican Party if at all possible from what he worries will be a debacle this fall. He will defend Richard Nixon whenever he can as long as he can, but Nixon's survival is secondary to the survival of the GOP."

The qualitative change in Ford's defense of Nixon didn't pass unnoticed at the White House, which began telling reporters that maybe the vice president wasn't as loyal as he professed. That prompted another celebrated Ford turnabout.

On April 24, a week after my fateful conversation with Ford in Palm Springs, Maggie Hunter in the *Times* broke a story that began, "Vice President Ford has confided to acquaintances in recent weeks that he is perplexed by what he senses to be the feeling of some White House aides that he is attempting to undercut President Nixon."

The story analyzed the schism between Ford and some of Nixon's more rabid assistants and noted, "Mr. Ford is said to be deeply concerned over the apparent feelings of some White House aides that he is intentionally trying to overshadow Mr. Nixon. He has told close friends that he has no desire to rupture his still close relationship with the

President, but he feels he is obliged to do all he can to keep his party from being swept away in a Democratic landslide this fall."

Maggie was a good reporter and a fabulous den mother for us rookies on the Ford beat, but her sourcing for this particular article was unusually impeccable: Jerry Ford himself. In this instance, we were "the acquaintances" in whom Ford had confided.

In fact, Ford had backgrounded all of us reporters traveling with him the week before between Monterey and Palm Springs. But he had insisted any stories we filed be held for a week so they would carry Washington datelines, a device he hoped would help disguise the true identity of our primary source.

Three decades later, it's clear in retrospect that *Air Force Two* was his private chamber, his flying safe house. It was the only place where he could really relax, and he often included us. "Anything that was on his mind," Phil Jones remembered, "we would usually know about it."

None of us in the press corps considered ourselves "close friends" of the veep, but we went along with Ford's ground rules to help cover his tracks—and facilitate our access to him in the future. Such phrases as "in recent weeks," "observed a few weeks ago," and "said to feel" were all standard camouflage language. That's the way the leak game is played in Washington, then and now.

It was apparent by then that while he was predisposed to give Nixon the benefit of the doubt, the more he learned about Watergate, the more he began to believe he was being lied to—a political mortal sin for a straight arrow like Jerry Ford. By early May, I was filing that Ford agreed with old friends in Congress that Nixon would be impeached.

Not coincidentally, his rhetorical distance from Nixon expanded significantly. Returning from a day trip to New York City on May 6, Ford wandered up to the press cabin and said he was now worried about Nixon's ability to conduct foreign policy because of the scandal.

In effect, he was suggesting that Nixon's political survival might no longer be in the national interest, a blockbuster notion coming from the guy who would have to pick up the pieces.

All of us immediately grasped the impact of what that meant; Nixon's foreign policy strengths were the bedrock of Ford's case against impeachment. In almost every speech he would say, "Richard Nixon is the greatest president in foreign affairs in my lifetime." Now Ford was *really* off the reservation.

The next afternoon, after his personal phone calls failed to persuade the regulars to hold off on publishing his damning remarks, Ford was in a rage when he came aboard for that day's trip back to New York.

"Good afternoon, gentlemen," he said, brushing past reporters without pausing. It was the only time in those eight months that I saw him struggle with his temper, and he told me coming back to Washington that night that he'd never hoist a round with us again. Typically, that embargo lasted a little more than twenty-four hours—which told me Ford was only annoyed his remarks were attributed to him, not that they were reported.

Four days later, on May 11, Ford was the commencement speaker at Texas A&M University, my alma mater. For a story previewing the vice president's visit, I was interviewed by a reporter from the student newspaper, *The Battalion*, where I had once been the editor.

The day before we arrived in College Station, *The Batt*, as it's known, ran a front-page story that began this way: "Those who hear U.S. Vice President Gerald R. Ford speak at Saturday's commencement exercises will probably be listening to the next President, said *Newsweek* writer Tom DeFrank."

The story was delicately modulated; I'd been careful in the interview not to say Nixon was a goner, only that Ford was "capable of stepping into the Presidency" if it came to that. I also talked about Ford's pleasing personality and opined, "I believe Ford is being honest when he says he will not run for President in 1976. At the same time, he is smart enough to know that if he is forced into the Presidency, it will be a different story."

But as all reporters quickly learn, often to their dismay, sometimes a story's headline is pithier and more lacking in nuance than the text.

That was certainly true in this case: "DeFrank Predicts Ford's Presidency," the headline trumpeted.

Not long after *Air Force Two* landed at Easterwood Airport, I was tipped off to the story by Mary Helen Bowers, the wife of my favorite journalism professor and faculty adviser, David Bowers. Unfortunately for me, several of my colleagues in the traveling press corps overheard our conversation.

After Ford's unmemorable address, which included a couple of local-color references about A&M traditions that I'd passed along to his chief of staff Bob Hartmann, the entourage returned to the airport and flew off to political events in Houston and Dallas before heading home.

As we boarded *Air Force Two*, it was instantly apparent the irrepressible pot-stirrer Phil Jones had been up to his usual mischief: every seat on the plane had a copy of the *Battalion* story talking about how Jerry Ford was going to be the next president. Their only source for this bombshell revelation, of course, was me.

As Ford walked through the press cabin, Jones helpfully pointed out a story in the local press that might be of interest. Ford picked up the paper, saw the headline, and winced, literally.

"You're gonna get me in trouble, Tom," he grumped, swiftly exiting our cabin before any of my gleeful colleagues could engage him further.

I knew he was annoyed; even though the story was complimentary to him, there was no doubt it added to the uncomfortable bind he'd been in since being sworn in. But I also knew I was right about my prediction; I'd heard him admit it himself just three weeks earlier in Palm Springs. I wondered if he remembered that conversation; perhaps that was why he didn't give me more of a hard time about it.

In fact, good sport as ever, he actually signed a copy of the offending article for me. It turned out to be the tersest autograph I have from him: "Thanks, Jerry Ford."

Two days later, Ford flew to New Orleans. Then he changed planes for the short hop to Baton Rouge for a speech to the Louisiana legislature. On that leg, *Air Force Two* was an ancient Naval Reserve C-54 propeller cargo plane that should have been in an air museum instead of hauling VIPs. The engine cowlings appeared a heartbeat away from metal fatigue. The interior, I wrote in my notebook, looked like the inside of a New York City subway station. There was no air-conditioning, leaving Ford's retinue to baste in the muggy eighty-degree climate. Instead of the vice presidential seal, the door of the plane carried its own distinctive logo: a smirking raccoon, its tail hoisted in the air.

This day, the vice president of the free world was being flown in a plane emblazoned with the ass of a raccoon.

The pilot apologized to Ford's military aide: "Commander, I know this is a cattle car. But you should have seen it yesterday before we cleaned it up."

That was a relative description for a plane whose normal mission was ferrying okra and snap beans around the Mississippi River delta. When Louisiana governor Edwin Edwards fastened his seat belt, his pristine vanilla ice cream suit got slathered with grease. Congressman F. Edward Hébert, powerful chairman of the House Armed Services Committee, was so incensed by the plane that he arranged alternative transportation back to New Orleans.

Ford, as usual, took it all in stride. But he later told an aide: "Don't ever let this happen again."

As he walked into the statehouse later, the resemblance to a president entering the House of Representatives for a State of the Union address was eerie, and the symbolism wasn't lost on the former House minority leader.

After being introduced by Edwards, Ford quipped—or did he: "I hope my friends in the press aren't getting the wrong impression that my speaking before a joint session of the legislature is any forerunner to what might happen in the future."

If that is the case, I thought to myself, the country will need to get used to a less than spellbinding orator. In that utterly pedestrian speech, Ford uttered one of the dopier lines of his vice presidency: "General revenue-sharing is as basic to the new federalism as shrimp is to the Creole."

Another week, more waffling. Nixon had turned over nineteen "edited" transcripts of his Oval Office conversations to the House Judiciary Committee. In Delaware on May 22, the same day the White House said it wouldn't give the committee anything more, Ford criticized the decision. "Let's get it all out there and the quicker the better," he argued.

Nixon was livid, and Ford was summoned to the White House the very next day for a private chat. It didn't go well; I know that because in an off-the-record interview that I was able to use only after it was heavily doctored, he told me so. A telltale sign, according to Ford: Nixon wasn't smoking a pipe, which he usually did when he and Ford were alone.

Ford confided that he'd told Nixon his hard line on the tapes was counterproductive and that by opposing Nixon's stand, he was giving his defense of Nixon's innocence more credibility. Nixon wasn't buying.

Then, Ford said, he'd warned Nixon that if he didn't turn over more tapes, he almost certainly would be impeached.

"I made my position clear and he made his position clear," Ford guardedly told me.

Ford always wore his emotions on his sleeve; on a trip to Lansing, Michigan, the next day, he appeared visibly tense and upset. It was apparent the meeting had thrown him off balance.

On May 28, Nixon singled Ford out for his "terrific job" at a hastily arranged cabinet meeting. The stroking worked; in Charlotte later that day, before playing golf with Billy Graham at the Kemper Open, Ford touted his bonds to the boss: "The president and I have had an excellent personal, social, political relationship, and I see no change whatsoever despite what some have speculated. We are firm friends."

The next day in Birmingham, he recanted his previous criticism, saying Nixon's decision to hold off on more tapes "is proper" for the time being.

It drove his staff crazy. They privately fretted to me and other reporters that Ford looked indecisive; his vacillating, one of his closest aides complained, could be fairly construed as a "commentary on his ability to command." Ford's aides knew Nixon was history, too.

Why another maddening reversal? His indiscriminate admission to me in April that Nixon was a goner had been proven out with each new round of revelations and stonewalling. He knew he would be president, and soon. As a wounded nation's new leader, he had to know that the beneficiary of Nixon's demise couldn't be seen as a party to the process that forced him out. If it looked like he was greasing the skids, Republicans would never forgive the man who liked to think of himself as Mr. Republican, and Democrats would surely suspect him of opportunism. His moral authority would be shredded.

I remembered what he'd said in April: When the pages of history are written, nobody can say I contributed to it. Nixon's doom was now certain; the loaded pistol was on the nightstand. Ford was determined not to have his fingerprints on the weapon.

One morning in early July, Mel Elfin called me into his office and laid a huge downer on my head: *Newsweek*'s White House correspondent, Hank Trewhitt, was leaving for the *Baltimore Sun*. I'd be replacing him.

I was crestfallen. I was having the time of my life on the Ford beat; now I was being banished to the Nixon bunker, which had become even more oppressive and hostile to the press as the president's prospects diminished.

I reminded Mel he'd assigned me to Ford in the first place so the magazine would have someone with connections to the new president and his staff. It made no sense to yank me off now, I argued.

Mel was adamant. I was now sufficiently well sourced with the Ford operation, he said, so whenever he took over, I'd be in good shape and already in place at the White House.

I figured Nixon was toast, but guessed he could hang on another six months. That would be pure hell for me, like a major-leaguer banished to the Double-A Texas League of my youth.

I had no choice, so with monumental unhappiness I did as ordered; you didn't say no to Mel Elfin. But I wangled one small concession. Ford had a trip coming up to New Mexico and California that included a meeting with Nixon, who was vacationing at his La Casa Pacifica compound in San Clemente. Mel agreed that I could fly out with Ford, make my goodbyes, and cover the Nixon meeting. But when Ford flew back to Washington, the torch would be passed: I would stick with Nixon.

So on July 12, I flew off on my last *Air Force Two* trip in a bleak mood. It had been such a blast—the most fun I've ever experienced in journalism—but it was over. Ford had been especially generous to me, and I wanted to thank him for that and also explain why he wouldn't see me around anymore. So somewhere between Washington and our first stop in Alamogordo, New Mexico, I wrote out a handwritten goodbye letter to Ford.

At the end, I couldn't resist a little snippet of reality. I said that since I was heading to the White House I expected to see him there before long. "So just consider me your advance man," I signed off.

The next day in California, I was the print pool reporter for the Nixon meeting. Nixon had sent his personal helicopter to pick Ford up, and that's the only time I've ever flown on *Marine One*. (Or maybe it was *Army One;* in those days the Army and Marines each had a helicopter squadron that rotated presidential transport missions.) Then Ford had a dinner speech in Orange County, and afterward he and my friends red-eyed back to Washington.

As I watched from the tarmac as they all flew off without me, my spirits couldn't have been lower. I took a cab to Laguna Beach and prepared to begin my exile on the Nixon death-watch beat.

By the time Ford landed at Andrews, he'd be observing his sixty-first birthday, so his staff had planned a party en route. My colleagues presented him with a rakish birthday card (which I'd signed on the flight between New Mexico and the coast) featuring the rear end of a mule stuck astride a fence and the caption "You're damned if you do and damned if you don't."

During the festivities, Ford mentioned he was sorry I was AWOL but that he'd gotten a letter from me he hadn't read. When he fished it from a pocket, my press colleagues talked him into sharing the letter to the assembled.

Memo to future vice presidents in waiting: never read in a public forum a private communication that you haven't vetted first.

All was well enough until he got to my last line. He paused, instinctively understanding the reaction he'd get. But he was in too far—my media pals goaded him to keep reading. Visibly uncomfortable, he did so, and lusty applause erupted from the audience over the advance man line.

Eleven days later, I received a very generous letter from Ford:

*Yours is one of the most touching letters I have ever received from anyone. It was with great appreciation that I read your comment that you "have never been around any politician for whom [you] have greater personal or professional respect."*

*It has been great having you cover me. I am most grateful for your fair and objective reporting and for your fine friendship. I will miss you very much.*

For my money, Ford buried the lead, as journalists like to say. His cryptic third paragraph had this to say: "I also appreciate your comments regarding another matter on which I will not quote you. Thank you very much."

Ah, I thought, Ford gets the joke. I remembered our momentous conversation of April 17, when he'd told me he knew he was going to be president. Now he was signaling me that he indeed knew he would be sitting in the Oval Office—and even sooner than I had feared when

I'd been reassigned. Suddenly my grim Nixon duty seemed a little more tolerable. As George W. Bush would say at every stop of his 2000 campaign, help is on the way.

A few days later, however, I heard from one of his aides that Ford was irritated about my letter. The implication was that I had sandbagged him by putting him on the spot in front of my colleagues. I remember saying, in my defense, that I'd never dreamed it would be seen by anyone but his staff, much less read aloud in a public setting. I did some more checking, and heard the same thing: he's irked with you.

Improbably, I brooded, Ford and I had now come full circle. We'd started out on a lousy footing, then developed a strong professional bond. Now I was back in the doghouse where I'd started, and he was about to become the next president.

History records what happened not long thereafter. The Supreme Court had ruled on July 24—the day before my letter from Ford was dated—that Nixon must hand over the tapes to Jaworski. Three days later, the House Judiciary Committee voted the first of three articles of impeachment against Nixon. On August 5, the White House reluctantly released the "smoking gun" tapes proving that Nixon had approved of the cover-up. I called Mel Elfin from the White House and read him a couple of sentences. It was over.

On August 8, Nixon told the nation he'd resign the next day. Watching his speech on a tiny black-and-white television in the basement of the press room, I heard a tumultuous roar of approval from the thousands of demonstrators across Pennsylvania Avenue in Lafayette Park.

The next morning, after an emotional farewell address to his distraught staff, Nixon walked to *Army One,* accompanied by his vice president and their spouses. At the top of the steps he waved goodbye; then, in almost an afterthought, he flashed that signature double-V salute that his enemies despised, and helicoptered off to exile to await history's judgment.

As I walked back into the White House to await Ford's swearing-in,

I noticed a hard-nosed, middle-aged guy with tears streaming down his cheeks. It was Dick Keiser, the head of Nixon's Secret Service detail.

Exactly one week later—Friday, August 16—Ford hosted his first state dinner, with King Hussein of Jordan.

I was shocked to receive an invitation to the dinner, but that was Jerry Ford. The *Air Force Two* regulars were invited guests that night.

I'd been in a couple of pools with the new president but hadn't gotten close enough to speak with him. As I stood in the East Room receiving line before the dinner, I was filled with trepidation. After the letter flap, I was sure he'd give me the cold shoulder.

Finally, it was my turn to be introduced by a young military social aide who had no idea that Ford and I had ever met.

"Mr. President, Mr. Thomas DeFrank of *Newsweek* magazine."

"Hello, Mr. President. Congratulations."

"Hello, Tom, nice to see you." (That was the standard Ford greeting; no tipoff to his mindset there.)

Then he turned to the king. "Your Majesty," he said, "I'd like you to meet Tom DeFrank. He's one of my advance men."

Before I could react, out came that hearty Midwest bellow that was another Ford trademark.

King Hussein didn't have a clue what was going down.

"My congratulations, sir." He smiled, earnestly shaking my hand.

It was a classic "gotcha" moment. But the real message, which I absorbed with enormous relief, was that Ford and I were back in business.

# THREE

# White House Years

A Nixon partisan once predicted that Watergate would eventually evaporate like an evanescent cloud. Instead it had cast a funereal pall over the country and the White House. That August evening in the East Room, the cloud began lifting.

That first Ford state dinner marked a seismic correction to the style of the arrogant, secretive, and oppressive attitude of the Nixon years. In just a couple of hours, the camaraderie and the conviviality of that dinner seemed to dissipate much of the angst and rancor that had turned the president's house into a fortress for the previous four years. The sea change was remarkable.

For instance, I'm confident in predicting that Jerry Ford will be the first, last, and only president of the United States to dance at the White House to Jim Croce's street-dude ballad "Bad, Bad Leroy Brown."

But long before the new president boogied with the wife of NBC News's Ron Nessen, later to become his press secretary, the new mood of the place was apparent to all.

At the predinner reception, Senator Mark Hatfield of Oregon walked up to a friend, stuck out his hand, and beamed. "Happy New Year," he said.

JFK and LBJ secretary of defense Robert McNamara, a fellow Michigander who had been added to the guest list by Ford himself, told fellow invitees that he'd returned from Venezuela the night before and had planned to fly to Aspen—until the invitation arrived.

Shocked and delighted at being included—McNamara was *persona non grata* in the Nixon regime—the former president of the Ford Motor Company was overcome by the high drama and emotion of the moment. Trembling, he pointed at Ford and said, "I wouldn't have missed it for anything. Civility had gotten lost in the country, but this man has America smiling again."

Henry Kissinger greeted McNamara warmly. "My God," he said, "you know things have changed when they let *you* in here."

They had indeed—but the new mood had been apparent even before Ford had taken the oath of office in the same room just a week before.

By design, the president-to-be strode into the East Room with a distinct absence of fanfare. It was a solemn, sad moment in our history, Ford had told his aides, not cause for celebration. So at his express order, the ubiquitous presidential anthem, "Hail to the Chief," wasn't played to herald his arrival.

Long ago, history settled on the operative sound bite from that inaugural address:

"My fellow Americans, our long national nightmare is over. Our Constitution works; our great Republic is a government of laws and not of men. Here, the people rule."

As I stood in a corner of the East Room watching him promise not to let America down, my mind kept returning to a line he had used all the time as vice president: "I'm a Ford, not a Lincoln." It was a clever device to lower expectations, but also a window into Ford's humility.

My most enduring memory of that historic day has nothing to do with Ford. As the audience assembled in the East Room, I was struck by the pathos of chief of staff Alexander Haig trying to comfort Nixon's personal secretary Rose Mary Woods as they waited for Ford to arrive. Haig kept patting Woods on the arm, as if to reassure her that life would go on without her former boss. A superloyalist until her last breath in 2005, Rose Woods was in no mood for consolation: she stared straight ahead, eyes fixed on the lectern, trying, I thought, to control her rage and grief. By outward appearances, her life was over.

In the next few days, Ford and his lieutenants set about reassuring the nation and the world that nothing had changed in America except presidents. They also worked overtime dismantling the stuffy and imperial Nixon aura.

It wasn't a behavioral stretch for the new president: he was as unimperial a politician as I've ever encountered.

He commuted to the Oval Office from his Alexandria home for a few weeks, for example, before finally settling in to the White House. After church services in Virginia one Sunday, the Fords swung by the house to check on the status of the packing. The new president saw an open carton in the living room. Reaching in, he discovered his World War II Navy uniforms—khakis, whites, blues—meticulously folded by Betty.

"Well, I guess we should send them to Goodwill," he observed.

Betty smiled. "Jerry, I think some of this stuff may be a little important now. We'd better keep them."

"Well, okay," her husband said. Those uniforms now reside in the Ford Museum in Grand Rapids.

The Ford takeover may have been the most stylistically jarring switch since John Quincy Adams and his Boston Brahmins were replaced by Andrew Jackson and his frontier ruffian pals.

Word was passed that the White House family quarters henceforth would be known as "the residence," instead of "the Executive Mansion." Nixon's grandiose name change for *Air Force One, The Spirit of '76,* was swiftly repealed. When he wasn't busy toasting his own English muffins or having cottage cheese and ketchup for lunch, Ford replaced the unpopular Ron Ziegler as press secretary with Jerald terHorst, a widely admired journalist. He also told his senior staff they could talk with reporters without having their contacts cleared by the press office.

To reinforce the image of bipartisanship he'd pledged in his inaugural speech, Ford decided not to attend any campaign fundraisers in the fall. He banned Nixon's practice of having church services at the White House; this president would come to God, not vice versa. He met guests at the door to the Oval Office instead of waiting at the imperial desk. He let his counselor Bob Hartmann use the private presidential toilet. When his golden retriever Liberty needed to answer nature's call in the middle of the night, Ford would grab his bathrobe and walk her to the South Lawn himself. And he decided to offer conditional amnesty to young men who'd fled the country to avoid being drafted for Vietnam.

"The real reason he likes living in the White House," a senior counselor joked, "is because he drops his laundry down a chute at night and it comes back clean in the morning."

But there was one serious new-life downside for a president religious about his daily aquatic regimen: his new home's swimming pool, favored by FDR and JFK, was underneath the briefing room and long sealed up.

"Fifteen minutes in the pool," he moaned to an aide, "are worth two martinis."

The humanity offensive worked. The *Washington Post*'s esteemed David Broder described Ford as "the most normal, sane, down-to-earth individual to work in the Oval Office since Harry Truman left." A holdover West Wing secretary told me at the end of Ford's first week, "I haven't seen so many smiles around here in a long, long time."

This cheery era of good Ford feeling abruptly imploded twenty-three days later, at 11:05 on the morning of Sunday, September 8.

At 8:30 A.M., press office staffers began alerting media regulars that Ford would have something to say in a couple of hours. Newsmagazine reporters got an extra bit of off-the-record guidance: might be a smart idea to stop your presses.

During his vice presidential confirmation hearings, Ford was asked about the possibility of pardoning Nixon, before he'd been indicted. "I do not think the public would stand for it," he'd replied. That was prophetic in the extreme.

Speaking on live national television from his desk in the Oval Office, Ford called Nixon's plight "an American tragedy" that was "threatening his health"—three words he inserted into the text his staff had prepared. "Someone must write the end to it. I have concluded that only I can do that."

He granted his predecessor a "full, free, and absolute pardon," signing it on the spot.

It wasn't as if he hadn't warned us. At his first press conference, on August 28, where he'd worn his congressional tie as a further reminder of his unimperial side, Ford was asked about the pardon more than once. Instead of brushing it aside as a hypothetical question, he said, "I'm not ruling it out. It is an option, and a proper option for any president." Listened to a third of a century later, those words leap off the videotape. We in the press hadn't been paying sufficient attention; it had sailed right past us all.

A few minutes after the bombshell announcement, I ran into Howard Kerr, who was now working for Ford counselor Jack Marsh in the West Wing. Kerr was standing near the Cabinet Room with Alexander Haig, who had replaced H. R. Haldeman as Nixon's chief of staff and was known to have favored the pardon.

Kerr asked me what I thought. "Howard, he just lost the 1976 election," I replied. Haig begged to differ. "He just made his first presidential decision," the general maintained.

Three decades later, I think Haig and I were both right. I'm still convinced the pardon finished Ford's chance to escape the historically unique status of being America's only unelected vice president and president, an anomaly that bothered him far more than he ever admitted.

In time, however, the pardon has also been judged a principled decision of statecraft that helped right a wounded and polarized nation after a profound constitutional crisis. Ford always believed that winning the Profile in Courage Award from the John F. Kennedy Library in 2001 for the pardon was not just one of the great honors of his life; it was historical vindication as well, an acknowledgment from onetime political foes that would embellish his legacy forever.

That was hardly apparent at the moment, to put it mildly.

Overnight, the healing stopped. Ford had sought to cauterize the wound of Watergate; instead, he'd ripped off the scab. In the process, he'd grievously damaged his own political prospects as well as his ability to pick up the pieces of government and craft a bipartisan agenda.

The enormous reservoir of goodwill Ford had enjoyed, especially with his Democratic cronies on Capitol Hill, swiftly dissipated. His popularity plummeted, making it easier for the Democrats who liked him personally to doubt him politically. In turn that made it harder for Ford to rally support for dealing with runaway inflation or the Vietnam War.

When he nominated George H. W. Bush director of the Central Intelligence Agency, Senate Democrats made Ford promise Bush wouldn't be his running mate in 1976. Before the pardon, that wouldn't have happened, but Ford had squandered his political leverage with the pardon.

Democrats said he was just another pol cutting just another deal for a discredited crony. The country appeared to agree: in the November elections, Republicans were obliterated. The Democrats gained forty-nine seats in Jerry Ford's House, giving them more than a two-to-one majority. The new president could kiss his legislative agenda goodbye in the 94th Congress.

With the party and Ford's moral authority in tatters, the conservative Republican wing was emboldened to abandon a leader they'd never much liked. By year's end, Ronald Reagan decided Ford was sufficiently weak to challenge a sitting president for his party's nomination in 1976.

Within hours, the collateral cost of his decision manifested itself in a very personal way for Ford. Not long before *Newsweek* closed its pardon package that Sunday afternoon, I called terHorst as a safety check. I simply wanted to make sure there was a "lid" for the day at the White House, a time-honored signal that reporters can safely stand down until the next news cycle.

I had no particular reason to say that I assumed nobody on the White House staff had resigned because of Ford's decision.

"What's your question?" Jerry asked.

"Has anybody on the president's staff resigned in protest over the pardon?"

"Yes," he said.

"Who?"

"Me."

Ford was stunned when he'd learned, but couldn't talk his press secretary into reconsidering. Ford wished him well, but their relationship never recovered.

The rapport between Ford and us *Air Force Two* alumni, whom he always went out of his way to recognize at press conferences, remained intact. Energized by our presence at the state dinner, the veep-beat regulars began planning an *Air Force Two* reunion for his Christmas trip to Vail. We knew he'd come; at a reunion barbecue at Ron Nessen's house nine days after becoming president, he'd been invited, and had accepted on the spot.

In planning for the party, we all got a quick lesson in how the logistical train required for every presidential movement complicates the spontaneity of any event. Instead of a handful of aides, social directors suddenly have to factor in personal aides, doctors, communications specialists, the military guy with the nuclear codes, and exponentially more Secret Service agents. It's far worse these days; the now routine hassle of magnetometers was still years away.

There was no way to duplicate the informality we'd taken for granted in the pre–August 9 universe, or so we thought until Ford blasted right through the institutional barriers.

He walked in the door of my rented condo, unannounced and unnoticed, made straight for the kitchen, and asked as heads swiveled, "Who needs a drink?" For a half hour or so, he wasn't the leader of the free world anymore. If he hadn't been on holiday, he might as well have been wearing one of his congressional ties.

He mixed and mingled with the two dozen guests, then took the seat of honor on a sofa and fired up his pipe. It was small talk, mainly; he remarked on how much easier the Christmas of 1973 had been. He described the seismic shift in his life with a simple "before things changed."

About five minutes before he was scheduled to leave, he shifted in his seat and crossed his legs, managing to plant a loafer dead in the center of a two-pound wheel of Brie on the coffee table.

It's not often that reporters are eyewitnesses to that sort of social faux pas, particularly when a president is the perpetrator, and here was a boatload of them, trying to keep from giggling as Ford puffed on his pipe and blithely chatted away.

I had nightmare visions of Ford standing to leave, accompanied by his new best Brie. No way that story would stay in the room. I'd probably be pressed to write something for the magazine. The gossips would have a field day. I'd be blamed by his staff, of course.

All eyes were on the cheese, except Ford's. So he didn't notice, as he stood up, that the cheese stuck to the bottom of his shoe for a heartstopping instant—before quietly plopping back onto the plate. He never knew. The reunion was a resounding success.

Later, when he started bumping his head on helicopter doors and fell down the steps of *Air Force One,* those of us who were graced by his generous company that night always said to ourselves: we've seen this movie before.

For the rest of his term, Ford was reduced to playing defense, fighting fires with the Soviets, the Democrats, and the Republican conservatives.

His White House staff was an uneasy amalgam of old-timers like Bob Hartmann, his congressional counselor and *über*-speechwriter, and new recruits like chief of staff Donald Rumsfeld and his young deputy Dick Cheney, whom Hartmann disdained as "the praetorians." For all Ford's geniality, the constant internecine warfare between the factions frequently got in the way of policymaking.

It was an unusually strong cabinet—Kissinger at State, Bill Simon at Treasury, Ed Levi at Justice, Bill Coleman at Transportation, Cap Weinberger at HEW, Jim Lynn and later Carla Hills at HUD—but because of the pardon, they were dealing with a weak hand, and time was short.

In a little more than two years, Ford confronted his share of governmental grief: runaway inflation and high unemployment, the traumatic end of a wrenching war in Vietnam, a major cabinet shake-up, a looming energy crisis, and escalating Cold War tensions with the Soviets and North Koreans.

He knew 1976 would be a bruising political year, so he crammed all his foreign travel into 1975 to keep the election year clear for maximum campaigning. Beginning with a trip to Japan, Korea, and Vladivostok in November 1974, he made seven foreign trips in thirteen months, including the People's Republic of China and three trips to Europe.

In his spare time, he welcomed the Emperor of Japan to the White House, dealt with his wife's breast cancer surgery, fired his CIA director and secretary of defense, named John Paul Stevens to the Supreme

Court, dumped Vice President Nelson Rockefeller, and juggled a bona fide international crisis.

On May 12, 1975, an American merchant ship, the *Mayagüez,* was seized off the coast of Cambodia and its thirty-nine civilian crew members were taken ashore by members of the Khmer Rouge. After three days of intense deliberation with his National Security Council, Ford ordered air strikes to retrieve the ship and rescue the crew.

The operation was a success; Ford got the word after being pulled from a black-tie dinner with the Dutch prime minister. He wanted to trumpet the good news and knew he shouldn't appear in the press room in his tuxedo. So he changed into a brown business suit, but forgot to replace his patent leather pumps.

At 12:30 in the morning, he exited the press room and walked down the colonnade that connects the West Wing to the state rooms and family quarters. Watching from behind, I thought he looked like a man with the world's weight still on his broad shoulders.

Just before he disappeared into the residence, he turned to an aide and posed a question. A couple of days later, I caught up with the aide and asked about his query.

Ford had merely asked, "Say, does anyone know who won the Bullets game?"

As he wrote in his memoirs, "Once I determine to move, I seldom, if ever, fret."

Four months later, Ford confronted an even greater crisis, this one personal. On the morning of September 5, 1975, Ford set out from Sacramento's Senator Hotel for a meeting in the Capitol with California Governor Jerry Brown and a speech to the legislature. It was a very short distance and it was a sunny day, so Ford decided to walk, something that would never happen today. The press pool accompanying Ford was about fifteen feet behind him on his right.

We crossed L Street and began a leisurely stroll up a curving walkway through the statehouse grounds. Spectators standing two or three deep lined both sides of the sidewalk, and Ford shook a few hands en route.

About a hundred yards from the rear entrance to the Capitol building, someone suddenly yelled, "Gun." I later learned it was Secret Service agent Larry Buendorf, who plunged into the crowd.

"Get down, let's go," barked Ernie Luzania, who had been the chief of Ford's vice presidential Secret Service detail and had followed him to the White House.

Simultaneously, the agents nearest Ford formed what reminded me of a football huddle around him. Luzania and a second agent grabbed the president by the scruff of his blue suit jacket and pushed him forward so forcefully that he buckled over almost to his knees. The protective cluster set out for the statehouse in a full gallop, with the press pool in hot pursuit.

We caught up with Ford on the steps of the Capitol. Just before the president disappeared inside, ABC's Steve Bell asked him, "Are you all right, sir?"

Ford's face was ashen, his demeanor grim. He was so shaken, in fact, that he could barely answer Steve's question. "Sure," he whispered, managing a nod that signaled the pool that he was okay.

As I described the moment in the pool report delivered verbally in a frenzied press room a few minutes later, "He seemed to me stunned, bewildered, dazed, something like that, and it was clear that he knew what had happened."

That's because he had stared squarely into the barrel of a .45-caliber handgun brandished by the now infamous Lady in Red: Lynette "Squeaky" Fromme, a twenty-six-year-old disciple of convicted murderer Charles Manson.

As Fromme famously noted when the agents handcuffed her, "It didn't go off." There were four rounds in the weapon, but none was in the firing chamber.

Press pools are a staple of news coverage, a vehicle used to keep a manageable number of journalists in proximity to a president in case he decides to commit news or something unexpected occurs. Poolers are charged with staying with the "body" at all times; we couldn't peel off to see what had caused all the commotion. By the time we'd finished briefing our absentee colleagues, Fromme was long gone, the crime scene secured, and the crowd dispersed.

That pool was a curious historical anomaly: we were all eyewitnesses to an assassination attempt against a sitting president—but never saw a thing until we reviewed the videotape later. Because we were behind and to Ford's right and Fromme was ahead on the left, the scrum of agents and staff blocked our view.

From outward appearances, Ford shrugged off the death-defying encounter; he didn't even mention it during a forty-five-minute chat with Brown. But a few days later, I encountered him at a social event, and he couldn't stop talking about nearly getting killed. It was clear he hadn't gotten it out of his system.

"I extended my left hand to her—that's when I saw the gun," he told me. "Then Ernie grabbed me, and I was gone."

Incredibly, it happened again in San Francisco, just seventeen days later. Ford was leaving the St. Francis Hotel on Union Square after a local television interview. He emerged from a side entrance and waved to a large crowd on the north side of Post Street.

Then the pop of a single gunshot rang out, clearly heard by those of us in the press bus, which was pulled up near Ford's limousine. Two agents flung Ford into the car and the motorcade tore away from the hotel. As the bus lurched forward, we could see a huddle of police and agents surrounding someone in the crowd. She later turned out to be Sara Jane Moore, who had fired a .38 revolver at Ford. Her errant shot slammed into the facing of the hotel.

By year's end, Ford had switched to full campaign mode to confront Ronald Reagan, who'd announced his Republican primary challenge just before Thanksgiving.

It was a grueling and divisive primary, with Reagan charging that

Ford was an ineffective leader who wanted to give away our Panama Canal and make too many deals with the Soviets, and Ford insisting, mainly through surrogates, that Reagan was naïve, inexperienced, and trigger-happy.

Along the way, there was time for a little fun—like the Saturday in San Antonio when after a speech at the Alamo he attended a reception in his honor given by the Daughters of the Republic of Texas and dug into a homemade tamale before remembering to remove the corn husk.

He and Dick Cheney were also the ringleaders of one of the more ambitious pranks in White House press lore. Unfortunately from my perspective, it was at my expense.

On March 5, 1976, Ford was in Peoria campaigning in the Illinois primary. His entourage spent the night at the Peoria Hilton.

I was already in bed when my phone rang around 11:30 P.M. It was press secretary Ron Nessen, my old comrade-in-arms from *Air Force Two*. He told me he had a great piece of gossip if I could meet him in the hotel bar. I wasn't thrilled and tried to get him to spill over the phone, but he was persistent; he wanted to do it in person. He promised his info would be perfect for *Newsweek*'s Periscope section. He'd found my soft underbelly: in those days, we were paid extra for Periscope items.

I trudged downstairs for a quick drink and Nessen's "hot tip," something so lame neither he nor I can remember it. Irked by being yanked from bed, I went back to my eighth-floor room to discover a dozen of my colleagues hiding in the bathroom, and a sheep so terrified that she kept depositing remembrances of her visit on the carpet.

What became known as The Sheep Incident was masterminded by *New York Times* beat reporter Jim Naughton, supposedly to honor my pedigree as a graduate of Texas A&M, renowned for its agricultural and military heritage.

Ford had bestowed his full blessing on the scheme and had given Cheney permission to make the arrangements. That wasn't a mere courtesy; livestock, after all, aren't ordinarily cleared by the Secret Service into hotels where a president is sleeping.

By coincidence, I was the magazine pool reporter for Ford's first "movement" the next morning. In those days, pool reporters were routinely allowed in actual physical proximity to a president; by contrast, these days President Bush is out of his limousine before the pool van rolls to a stop at the rear of his motorcade.

Ford popped out of an elevator and saw me: roadkill.

He had so much fun with this that he put the tale in his memoirs. "How's your friend?" he has himself gleefully wondering.

Another published version of our encounter quotes him asking, "Did you boys play well in Peoria?"

After he managed to stop giggling, what he actually said was, "I understand you had company last night."

Nessen had the last word, and best line; just before the motorcade pulled away from the Hilton, he appeared at the door of the press bus and chortled. "Tommy, there's a sheep in the lobby crying her eyes out."

That was one of the few mirthful interludes in that bitterly contested campaign. After months of mortal combat, Ford had just barely beat back Reagan's challenge at the Kansas City convention, winning renomination by a couple of dozen delegates. But he was left with a horribly fractured party and the Nixon pardon dragging him down. In the general election, he started out dead in the water, nearly thirty points behind former Georgia governor Jimmy Carter.

He wasn't a particularly effective campaigner. Until Ronald Reagan and the Presidents Bush came along to trump him, Ford's verbal bloopers were the gold standard for rhetorical malapropisms:

Uran-um. Beverly Stills. Ma-*zell*-tov. Judga-ment. Geothermer energy. And his thanks to a priest who'd delivered an invocation: *"Merci, garçon."*

Gradually, however, he managed to narrow Carter's once impregnable margin. In an Oval Office interview five weeks before the election, Ford was sounding more bullish about his prospects.

"I'm optimistic, I really am," he told me, "on the basis that we have the momentum and they have been dropping off. Number two, they are getting very strident, very partisan and very personal"— characteristics Ford believed were always symptoms of a campaign in trouble.

The optimism of that interview was rendered obsolete exactly one week later at the Palace of Fine Arts in San Francisco, when at the second debate with Jimmy Carter, Ford uttered a memorable election gaffe: "There is no Soviet domination of Eastern Europe, and there never will be under a Ford administration."

With that one sentence, momentum abruptly shifted back to the challenger. Carter's handlers gleefully exploited their opening, saying Ford had shown he really didn't have a firm grasp on foreign policy. It took twenty-four hours of fighting with an unusually stubborn president before Cheney, in a southern California parking lot, finally persuaded a recalcitrant Ford that he had to issue a "clarification" to stop the bleeding.

Many of Ford's senior campaign hands still believe the contretemps threw Ford onto the defensive for just long enough to make a lethal difference.

His handlers had kept him bottled up in the Rose Garden for most of the campaign because, as chief strategist Stu Spencer immortally told him to his face one day in the Oval Office, "Forgive me, Mr. President, but you're a fucked-up campaigner." They finally let him out for a final ten-day blitz, and to the surprise of some of his aides he rose to the rhetorical occasion. To nobody's surprise, he ended his surge with a rally in Grand Rapids.

After voting at an elementary school near his old home next morning, an exhausted Ford kept to his tradition and ate blueberry pancakes at Granny's Kitchen, as he had after voting in each of his thirteen congressional elections. He paid $4.37 for himself and Betty. Then he flew back to the White House for the denouement, convinced that his strong performance down the stretch would pull him through, if barely.

To chart the eleventh-hour ebb and flow of Ford's fortunes, I'd asked

Dick Cheney to let me spend the evening in his corner West Wing office, just a handful of steps from where he operates today. The chief of staff had graciously agreed.

As the polls began closing, I was struck by the absence of much emotion among Ford's chief lieutenants, which I read as a bit of a down indicator.

Throughout the evening, as returns rolled in on two color television sets and three miniature black-and-whites, the staff mood began to worsen and their comments, though largely matter-of-fact, reflected an erosion in confidence.

At 8:40 P.M., Cheney mused, "If we're going to do it, we'll do it by an eyelash in the big states."

Twenty minutes later, he was theorizing that Ford might win the electoral vote but lose the popular vote.

By 9:40, when an aide delivered the bad news that Ford would lose Philadelphia by 270,000 votes, Cheney grimaced.

"We can do it without Pennsylvania, but it's awful tough."

Just before ten o'clock, Cheney looked over at his wife Lynne and warned, "It's gonna be a long night, baby."

Hard to imagine Vice President Cheney saying anything like that, but I was there.

He was certainly right about that.

At 12:30 on Wednesday morning, pollster Bob Teeter got strategist Stu Spencer on the phone and ran through four possible combinations that might still produce a win. They were all a stretch. "The possibilities are getting pretty extreme," admitted Teeter, always an honest guy with the numbers.

Cheney looked up from his calculator and legal pad to announce at 1:03, "Without Texas or New York, we're at 266—if we take Ohio, Michigan, Illinois, and California. Then Hawaii could give us 270," the magic number.

Reliably Democratic Hawaii? Not likely, and Cheney knew it.

Over in the residence, Ford decided he'd had enough. "If I'm going to be worth a damn tomorrow," he told an aide at 3:15, "I'd better go to bed."

At 3:55 A.M., with the outcome still hypothetically in doubt, Cheney announced, "Gentlemen, I'm going to close up the shop."

Although aides knew the signs were ominous, Ford went to bed not knowing if he'd still be president when he awoke. Just before that, Ron Nessen arrived in the residence, carrying the United Press International flash giving the election to Carter. Not seeing Ford, he didn't have the heart to pass it along.

Somehow, it made psychic sense for Ford to learn the news from photographer Dave Kennerly, who'd become his de facto fourth son.

"I'm afraid we've had it," the usually irrepressible photographer told him at 9:00 A.M.

My final image of that long night was Kennerly, his feet propped up on Cheney's conference table.

"You know," he said, "I'll bet the pardon had a lot to do with this. I don't think he ever really got over the effects of it."

At 12:14 Wednesday afternoon, the Ford clan trooped into the press room. They all looked stricken except Betty, whose cheerfulness seemed to say that her side may have been vanquished but she'd won, because she was about to see a lot more of her husband.

Ford had lost his voice and could barely rasp out a few painful words:

"It is perfectly obvious that my voice isn't up to par, and I shouldn't be making very many comments, and I won't. But I did want Betty, Mike, Jack, Steve, Susan, and [daughter-in-law] Gayle to come down with me and to listen while Betty reads a statement that I have sent to Governor Carter. . . .

"But I do want to express on a personal basis my appreciation and that of my family for the friendship that all of us have had. And after Betty reads the statement that was sent to Governor Carter by me, I think all of us—Betty, the children, and myself—would like to just come down and shake hands and express our appreciation personally."

Betty, whom he'd introduced as "the real spokesman for the family," read a poignant statement that, given the pain on his face, was mercifully brief.

"It has been the greatest honor of my husband's life to have served his fellow Americans during two of the most difficult years in our history," she said, thanking his supporters and urging the country to give "your united support" to the president-elect.

Then she read the "Dear Jimmy" concession telegram, which said in part, "Although there will continue to be disagreements over the best means to use in pursuing our goals, I want to assure you that you will have my complete and wholehearted support as you take the oath of office this January."

Then, as advertised, all seven of the Fords stepped down from the podium and circulated through the press room, case studies of grace under emotional strain. I can't remember what Mrs. Ford said as she grasped my hand, but the president's tortured words are seared into my consciousness, as vivid and painful as I write them now as they were at the moment he uttered them.

"Well, Tom, we had a great time on *Air Force Two*, didn't we?"

I told him those times had been the most fun I'd ever experienced in journalism, and among the best moments of my life. I thanked him for his generosity and said I was sure we'd see each other in the years ahead.

"Don't forget us when we're gone," he whispered in his shredded voice.

I struggled to keep my composure as I managed to reply, "Mr. President, I'll have to live a very long time to be able to reciprocate all the nice things you've done for me."

"Okay, Tom," he said, moving away to work the room.

For another ten or fifteen minutes, he circumnavigated the briefing room, greeting everyone, the film crews, the techs, even a couple of reporters he didn't like.

Gradually, he worked his way back to the front to return to the

Oval Office. He saw me again, and walked over to where I was standing. So numbed by the raw emotion of the moment, I guess, he didn't realize we'd played this scene minutes before. So we both had to struggle through the sorrowful minuet a second time.

"Those were great times on *Air Force Two,* weren't they?" he said.

It could not have been over soon enough for me. I've spent thousands of days in that room, more than any other professional venue; those two fleeting exchanges were the most wrenching moments I've ever endured there.

Presidential transitions are always the worst of ordeals for the departing. They've suddenly become yesterday's people. The national spotlight obsesses with the president-elect, his transition team, his cabinet and White House appointments, his every utterance. Overnight, the White House is a death-watch beat, where everyone but the president himself is worrying about the next paycheck.

Ford flew off to California for a week of golf and emotional rehab. To the alarm of his retainers, the vacation didn't get him out of the doldrums. He was so down that when the *New York Times* asked to interview him for his obituary, Ford got unusually agitated. "I'm not interested in obit interviews," he snapped. The very idea made him feel like a has-been.

In late November, *Newsweek* ran a story reporting that Ford was taking his defeat exceptionally hard—so hard that a naturally gregarious guy had become something of a recluse.

"He's just unbelievably disgusted with himself for losing," one old friend told me, "and every day, as he hands over more power, it drives the point home deeper."

After Jimmy and Rosalynn Carter visited the Fords, a top Ford aide scathingly complained to me, "He'll probably take Carter through the residence next time to see if there are any coats or ties or anything else he wants. That's probably why he lost the election."

The story was headlined "Jerry Ford's Blues," but around the West Wing it became universally known as "The Sulking Story." Dick

Growald of UPI did a clever cartoon of Ford skiing at Vail with a Cheshire-cat grin plastered across his face. "He doesn't want DeFrank reporting he's sulking," the caption read.

I heard he was irked about the piece, especially the wardrobe line. But nobody told me I was wrong. Nearly all his closest aides, in fact, including several who personally assured him they hadn't helped me, were my sources.

In time, he recovered his emotional balance and reconciled himself to building his new life in the desert and presiding over a graceful if unwelcome transition of power.

To commemorate another Ford passage, we in the remaining *Air Force Two* press corps decided to have an Auld Lang Syne reunion on New Year's Eve. Just five Slingshot Airlines alumni were along on that bittersweet vacation for Ford, and only three of the originals: CBS's Phil Jones, the VOA's Bob Leonard, and me. The venue was the same as the first in December 1974, my rented Vail condo overlooking the creek in the center of town.

Even before we heard back, we knew Ford would show up; he'd come to the second, at Maggie Hunter's home in the winter of 1975, and there was no way he'd skip the finale. That's just the way he was.

He arrived on time and stayed nearly an hour, reminiscing about those halcyon days of yore. He remembered that night returning to Palm Springs when the plane hit an air pocket and plunged downward, dumping a gin and tonic onto his head and scaring the hell out of all of us.

He was in high spirits that night; the blues that had seized him for several weeks after losing had vanished completely. Curiously, he wanted to know about life in Plains, Georgia, his successor's hometown. I remember him roaring with glee when I said that the British must have had Plains in mind when they envisioned Georgia as a penal colony in the eighteenth century.

Solicitous as ever, he wanted to know how I'd dislocated my right shoulder playing tennis early that morning. He told a long story about how he'd done the same thing courting Betty during a ski vacation in Michigan.

"You're going to have problems with it for the rest of your life," he warned.

My colleagues and I were struck by Ford's liberal use of profanity. Even in those private sessions aboard *Air Force Two* when he'd loosen his tie and unload on political opponents, he'd never curse. But this night the hells and damns and craps flew off his tongue; hardly Nixonesque blue-streak profanity, but out of character for Ford. The conclusion was obvious: as a soon-to-be unemployed politician, he no longer felt any need to watch his language.

At the end, we presented him with a plaque featuring an engraving of our aging propeller plane and this inscription: "From the bright-eyed and bushy-tailed survivors of *Air Force Two*—'Slingshot Airlines'— in appreciation for good times. Best wishes for clear skies and tailwinds."*

His eyes misted a bit as he said that while he'd enjoyed every moment of being president, he likewise remembered the *Air Force Two* era with special affection. He posed for a farewell group photo and went back home to get ready for his own New Year's Eve party, to which the *Air Force Two* charter members were also invited.

That's where he laughed uproariously over a gag gift—a Ski Poland travel poster. UPI's Growald had altered the headline to read "Ski Free Poland," a witty reference to Ford's calamitous remark in the second debate.

---

*That cozy little plane, whose Air Force tail number was 42815, still flies. After being used successively by the Air Force, the Navy, the State Department, and the Peruvian national police, it was rescued from a military boneyard in Arizona by a commercial cargo outfit in 1999. Its latest incarnation: in the spring of 2008, the Canadian government will begin using it as a "water bomber" fighting forest fires in the province of Saskatchewan.

W hen I returned to Washington, I retrieved the *Air Force Two* class photo from the first reunion to compare with the new one. The contrast was astounding; in 1974 he looked a decade younger. Maybe he hadn't enjoyed every minute of being president after all; in any event, the rigors of the job had aged him dramatically in just two years. Presidencies have a way of doing that, even with younger men. Just compare the photographs of George W. Bush in his first year with today's images.

On January 20, 1977, Ford reluctantly passed the baton to Jimmy Carter and flew off to retirement in southern California, where Richard Nixon had also begun his political rehabilitation.

By the time Ford reached Andrews Air Force Base, the trappings of executive power were already slipping away. Left behind at the Capitol were two men never far from his side when traveling—his personal physician, Rear Admiral William Lukash, and a military aide with the "football"—the satchel of ultrasecret codes triggering nuclear attacks against enemy targets only on the commander in chief's personal order.

Departing his *Marine One* chopper for the last time, Ford was greeted with a nineteen-gun salute, not the twenty-one he would have rated two hours earlier. Even the backup *Air Force One* he was flying— the same plane that had brought John F. Kennedy back from Dallas— was now simply a more prosaic *Air Force 26000*.

Normally, presidential pools are assigned by a long-standing formula: wires, networks, print, magazine, photo dogs. On this bittersweet occasion for him, however, Ford ended his presidency the same way he had begun it—with a thoughtful gesture toward the media.

This particular pool was an Auld Lang Syne lineup, handpicked personally by Ford. It included all the *Air Force Two* regulars still in journalism, plus some other Ford family favorites, like Growald.

For the first ninety minutes, the former president and Betty were alone with their memories and their golden retrievers, Liberty and Misty. After his customary brace of martinis, Ford ordered the low-calorie plate: canned salmon, cottage cheese, and raw onion slices. But he indulged himself a final time with two scoops of butter pecan ice cream, his favorite dessert.

Then, coatless and with tie askew, he wandered to the rear of the aircraft for his last airborne interview.

"Do you have anything to tell us?" a reporter asked.

"Well, anything I say isn't very important anymore."

The sting of his defeat had momentarily evaporated. Jerry Ford was his gregarious, bluff, genial self again.

He praised Carter's inaugural speech, shocked his aides by describing the new president as a friend, and offered to help the victor however he could.

"I don't deny I got a little sentimental," he added, "but I tried not to expose it, to keep it within myself. But we've had two and a half great years and you can't help but be a little emotional and sentimental. I'm human, like anybody else."

Later in the flight, Ford invited Dick Growald, Phil Jones, Maggie Hunter, and me up to his cabin for a private adios. My notes record him saying his loneliest day was the Friday evening when Betty was at Bethesda, preparing for cancer surgery. His tensest moments were the *Mayagüez* crisis. He wasn't ruling out running against Carter again in 1980.

The truth is, I remember almost nothing about that moment, except for his parting words.

"It's been great, Tom. Tell your wife hello. Come see us in the desert."

As the ex-president and his wife returned to their memories, the most embarrassing spectacle I've ever witnessed in three decades of flying *Air Force One* was playing out in the press cabin.

Reporters are notorious pack rats, of course, but the wholesale looting by the pool was breathtaking. I should have known what was coming when a pool photographer showed up with two camera bags, one brimming with gear, the other empty.

The keepsakes that passengers grab on every presidential flight went first—the notepads, the matchbooks, the menus, the cigarettes, which were replaced by small boxes of M&M's chocolate candies during the Reagan years.

The grand theft didn't end there. Nothing was safe: pillows, blankets, silverware, napkins, candy dishes—gone. One reporter swiped an entire set of glasses with the presidential seal. Another even took the made-in-Taiwan wicker fruit basket. The feeding frenzy didn't stop until we landed in California. To this day, I still cringe when I think about it.

In a tableau tinged with pathos, Ford bounded from the Boeing 707 after landing in Monterey and instinctively moved toward the fence to work the crowd of two thousand who'd come to bid him farewell. Suddenly, he seemed to remember: it's all over. He was just Good Old Jerry again. He stopped in mid-stride, climbed into a black Cadillac Fleetwood limousine without the trademark presidential seal and flags, and rode away in a six-car motorcade that the day before would have been at least triple the size. By day's end, Citizen Ford was golfing at Pebble Beach with Arnold Palmer.

I was too neurotic to stay and enjoy the Monterey Peninsula. I'd spent only a couple of weeks covering candidate Carter and felt woefully behind the curve with the new president. So I asked Colonel Les McClelland, the presidential pilot, for permission to deadhead back to Andrews. He graciously obliged, and after a brief refueling stop, we flew back to Washington. It was a surreal feeling: I was the only passenger on the most famous aircraft in the world, now empty and darkened.

In an hour or so I'd banged out a file on my portable typewriter, then settled in for a few hours of decompression before worrying about President Carter. In due course, I struck up a conversation with a friendly Air Force flight attendant. After a couple of drinks, I confessed I was mortified at the media thievery.

He didn't seem perturbed at all. "We're used to it," he said cheerfully. "It happens all the time. As a matter of fact, senators and congressmen are the worst. They steal everything that isn't bolted down."

Just as I was starting to feel a little better about the whole squalid affair, he politely inquired, "Incidentally, what did you take?"

I gulped. I blushed. I squirmed. Consumed by guilt, I decided to come clean.

"I only took one thing," I protested. Sheepishly, I pulled from my briefcase a white cotton hand towel I'd lifted from the lavatory on the outbound leg. It had the words "Air Force One" embroidered in royal blue script along the border. A keeper of a souvenir: these days the lav towels are paper in the press cabin.

"Is that *all* you took?" he persisted.

"I promise; I swear, nothing more."

"Well, if that's *really* all you took, you deserve to be rewarded. Come with me."

He led me up to the front of the plane, past deserted cabins that hours before had been crammed with Ford's friends, aides, ex-staffers, and Secret Service agents, past David Kennerly's color portraits of the Fords, now garishly out of place. We entered the former president's private cabin, the inner sanctum ordinarily off-limits to all but the closest presidential intimates. He invited me to sit in Ford's blue, high-backed executive chair while he rooted around in a side cabinet. The very same chair where, a few hours before, Ford had bade farewell to the *Air Force Two* regulars.

After a few seconds, the steward handed me my prize. It was a double bridge deck of genuine Gerald R. Ford autographed playing cards in a blue suede slipcase.

"I guess we won't be needing these anymore," he said. It was the only memento come by honestly that Inaugural Day thirty years ago.

"I think Carter's going to be okay," he said as I was ushered back to the cheap seats, "but it's going to be a helluva long time before we fly any finer man than Ford."

# FOUR

# New Life/
# Jerry Ford Inc.

THE DAY HE LEFT OFFICE in January 1953, Harry Truman boarded a train at Union Station without a penny in federal largesse except a microscopic Army pension. Back home in Independence, Missouri, the newly retired president soon discovered that he couldn't even answer his mail—biographer David McCullough reports he got 72,000 pieces in the first two weeks alone—without dipping deep into his own pocket. Even after selling some property and signing a book deal for his memoirs, Truman complained that he was financially squeezed.

Because of Truman's predicament and some personal lobbying by the 33rd president with former Capitol Hill cronies, Congress eventually passed the Former Presidents Act in 1958. It gave Truman and his successors a $25,000 yearly pension, plus annual stipends for staff, office space, and free use of the mails.

A half-century later, those modest emoluments have escalated dramatically into a massive financial safety net; these days a former president, regardless of his length of service, draws a $191,000 annual pension for life, regularly increased, plus generous appropriations for expenses, travel, staff, office space, and Secret Service protection for at least ten years.

These regal sums, however, are but the tip of the buckraking iceberg available to retired chief executives. In his first year out of office, Bill Clinton earned $9.2 million from speechmaking, delivering a paid lecture every six days on average. More than two-thirds of that income was to audiences in nineteen foreign countries. He earned $350,000, nearly double his presidential salary, for a single talk in Milan. With the help of the international date line, he even managed speeches in New York and Hong Kong on the same day, at a breathtaking $250,000 apiece.

For better or worse, this eye-popping earnings potential exists because of Jerry Ford and his lifelong devotion to free-market, capitalist philosophy.

As an early order of business, in fact, every future president should visit Ford's grave in Grand Rapids and thank him personally for ensuring that each of them will be multimillionaires in perpetuity.

Before Ford's involuntary retirement, the primary income-generating opportunity for ex-presidents was a written memoir of their White House years. At the time it was considered unseemly for them to accept speaking fees, have consulting contracts with corporations or go on their boards. There were occasional exceptions; Dwight Eisenhower decided to supplement his government pensions by becoming president of Columbia. But Congress presumed that anyone who once was the most powerful leader in the universe had sufficient means to live out his days comfortably.

Ford single-handedly rewrote those rules, and always deeply resented critics who accused him of moneygrubbing. The financially strapped college kid who sold his blood to a hospital for $25 a pop was determined to live well in retirement and provide for his four kids and his grandchildren, and made no apologies.

He was enraged, in fact, with his first White House press secretary,

Jerald terHorst (who had resigned after a month on the job the very day Ford pardoned Richard Nixon), after terHorst, an old Michigan friend and veteran journalist, wrote that Ford was making so much money he should be required to have his government pension reduced by a dollar for every two dollars he was making in the private sector.

"Dammit, Tom," he told me a few years into retirement, "it's the free-enterprise system at its finest," pounding his fist on his desk for emphasis.

He certainly practiced what he preached. Between 1977 and 2001, for instance, Ford averaged two trips a year to Las Vegas, and he wasn't a gambler. They were speaking gigs, mostly to well-heeled conventioneers.

Not all his enterprises were income-generating. In a given year he always made far more pro bono appearances, and raised millions for charitable causes. He estimated that he turned down three or four paying propositions for every one he accepted.

Still, he earned boxcars of cash, well beyond his expectations. At the age of sixty-four he was the first former president with both the esteem and the energy to pursue an aggressive agenda of retirement opportunities. Roosevelt and Kennedy had died in office; Truman had left Washington with his reputation and popularity in tatters; Lyndon Johnson, already independently wealthy, was in poor health and saddled by Vietnam; Nixon was in abject disgrace. Ford also had the good fortune to become a commodity in the marketplace at a moment when speaking fees available to big-name public figures were exploding.

At the peak of his commercial activities, Ford was earning $3 million to $4 million every year. The first decade after leaving Washington, he averaged twenty-three travel days a month, and a normal day on the road involved five separate events. He was so flush with cash that he paid off the mortgage on his Rancho Mirage home in a mere eighteen months. At his death, informed estimates of his net worth were in the $25 million range.

"I was young enough when I left and I was healthy enough," he explained to me in 1992. "I wanted to have some ongoing interests. I didn't feel like coming out here and playing golf seven days a week, and I didn't want a full-time job. So I developed a broad-based list of activities."

At 7:33 on a sun-splashed July morning in 1977, Gerald R. Ford emerged from the kitchen of his rented chalet in Vail, Colorado. Wearing a white terrycloth bathrobe emblazoned with blue tennis rackets crossed like sabers, he sauntered past strawberry plants showing signs of chipmunk damage.

"This is the earliest Barrett has been up in months," he twitted a distinctly slit-eyed Bob Barrett, his White House military aide who'd resigned his Army commission to journey westward with the ex-president as his retirement chief of staff.

Then Ford plunged into a covered, heated swimming pool for the first of his two daily swims. A dozen hard laps later he pulled himself from the water and onto an aquamarine scale. "One-ninety-seven," he said, only two pounds more than his best weight during the White House years. "Not bad."

Six months after he left Washington, the bitterness of his narrow loss to Jimmy Carter seemed to have largely dissipated. "It's been an exhilarating experience," he told me, toweling himself dry. "It's a wonderful new life, and I love it." Then, unable to suppress a twinkle in his blue eyes, he mischievously added, "But I certainly wouldn't want this nice life to preclude my taking a look at political opportunities in the future."

Ford was so gushing about his new life-after-political-death that I couldn't resist suggesting that he almost seemed happy to have lost the election.

"I don't want you to get that impression," he quickly interjected. "All I'm saying is we lost, the term ended, and we've had a most enjoyable six months. I'm a pragmatist; I prefer thinking about the future."

From the moment he finally reconciled himself to the reality that his political career had first been unexpectedly extended and then, to his mind, cruelly truncated by fate, Ford had set himself three parallel goals for his post-presidential life. First, the cash-poor congressman who took out loans on all his insurance policies to buy a modest condominium in Vail resolved to get unflinchingly rich, at least to the extent of providing permanent financial security for Betty, the four kids, and the grandchildren.

He also wanted to assemble a package of philanthropic, educational, and political endeavors to burnish his legacy as an elder statesman and certified national asset. Simultaneously, he quietly began plotting a grudge rematch against Jimmy Carter in the 1980 presidential election, a contest Ford was convinced he would win easily if given the chance by other Republican hopefuls—namely, his implacable nemesis Ronald Reagan.

Whatever Ford's choices, it was certain to be a comfortable existence. For openers, he had lifetime Secret Service protection, which was more of a huge and extremely welcome transportation and logistics benefit than anything else: the threat level largely evaporates once a president leaves office. There was also government money for staff, office space, postage, and travel, and his two pensions, for his congressional and presidential tenures. As it turned out, those cushions would amount to pocket change for the president-turned-entrepreneur.

"He's going to have most of the perquisites and none of the grief of being president," Dick Cheney, his last chief of staff, observed to me early in Ford's retirement years.

One of those perks was far more privacy. I once asked Ford what he enjoyed most about retirement. "Oh, lots of things," he replied with a broad grin. "And you don't have to release your tax returns every year." (The only reason anyone knows about Bill Clinton's postpresidential cash windfall is that such information must be listed on his wife's financial disclosure forms as a senator.)

His selection of venues was the easiest of all his post-Washington lifestyle choices. He and Betty already owned a condo free and clear at

The Lodge in the center of Vail, and for years had rented a place in Palm Springs, where the dry desert air favored his passion for golf and tennis and her arthritic neck. That much was settled early: the California desert for most of the year, the mountains in the summer and ski season. Jerry and Betty sold their home in suburban Alexandria, Virginia, for a $115,000 profit and headed for the coast.

The Fords had been aficionados of the Palm Springs life since the 1960s; they'd been hooked on the charms of the desert by Earl (Red) Blaik, the legendary football coach at the U.S. Military Academy from 1941 to 1958. He and Ford had met in the thirties, when Blaik was coaching football at Dartmouth and Ford was scouting Ivy League opponents for the Yale football team while getting his law degree. "When I was going up to Hanover to scout, after the game I would drop by and say hello as an old Michigan football player," he recalled in 2000, "so that's how our friendship developed."

After leading West Point to two national championships and producing two Heisman Trophy running backs, Blaik retired in 1958 and signed on as the Washington representative of Avco Corporation. In that capacity he'd call regularly on Ford, who was then a rising House power and in a position to be useful. Blaik's company had a condo in Palm Springs, and the old coach had often suggested that Jerry and Betty stay there over Easter. They took him up on the offer during a trip to San Diego one year; as Blaik had predicted, they loved it and succumbed swiftly. The following year they rented another condo for a week with their friends Leon and Barbara Parma, a tradition that remained intact until he became vice president.

At the urging of his old friend and major Republican moneyman Leonard Firestone and to the surprise of nobody, Ford quickly decided to make Rancho Mirage his formal base of operations. He accepted Firestone's offer to rent out a home once owned by Ginger Rogers's mother on the Thunderbird Country Club golf course as his permanent office. (The Secret Service and the General Services Administration, which by law provide office space for every former president, paid the rental tab to Firestone.) He also bought a lot from Firestone next to the office on Sand Dune Road and commissioned architects to begin planning his dream retirement home.

For the first thirty days, he decompressed—no public engagements, only marathon bouts of golf—and mulled a blizzard of offers, most of them for pay. It was a given that he'd land a multimillion-dollar contract to write his memoirs; every former president was in demand that way as a prestige author, even though most of them produced prosaic, ghostwritten apologias that sugarcoated and frequently skirted the truth. Ford's, titled *A Time to Heal,* didn't break the mold when it debuted in 1979.

Even before he'd left the White House, Ford had been approached by a Washington law firm eager to land his services. Actually, they just wanted his name: they were willing to pay him a quarter-million dollars a year just for the privilege of listing him as "of counsel," with no legal duties whatever. He declined.

Within two weeks of leaving the White House, Ford became a millionaire overnight when he signed a seven-figure deal with Harper & Row for him and Betty to write memoirs. He was financially set for life, and hundreds of thousands of other dollars began rolling in.

He received requests to make speeches, write newspaper columns, cut ribbons opening shopping malls, join corporate boards, and affiliate with colleges and universities; those latter offers multiplied after he mentioned to me in a *Newsweek* interview that he'd be interested in doing some teaching. Before long, he was lecturing before trade associations and major corporations for $10,000 a pop, a princely sum three decades ago but chump change for ex-presidents today and even for Ford himself in his latter moneymaking years, when he had the luxury of rejecting engagements paying $100,000 and more.

Though he aggressively pursued his wealth-building enterprises, Ford was always a little in awe of the huge amounts of cash he could make—and spend. When his home was being built in the desert, he'd inspect the construction once a week. On one of those visits, workers had just finished a large concrete slab for his golden retrievers.

"That dog run," he told a companion, "cost more than my first house."

In 1978, in a deal that some of his most ardent loyalists thought tacky, he signed a contract with the Franklin Mint to hawk commemorative medals depicting the hundred most significant events in the American presidency, ranging from George Washington's first inaugural to Ford's speech in Philadelphia honoring the country's Bicentennial. He sent off "Dear Fellow American" letters hustling the medals, which could be had in gold or silver for $1,950 to $2,750.

Early into retirement, he warmed to Barrett's idea of hosting two annual events in Vail to raise his profile: a charity golf tournament, the Jerry Ford Invitational, and the World Affairs Forum, where Ford enticed political leaders and old global cronies like Germany's Helmut Schmidt and Britain's James Callaghan to enjoy the crisp mountain air while opining on geopolitics. It was a Rocky Mountain version of the Bohemian Grove for the towel-slapping political and corporate elite.

After the book deals, Ford's most lucrative arrangement was a $1.25 million contract with NBC to collaborate on documentary programs and take two round-the-world trips as a goodwill ambassador for the network. He also drew stipends from the American Enterprise Institute, a conservative Washington think tank, and the Eisenhower Fellowships program.

Before long, he was also raising millions of dollars for charity. An early passion was the Betty Ford Center in Rancho Mirage, a world-class detox center to help people with the same sort of alcohol- and substance-abuse maladies that Betty Ford had battled for decades and finally conquered. He helped bring in millions more to endow his presidential library in Ann Arbor and his museum in Grand Rapids.

Mixed in were a steady stream of foreign trips, college seminars, and fundraising appearances for Republican candidates, and the occasional pleasure cruise. He temporarily decided against doing corporate work and permanently ruled out lobbying and consultant offers; he didn't ever want to be in a position, he told associates, of being paid to put the arm on former congressional colleagues. There was a has-been, opportunistic quality to that line of work that had always bothered him. He didn't want a full-time job, either, turning down a feeler from Pepperdine University to become its chancellor.

Anyone who thought Ford would enter meekly into his forced retirement had never studied his record. In twenty-eight years of elected and appointed federal service, Ford had never demonstrated any predilection toward repose. Even as president, he'd traveled so much that aides sometimes grumped he was on the road more than a Fuller Brush man. He wasn't about to change; approaching his sixty-fourth birthday, he showed no symptoms of slowing down. His vigor was even more extraordinary when compared with the reclusiveness of Richard Nixon at his La Casa Pacifica exile in San Clemente.

"Look at him. He's sixty-four going on fifty, the bastard," muttered Bob Barrett in the summer of 1977.

In the first six months of his so-called retirement, the former president logged 103,000 travel miles, spending eighty-seven days, or almost every other day, on the road. In May of 1977 alone, he was out of town twenty-seven of thirty-one days, an even more madcap pace than his peripatetic days as Republican minority leader. His logs showed that he'd answered more than one thousand questions from students attending his lectures and seminars on five college campuses and made dozens of public appearances. He received 120,000 pieces of mail and a whopping 5,000 invitations for personal appearances.

His projected schedule for 1978 was just as hectic, beginning with serving as grand marshal of the Tournament of Roses Parade in Pasadena on New Year's Day, a special thrill for an old Big Ten football jock. His public agenda for the indefinite future was so extensive, in fact, that Ford, a longtime advocate of fiscal austerity, ironically busted the budget for former presidents in his first year in the Exes' Club.

The Former Presidents Act simply hadn't envisioned a retired chief executive with the personal energy and, his defenders argued, the national esteem to generate and handle that level of public interest. The Carter administration agreed. When Ford's transition budget ran out on September 30, 1977, the White House asked Ford's old Capitol Hill cronies to increase his annual staffing allowance by more than half, from $96,000 to $146,000.

In the immortal phrase of one of his retainers, in less than a year Ford had become a one-man mini-corporation—and his most prodigious income-generating opportunities were then still several years away.

One of his closest political confidants, a former member of Congress with Ford, was even more pointed in his eyebrow-raising. "Ford has commercialized the former presidency," he would say disapprovingly—but never to his old comrade, who wouldn't have listened anyway.

It wasn't long before friends and staffers were grumbling about how Ford, who spent two hundred days a year on the rubber-chicken circuit as a Republican leader, was spreading himself too thin for no particular reason other than his always impressive energy level. By the 1980 election, he had logged three million travel miles.

One old friend who always thought Ford was overextended lamented to me in 1977, "If Adolf Hitler liked Jerry Ford and was loyal to him, Jerry would probably think Hitler was a pretty good guy who was just misunderstood."

That was obviously a tactless exaggeration, but there's no question Ford was a hopeless soft touch. At a convention where he was the featured speaker, Ford was introduced to a corporate CEO from Connecticut who asked about retaining his services at an upcoming event in Palm Springs. That invitation was an oratorical chip shot long favored by show-for-dough thespians: no travel involved. When the exec asked whom to contact at his speakers' bureau, Ford replied, "Those scoundrels? They'll charge you twenty-five thousand. Call me direct. I'll do it for five thousand." And so he did.

When I spent a few days with him in July of his first summer-in-exile, Ford's financial situation was sufficiently comfortable that he'd already stockpiled a quarter of a million dollars into his savings account even after paying from his own pocket the salaries of a full-time cook, a personal steward, and a valet, plus a personal assistant for Betty and a cleaning lady. He was living in a rented home in Rancho Mirage's Thunderbird Heights subdivision while his own ranch-style place was being built. When the 115-degree desert heat got to be too much, the Fords fled to the Colorado Rockies, renting the same house near the foot of Vail Mountain from Texas businessman Dick Bass he'd leased when he was president.

In either location, a typical at-home day for the former president began at 6:30, just an hour later than his usual rising time during the White House years. He didn't need a mechanical alarm clock to wake up and begin twenty minutes of sit-ups and leg lifts designed to strengthen his gimpy knees, never the same after football injuries in college.

After his first round of laps, Ford showered, shaved, and changed into casual slacks and a golf shirt. Betty was never a morning person, so while she slept in he ate breakfast alone—half a honeydew melon, orange juice, bran flakes with bananas, and an English muffin or two, depending on whether he was dieting

By 8:30, he'd finished breakfast, scanned the papers, and begun two hours of never-ending paperwork: correspondence, autographs, speech contracts. Four days a week, he'd play a round of golf, gobbling a sandwich on the run between the front and back nines. On non–links days he'd play tennis doubles, his knees propped up by braces concealed beneath sweatpants. A couple of hours with his memoirs was followed by another bout of paperwork, usually while nursing a double martini.

He spent at least half an hour each weekday kibitzing with Washington pals, even House Speaker Tip O'Neill, one of his closest political friends despite their monumental ideological differences.

"Tip and I have great rapport," he said of their odd-couple relationship. "He gives me hell and I give him hell. He's an old rascal."

"I get restless if I just sit around the swimming pool," he added.

"That's not my nature. It'll never be my lifestyle. I'm going to be busy in some way all the rest of my life. Betty accuses me of being busier now than when I was in the White House." Not really so, he added, since morning intelligence briefings and managing foreign crises happily weren't part of his portfolio any longer.

"But right now the truth is I work a minimum of eight hours a day, six days a week," he boasted, a testament to his Calvinist upbringing and devotion to the work ethic. "I drive myself because I've done it all my life. It's just natural for me to keep working."

Despite protestations to the contrary, even then Ford was extraordinarily sensitive to, and eternally peeved about, whispers that he was profiteering from an accidental presidency. It simply drove him crazy. In his view, he'd never earned a cheap dollar in his life, much less accepted a freebie. He was absolutely furious with me after a story on his moneymaking enterprises ran in *Newsweek* in 1981.

"It's important for a former president to write a book," he explained to me. "It's constructive to do television documentaries. It's constructive to meet with students. Everything I'm doing is constructive, and the compensation I get is very proper. I think I earn the money I'm being paid. Over the years I got used to cheap shots. So I just don't pay any attention to these cheap shots."

That was the high-toned, defensive version of what he really thought. More like it: "I'm a private citizen now," he added, bridling at the memory of some reporter who'd recently asked him how much he was worth now. "It's nobody else's business."

He'd telegraphed his true feelings just two months after leaving office, when he was back in town for a few days. During that visit he met with the Sperling breakfast club of reporters, a Washington fixture run for more than forty years by the *Christian Science Monitor*.

He was circumspect about his view of the new president and for the most part was his usual cheerful self—except when a *Los Angeles Times* reporter asked him how much money he expected to earn from outside activities in 1977.

"I'm a retired public figure," he snapped. "I don't intend to discuss it." But he went on to defend his intention to make money, uttering a classic Jerry Fordism.

"That's what the free-enterprise system's all about," he said.

Besides, he always maintained, he always bent over backwards to be careful.

"I'm a lot more cautious, responsible, and careful than some of the others," he said in 1991. "Some news media have given me the devil that I've been too business-oriented. I feel very strongly that I've been extremely discreet. The facts are I've turned down ten for every business opportunity I've had, and I've done it [selectively] to be scrupulously careful. I have no apologies for business connections I've made, because I've worked at whatever my responsibilities are.

"I never take money for not doing anything. What I do I think I earn, and the people who pay me think I'm worth it. But I turn down many, many more. I've been to almost 180 college and university campuses. I've taught more than 700 classes, answered 7,000 questions from students and faculty, and most of those are for minimum compensation. They can't afford to pay [more, and] I enjoy the opportunity."

As for his corporate boards, "I turned down about seven for every one I accepted," he said a year later. "Over a span of time I have served on about ten; I have now reduced that to four.

"I've been offered financial opportunities I might have pursued, but as a former president I was reluctant. You have to be even more cautious when something involves foreign interests. I've been very careful and scrupulous in what I have done."

In his rare hours of postpresidential repose, Ford spent considerable psychic energy preparing to run against his successor in 1980. Though reluctant to engage in analyzing the incumbent president, Ford wasn't able to resist telegraphing his belief that Jimmy Carter was messing up just about every issue he touched. "They had historic opportunities to move to a SALT II agreement," he lamented in 1977. "They had the best atmosphere in the Middle East in recent years for a major move for peace. They had an exceptional opportunity to make real progress in southern Africa. I just hope they can make progress, but time is slipping away."

It was also clear that Ford would have worked Carter over far more vigorously if the Georgian hadn't now joined the most exclusive fraternity in America.

"I have a certain obligation to speak out on major issues when I think the national interest demands it," Ford confirmed. "Other than that, I'm not going to be nitpicking on a daily basis. A president's got enough troubles without an ex-president beating him over the head every day in the political arena. I just don't intend to do that.

"I am not obsessed with the idea of running for president, but I'm not going to neglect my civic responsibilities if I think my party or the political arena need my participation.

"I'm deeply dedicated to certain economic and foreign policy principles that affect this country. If I believe that the choice in the Republican Party is going to be preempted by somebody who strays wildly off or away from those principles, I'm going to be active."

Translation: The thought of Ronald Reagan becoming my party's nominee makes me want to puke.

Ford's flirtation with running again in 1980 was fueled by three imperatives, all largely emotional. He wanted to avenge his loss to a president he thought had become a disaster; he also desperately longed to exorcise the Accidental President chatter, the whispers, galling him no end, that he simply never had what it took to be elected in his own right and had only gained the White House via a monumental fluke of history. By no means a minor consideration: he also relished the payback prospect of denying the Oval Office to Reagan, whom he considered a lazy and unfit pretender.

Ford was convinced he could beat Carter and sure that Reagan couldn't, a judgment that would of course ultimately prove erroneous. He further believed that the 48 percent of Americans who'd voted for him in 1976 would still be there four years later. Carter's rising unpopularity, he thought, would bring along enough other voters to make Ford another Grover Cleveland, who'd been defeated for reelection in 1888 by Benjamin Harrison but regained the presidency by beating Harrison four years later.

By the fall of 1979, Ford had traveled more than a million miles, basking at every step in the adulation of audiences who convinced him he was still politically viable. More than once, he'd be introduced by a university president or captain of industry who confessed he was embarrassed to admit he'd voted against Ford in 1976 and urged him to run again in 1980. Ford ate it up, and invariably pronounced absolution. "I am a very forgiving person," he told one such remorseful patron.

It wasn't all tease. By his own reckoning, he was a known quantity; his experience and integrity were a given, and Carter's missteps made Ford look progressively better. He was the single candidate, Ford thought, who neutralized Carter's positives and accentuated his negatives.

Longtime loyalists like Henry Kissinger and other former retainers urged him to run. Thomas Reed, a former secretary of the Air Force, formed a Draft Ford Committee. Two governors of megastates whose electoral votes were crucial, Jim Rhodes of Ohio and Bill Clements of Texas, lobbied him hard to make the race.

Ford wanted to believe, and so he did—up to a point. He was a totally conventional politician, as white-bread as they come, but his career had been propelled to heights he'd never aspired to by the most unconventional of circumstances. Even aides who were sure the idea was a disaster waiting to happen agreed that Ford couldn't be faulted for wondering whether destiny might work its magic with him one last election.

"For a guy who got to be president the way he did," one of the realists told me at the time, "he's one of those people who believes anything can happen."

But not all of his onetime inner circle were counted among the resurrectionist romantics. Loyalists like Dick Cheney, pollster Bob Teeter, and strategist par excellence Stu Spencer were all distinctly skeptical. To them, a renaissance race was theoretically doable but very tough. Everything would have to break Ford's way. Moreover, as one of them put it, "his only chance is to rip Ronald Reagan to shreds."

Understandably, Ford had a problem with that; he thought playing the spoiler would tarnish his cachet, not to mention possibly reelecting Carter by splitting the Republican vote. Carter with another four years was even more anathema to Ford than Reagan winning.

By early March, with important filing deadlines looming, Ford convened councils of war in Washington and Rancho Mirage with his closest advisers. Their judgment was sobering: the best-case scenario pegged Ford 150 delegates short of catching Reagan. They'd all be there for him if he decided to go, but he needed to recognize how iffy a proposition they thought it would be. "The math isn't there," Ford glumly told one of his true believers. Psychologically, he was desperate to run, but he wasn't totally crazy.

On the afternoon of Saturday, March 15, 1980, a sunny day as usual in the desert, Ford pulled on a gray suit and blue button-down shirt and walked out to meet a handful of reporters near the grapefruit tree in the front yard of his office complex. In what he'd later call the toughest decision of his life, he took himself out of the race.

"America needs a new president," he said, Betty smiling at his side. "I have determined that I can best help that cause by not being a candidate for president, which might further divide my party. I am not a candidate. I will not become a candidate. I will support the nominee of my party with all the energy I have."

Just before he walked back inside, his political career irrevocably ended, I caught his eye. He looked right through me; it was as though we didn't know each other. He was that upset over his "final and certain decision."

With Betty hugging him for dear life, he walked into his office and announced with a raucous laugh, "If I were a drinking man, I'd have myself a drink."

Instead, he changed out of his television clothes and immediately headed off for a therapeutic round of golf with Leonard Firestone, Darius (Dee) Keaton, and Alan Greenspan.

For the next twenty-four hours after ceding the Republican nomination to his archenemy, Ford was at war with the world. He charged out onto the Thunderbird Country Club course adjoining his home and took out his frustration on his golf game. He played some of his worst golf ever, spraying tee shots all over the course, clobbering palm trees, and missing easy chip shots, finishing his round literally in the dark.

He told aides he didn't want to take any phone calls. Even the dearest of friends who wanted to console him were urged to steer clear for a while, lest they absorb indiscriminate shrapnel. "Stay the hell away from him," Bob Barrett warned one old pal, "and make sure anybody you care about does the same."

By Monday, however, Ford had expunged his demons. He was as cheerful and upbeat as usual, his raucous laugh reverberating around his office-in-exile.

On Tuesday, three days after taking himself out of the race, Ford finally agreed to give me a brief interview in his office. His mood was markedly sunnier. After massacring Thunderbird on Saturday, he said he'd played the tough Mission Hills course on Sunday. "I played the best golf of my life," he boasted. "An 81 at Mission Hills—and it should have been 78."

He confirmed, however, that he'd been in a vile mood right after ending his political career and had needed a little time to decompress.

"I was still uptight and tense, but I feel good about it now. It was the right thing to do, and Betty is behind it 110 percent," he told me.

"This country has to get rid of Carter. To jeopardize that for the sake of personal ambition would have been irresponsible. Besides, you have to be realistic. I'm a realist—the numbers just weren't there."

Had he opted in, Ford added, he was convinced he'd be accused of being an egotistical party wrecker, a mortal sin for the ultimate party man: "You could see it coming; as soon as I got in I was gonna be torn apart, by Carter *and* Reagan."

"Now we're gonna enjoy the good life," he vowed. "I'm gonna do some things I've never done. We're going to the Kentucky Derby with friends, and I'm gonna play at Augusta National."

And make some *real* money in the bargain.



Closing that door simultaneously opened another, less fulfilling psychologically but infinitely more lucrative: a robust sellers' market for his services even his most aggressive financial advisers hadn't imagined. Literally overnight, Jerry Ford's earnings potential exploded, and that suited him just fine.

"This is my last political hurrah," he told me toward the end of the 1980 campaign. "I'm going to reduce my political activity ninety percent and concentrate on my business interests." For a man given to understatement, that was a whopper.

By then Ford was already a millionaire several times over, but he had consciously avoided the corporate world lest some business affiliation could present a practical problem if he ran for president again in 1980. When your name is on the door, Ford once told an associate, you're part of the problem if there ever is one. He worried about potential conflict-of-interest allegations if he challenged Jimmy Carter—a race he wanted to make, badly.

It was only after he reluctantly decided not to launch that rematch that he embraced his beloved free-enterprise system headlong and ratcheted up the buckraking machine.

"The first four years, I kept my options open for '80," he told me in 1993. "I didn't join any corporate boards, I affiliated with the

American Enterprise Institute, and taught at about sixty colleges and universities; made a few honorarium speeches; but I never got affiliated with any business organizations, so that if I ran in '80, people couldn't say, 'Well, look what he did with Corporation X or Corporation Y.' After '80, when I decided not to be a candidate ever again, I changed my focus to things that I thought I would enjoy."

Suddenly, the corporations who had eagerly sought his services even while he was still in office renewed their sales pitches, having been alerted that this time the response might be more favorable. Two weeks after ending his political career by his own reluctant hand, Ford was elected to the board of directors of Santa Fe International Corporation, an international oil-drilling company. Within a year, when *Newsweek* ran a story headlined "Jerry Ford, Incorporated," which he hated even though he was my source for much of the reporting, Ford was a director in six other corporations: Shearson Loeb Rhoades, the investment banking giant; AMAX, a mining and metals conglomerate; Tiger International, the international air cargo operation later subsumed into Federal Express; GK Technologies, a fiber optics and electronics firm; Texas Commerce Bancshares, a Houston bank holding company; and the Pebble Beach Corporation, a California real estate and resort development company whose board included his old friends Leonard Firestone and Dee Keaton.

In another year, Ford's director's portfolio had bulked up to include American Express and 20th Century–Fox Film Corporation, which had been acquired by his oilman pal Marvin Davis. Until mandatory age-limit regulations began forcing him off most of his boards, Ford was a director of more than a dozen major corporations. He was such a prolific corporate titan that one aide estimated it was costing his benefactors a million dollars a year in aircraft expenses for his services. That was another new, felicitous perk: more corporate jets, fewer commercial flights.

He also received thousands of shares of stock as compensation from some of those corporations. His friend Sandy Weill made sure that Ford held on to those shares, arguing, correctly, that over time they would increase in value handsomely.

Like other board members, Ford collected director's fees in the $20,000 range. But he was in such demand as a trophy hire that he asked for, and got, a separate consulting deal for most if not all of these firms. Those fees were estimated at between $35,000 and $100,000 each by Ford associates.

In a deal that some close associates thought crept right up to the top of the smell-test chart, he also inked a consulting deal with the Charter Corporation, a Florida conglomerate that had once retained President Carter's brother Billy to help lobby oil deals with the Libyan government.

For the handsome compensation they paid him, Ford's business colleagues gained a high-profile, prestige partner, one of the globe's most recognizable and formerly powerful individuals, who imparted an instant aura of legitimacy and respectability. He wasn't a rainmaker and still ruled out any lobbying chores. He consciously turned down all entreaties from defense companies, wary of conflict-of-interest charges, since those firms did billions of dollars' worth of business with the federal government.

So what did he actually do as a boardman?

"The chairman or the president will call me and ask for my appraisal of the domestic and international situation," he told me a month after opting out of the 1980 presidential race, "and at board meetings I'm usually called upon to give a review of the political, economic, and international situation as I see it. I never involve myself in actual business operations."

Even so, he was an eager corporate cheerleader, willing to inspire, schmooze, and entertain clients and employees alike. He was the star attraction, for instance, at the 1981 opening of Shearson's new branch in Singapore and later spoke to the firm's top six hundred salesmen in Honolulu in October. That same year he flew to Brazil with other GK Technologies directors and made an eleven-country around-the-world tour in a Charter corporate jet, mixing business activities with official duties as a high-level emissary to the Chinese and Saudi Arabian governments at President Reagan's behest.

Below the radar, Ford also aggressively pursued a variety of private investment ventures. In 1979 he and neighbor Firestone had formed Fordstone Incorporated. Among their early investments were radio stations in Durango, Colorado, and a local hotel and residential project opposed by environmentalists. Ford was one of several partners with golfing legend Jack Nicklaus in a golf course and had real estate holdings in the Midwest and California, including a piece of a San Jose shopping center.

Ford was a dutiful board member, faithfully attending quarterly meetings and making a dozen trips to New York City every year just for corporate work. Even when he couldn't handle the flying anymore, he participated in board sessions via teleconference from Rancho Mirage.

A quarter-century after he joined his first board, what some critics still denounce as his selling of the presidency arguably remains the most controversial aspect of Ford's career. There's little doubt that Ford's business dealings at the very least lacked some sensitivity to the appearance of impropriety. It was a blind spot even his defenders fretted about.

Predictably, he never saw it that way. To him, his reputation for personal integrity, not to mention a prodigious work ethic, should have been sufficient to insulate him from criticism. When he wasn't irked about the naysayers, he always seemed to me almost hurt by the suggestion he'd cheapened the presidential aura.

He was particularly irritated that Richard Nixon, Jimmy Carter, and Ronald Reagan were reliably reported to have accused him of unseemly profiteering. Carter even said so at a 1981 press conference: "I think it's inappropriate for an ex-president to be involved in the commercial world."

Those who decried his entrepreneurial excess never recognized, he often complained, that he did a huge amount of pro bono work. He never quite understood what the fuss was all about.

On his 1981 trip for both Carter and Reagan, he was at pains to point out, he'd refused to do any corporate work with the Chinese and Saudis despite plenty of openings to do precisely that.

"I kept the missions President Reagan gave me totally separate from the things I was doing otherwise," he told me in April 1981, betraying a sense of weariness as well as defensiveness at my questions. "I was very scrupulous in that regard."

As he got older, and wealthier, Ford steadily dialed back on his business operations. In 1995, when he celebrated his eighty-second birthday, he pointed out a new policy: "I won't take a speech in New York, even for a big fee, unless I'm out there [anyway]. That's a three-day commitment." At long last, Ford was slowing down.

"I used to speak three to five times a month for honorariums," he told me in 1998. "I now do probably one a month or less for honorariums. I just turned down this morning a $100,000 fee to go to Egypt. They wanted me to speak to two thousand people. I just don't do that anymore. It literally ends up into a four- or five-day trip. I'm finding that long-distance travel takes a lot out of me.

"I've cut back to three boards: Texas Commerce Bancshares; it's now Texas Chase, American Express, and Travelers."

He expected that the Travelers-Amex merger might result in his getting bounced from the new combined board of directors. "We don't need the money, and if I'm not on the board, we'll survive," he shrugged. "That's just five less trips to New York every year, which is fine."

Even as he scaled back, the questions never went away, nor his pained defenses. In his mind, they all boiled down to two simple sentences he uttered in 1981:

"I'm a private citizen now. As long as I work for what I get, and as long as I behave in an honorable fashion, it's my business."

At its peak, quite a business.

# FIVE

# 1991—The First
# Interview/Nixon

A T ELEVEN O'CLOCK on the morning of August 26, 1991, I arrived at Gerald Ford's mountain hideaway in Beaver Creek, Colorado, a few miles from the ersatz Bavarian-style village of Vail, where he'd been going to ski for decades. That inaugural off-the-record interview lasted for two hours and ten minutes, the longest we ever had.

He greeted me at the front door of the home at 65 Elk Track Court that I later learned he'd built for $5 million, complaining it had cost him way too much but pleased that his profitable commercial enterprises had enabled him to pay for it in cash.

Ford was wearing a handsome blue cable-knit sweater, white dress shirt with only the collar visible, gray cotton slacks, black socks, and black soft-soled shoes. As he walked me to his study just off the entrance foyer, I noticed he was walking with a pronounced limp, the result of his old football injuries from his years as a center for the Michigan

Wolverines. He told me his cartilage was totally gone. He'd have replacement surgery on his gimpy right knee later in the year; the same surgery on his left knee the year before had been wholly successful. Before I left he'd proudly show off the surgical scar, à la Lyndon Johnson baring the memento from his gallbladder removal to White House photographers.

We settled in for the first of sessions that would continue for sixteen years. I quickly reviewed the simple ground rules we'd already established: nothing he said could be printed until after his death. I also promised I wouldn't tell anyone else what he'd said. I wanted him to be reassured that just because I wasn't putting something into print didn't give me the license to dine out on his candor with friends.

Reporters have been known to do just that. I once attended an off-the-record *Newsweek* dinner where a senior aide to President George H.W. Bush made a modestly disparaging remark about Vice President Dan Quayle. Three days later, I was called on the carpet by the aide's press officer, who repeated the offending epithet to me verbatim. It turned out that one of my superiors had relayed the story to pals at the *Washington Post*, who were gleefully peddling it around their newsroom. When I told the perpetrator that the magazine's good name was being hammered because of his loose lips, he was unapologetic: "Screw 'em; we didn't print it."

"I trust you," Ford said. "Why don't we get started?"

Like most reporters, I opened with a couple of softballs. First, I asked if there were policies from his presidency that seemed to have gained more respectability with the passage of time. I thought he might raise the Nixon pardon. Instead, he opened with his participation in the 1975 Helsinki Accords, which conservatives had denounced as a sellout to the Soviet Union.

"You will remember the hell we caught from Reagan and all kinds of individuals and organizations that said it was wrong to participate. Well, the Helsinki Accords I honestly believe were a major factor in bringing about the human rights revolt in Poland, Czechoslovakia, [and] Hungary and current ramifications in the Soviet Union. The longer time passes, the better the Helsinki Accords appear.

"But there's no doubt that the greatest policy achievement of the Ford administration was restoring some confidence in government after the disasters of Watergate and Vietnam. You were there; you know how terrible the atmosphere was in the nation's capital and throughout the country. Younger people today who were not living or not old enough to know have no comprehension of the tension and the bitterness that existed throughout the United States. To turn that around—not that everybody agreed with me—the evidence is clear that at least we restored integrity in the White House and in our government. I think by any measurement, that was the most important thing, the biggest plus in my administration."

Among his disappointments, a troubled economy topped the list.

"I wish I could have turned the economy around more quickly. You know, I inherited the worst recession in the post–World War II period. Inflation was high, interest rates were high, we had the first oil crisis, unemployment rose. We had a tough time. We did get it turned around, but it came about too slowly, for humanitarian and political purposes. But I've learned one thing: a president can't turn a switch and overnight fix an economy as big and diverse as ours. It won't react in twenty-four hours or thirty days.

"In foreign policy, I was disappointed that we did not conclude a SALT II agreement. We came close. If I had been elected in '76, there's no doubt in my mind: I would have negotiated a SALT II agreement, and I'm confident it would have been ratified by the United States Senate."

"Even with Reagan bitching about it?"

"Well, having beaten him at the convention and if I had [then] beaten Carter, I'm confident that an agreement that I could have ne-gotiated would have been ratified."

Parenthetically, he also cited his decision to take away Henry

Kissinger's dual role as secretary of state and national security adviser as critical to restoring the proper functioning of the government's foreign policy apparatus. The turf-conscious Kissinger didn't enjoy losing a major piece of his portfolio, but Ford felt from an institutional standpoint it was long overdue.

"The National Security Council was set up in 1947 so that a president would have an independent think tank in the White House that could make independent evaluations from the Pentagon and State Department and elsewhere so that the president wouldn't be captive of the bureaucracy.

"When Kissinger had both State and NSC, there was not an independent evaluation of proposals, and I never liked that arrangement that I inherited. And when the time came to make some [other] changes at the Pentagon and CIA, it was logical to tell Henry, 'I'm gonna just leave you as secretary of state and upgrade Brent Scowcroft,'" who was Kissinger's NSC deputy.

The wisdom of Ford's reasoning was borne out, he argued, by the Iran-Contra mess in the Reagan administration:

"If I can add a little postscript, one of the fundamental problems of the Iran-Contra affair is that the NSC got into some action areas where they had no authority under the law. The NSC is a think tank, not a field operating organization, and during Iran-Contra they became a field operating organization, totally contrary to their charter. That's where they got their ass in a wringer.

"[Oliver] North and his people analyzing political pros and cons—that's a total undercutting. . . . The president [Reagan] had a fundamental responsibility and they allowed a terrible example of mismanagement. . . ."

As he did until our final interview in May 2006, Ford doted on the wealth of talent he'd recruited for his government. He was always proud that many of his alumni were a Who's Who of public service in successive Republican administrations: Alan Greenspan, Dick Cheney,

Don Rumsfeld, Paul O'Neill, Brent Scowcroft, Jim Baker, Bill Coleman, Carla Hills, Dick Thornburgh, Roger Porter, David Gergen.

He resisted naming his best subordinates, but when I pressed he finally conceded, "The best have to be Dick Cheney and Brent Scowcroft"—an ironic tandem, since the two old friends have fallen out over the Iraq War and have a civil relationship at best.

He didn't have to agonize when picking his worst cabinet officer: Secretary of Defense James Schlesinger, whom he inherited from Nixon and fired in 1975.

Ford never liked Schlesinger, considering him an egghead who liked to talk down to him. "He was the one that I was not comfortable with," he said. "He was a talented guy, but we just didn't fit."

But far worse in Ford's telling, Schlesinger was also at times insubordinate: "There were several instances where, if I had really felt it was worthwhile, I think I could have found where Schlesinger did not carry out orders issued from the White House," he told me.

For example:

"During the [1975] *Mayagüez* incident, I ordered that the aircraft carrier [USS *Coral Sea*] that we had turned around, that was on its way to Australia, to make air strikes against the [Cambodian] mainland. And the facts are after one strike, [Schlesinger] terminated them without getting further orders from me. It was a deliberate case, as I understand it, of not carrying out the order of the commander in chief. I don't know why.

"Secondly, at the time of the evacuation from Vietnam—you may not remember this, but I do—in the four or five days leading up to the actual evacuation, I had ordered the evacuation of as many Vietnamese civilians, military, et cetera [as possible], along with our U.S. personnel. I later found out that many of those planes that I thought were being loaded were flown out empty—and that, according to my sources, that order came from Schlesinger."

I asked another one of those journalistic bromides: What was your biggest mistake?

In his memoirs, Ford had written that he was "angry with myself for showing cowardice" by not telling the ultraconservatives in his party that he was sticking with Nelson Rockefeller as his 1976 running mate. Instead, he dumped Rocky, and was still upset about it.

"Well, I'm embarrassed by the fact that I did not stick with Nelson Rockefeller. I don't want to imply that Bob Dole was not a good candidate; I'm embarrassed that I didn't tell hard right-wingers that Rockefeller had done a good job and would be a good vice president for a four-year period. I'm embarrassed that I didn't fight it through, but the truth is Nelson and I had a long talk—very private—and after we got through, it was his view, as well as mine, that his candidacy as vice president at the convention could very well have resulted in my not being nominated for president.*

"We weren't worried about the election, but if you don't get nominated . . ." He chuckled at the grim recollection of just how close he had been to losing his party's nomination to Ronald Reagan.

"That was the key reason that both of us agreed [Rockefeller should step down], and he was as firm as I. Now, you know you can speculate if I had fought it through, but we only won that convention by about 150 votes out of 2,300 [actually 117 of 2,257]."

I wanted to know who had pushed him hardest to dump Rockefeller, and Ford confirmed my suspicion that Rumsfeld, his chief of staff who was hoping to succeed Rocky on the ticket, was first among equals: "Don was a major factor. I think Don did it from purely pragmatic points of view—not because he didn't like or admire Rockefeller."

Ford was pleased to report that his relationship with Rockefeller had weathered Rocky's ignominious dumping. He and Betty had spent a "wonderful time up there" with Nelson and Happy at Kykuit, their Pocantico Hills family estate in Westchester County, New York.

"Our friendship continued right up until his death, and our friend-

---

*Actually, Rocky was furious at being dumped, but fingered Don Rumsfeld and his deputy Dick Cheney for undercutting him with Ford.

ship with Happy has also been continued. So there's never been any backing off in our relationship, and I suspect, that [even] if I didn't say it directly, he understood that I was embarrassed."

I nevitably, we got around to what we both recognized was still Topic A seventeen years after the fact: Richard Nixon and Watergate. I asked him to explain about the tightrope he'd maneuvered between defending his former House colleague and growing increasingly suspicious that he was being lied to about Nixon's involvement.

"I never honestly hoped I would be president," he said. "I wanted Dick Nixon to survive, and therefore I was always trying to be protective of the presidency and to make it appear that I wasn't lifting a finger to undercut him and to become president; therefore I really never anticipated I would be president until the Thursday or Friday before I actually became president."

("I was hoping Nixon could stay on," he echoed in our 1997 interview, "because then I would quit as vice president and that was it. So my goal was to bolster Nixon as long as I could without compromising my conscience.")

"Until I saw or heard the evidence of the smoking gun, I always hoped, and based on Nixon's assurance to me, I didn't think he would be impeached—and if he wasn't gonna be impeached, I doubted if he would resign."

After years of reflecting on his conduct, Ford admitted, he could be fairly faulted for giving Nixon too much benefit of the doubt. On some level, perhaps Ford may not have wanted to know the truth; that certainly would have made his defensive duties far more difficult to pull off. Regardless, he didn't press Nixon for a just-between-old-friends accounting of the facts, and regretted his timidity.

"All the time that this thing kept getting hotter and hotter and hotter, whenever I would see him alone, I'd try to find out whether I was being fully informed. To be honest with you, Tom, I never said, 'Mr. President, were you involved? Did you know?' In retrospect, I probably should have.

"But whenever I would be alone with him, and we would talk about what was happening, he would frequently say, 'You know, Jerry, I've been so involved in foreign policy trips abroad, with the Middle East, with Brezhnev, et cetera, I never had time to get involved in these domestic matters and things of this kind.' And the clear inference was he neither was involved [n]or knew about it. And I accepted that, because it was a clear statement from him telling me what he was doing and he was not involved in either the planning, the execution, or otherwise."

"So he lied to you, but he wasn't the only one," I suggested.

"No," Ford agreed, distinctly remembering a meeting he and Senate Minority Leader Hugh Scott had with John Mitchell and Jeb Magruder to complain that Nixon's 1972 reelection committee was cutting Republican campaign officials out of the loop. It was a breakfast meeting only two days after the infamous break-in of Democratic National Committee headquarters that launched the Watergate crisis.

"I got there early, walked into Mitchell's office, and I said, 'John, that was a stupid thing that happened last Saturday night. Did you know about it, were you involved?' And John Mitchell looked me right in the eye and said, 'I didn't know about it; I wasn't involved.' So on the basis of that and the assurances from Nixon, I assumed the White House and the Department of Justice were in no way involved."

Ford's pique with Mitchell reflected his strong disdain for the palace guard that surrounded Nixon. He considered them arrogant Californians who fed Nixon's paranoia against political enemies and the media. In a 1997 interview, he didn't mince words about Nixon's handlers—and the stupidity of the cover-up that doomed Nixon:

"My biggest problem with the Nixon administration was the attitude of Haldeman, Ehrlichman, and Colson when I was the Republican leader. They were really obnoxious, Tom. They used to come up to my leadership office and meet with me and my Republican leadership and say, 'The president wants this, the president wants that.' I would sit there and I would say to myself, I've known Dick Nixon better than any one of you, and that's *not* what he wants. You're exaggerating his comments for your own self-aggrandizement. I used to detest those people. Of course, by the time I became vice president they were all gone."

Ford singled out for special disdain John Dean, the White House lawyer who helped blow the lid off the cover-up he had once helped perpetrate. Long before Watergate, he hadn't liked the brash young lawyer.

"I knew John Dean when he was chief clerk for Bill McCulloch," ranking Republican on the House Judiciary Committee. "I developed a suspicion and a dislike for John Dean then, because I just didn't like the way he operated. And I was shocked when the Nixon people took him over to the White House . . . [where] he tried to protect his own ass. The case against Dean is ironclad."

Mitchell's lying hardly exonerated Nixon, Ford readily agreed. That led him into a philosophical discussion whose centerpiece was the observation, hardly novel with him, that has become a fixture of Washington's scandal firmament: it's the covering up of political chicanery, not the original act, that usually dooms politicians.

"It was not a big deal," he said, referring only to the break-in of DNC headquarters at the Watergate Office Building. "Those kind[s] of spying on political opponents or political parties—that was kind of the atmosphere in those days.

"Now, what happens after the break-in is more significant. If Nixon had said, 'I knew nothing about it, people that I trusted were involved, I'm firing those who knew about it,' the whole damn thing would have been washed out and Nixon would have beaten McGovern just as badly. From that point of view it *was* something, it wasn't a nothing. It's tragic, and if the tapes hadn't been made, if the cover-up hadn't been carried out, I think Nixon could have survived. It was the after-the-fact manipulation, the cover-up, that created the disaster."

At several junctures in our relationship, chance has intervened in mysterious ways. The April 1974 interview is the prime example. Who could have choreographed a confluence of events where I interviewed Gerald Ford on the very day he was seething about White House criticism—and his press secretary was asleep on a sofa in an adjoining room?

More recently, on May 11, 2007, I delivered a commencement speech at my alma mater, Texas A&M University. That was the thirty-third anniversary, to the very day, that Vice President Ford made the commencement address at Texas A&M, accompanied by a twenty-eight-year-old journeyman journalist. The 2007 commencement marked another milestone, more bittersweet: the first anniversary of our last interview and first lunch.

In terms of sheer historical serendipity, however, it's hard to ignore this piece of destiny:

In the summer of 1994, I was invited to make a speech in Beaver Creek, Colorado. That venue was coincidence enough, but the timing was doubly karmic: August 9, the twentieth anniversary of Richard Nixon's resignation and Jerry Ford's accession.

Knowing Ford would be there on his summer hiatus, I called his house the day the speech contract was signed and asked to see him. Even though we'd just had an interview in May in California, the happenstance was too exquisite to ignore, I argued.

"Sure, I think we can work that out," he said. True to his word, he did. It was the only anniversary interview he ever gave.

Our meeting was subsequently scheduled for 2:00 P.M., immediately following my speech. The logistics were a trifle tight; I hurried through a posttalk question-and-answer session and rushed out a side entrance of the Hyatt Regency, hustling the few hundred yards uphill to his Elk Track Court chalet. As usual, he greeted me at the door.

"Hard to believe—twenty years ago." He smiled. "It wasn't what you'd call an ordinary day at the office."

Once we'd settled into his study, I began by asking if there was a memory that stuck in his head from that momentous day.

"Probably the most intimate and dramatic was when I went in to see Nixon. He told me that that night he was gonna announce publicly that he was resigning and would do so the next day. As I recall, that was around eleven, eleven-thirty in the morning on the eighth. It was a pretty dramatic meeting of two old friends, who for twenty-five years never suspected something like this would develop.

"I was surprised about how cool and composed he was. He said he was doing it because it was in the best interests of the country and knew I was capable of handling the job. He urged me to keep Henry Kissinger on as secretary of state. He was very emphatic about Henry.

"It was a warm but, you know, obviously an emotional meeting. I think I said, 'I'm sorry it all happened.'

"As you know, I didn't have any ambition to be president; I had hoped to be speaker. But I also was very confident I could handle the job. I had no reservations at all. I didn't want to brag about that, but I'd had experience in the House, on the right committees, the leadership, dealing with [Lyndon] Johnson, with Nixon—so that the White House was no strange place for me."

He couldn't remember either of them analyzing the reasons for Nixon's demise, "although I will say on several other occasions prior to this, he said that he was so preoccupied with major foreign policy problems he did not have time to pay attention to something like the details of Watergate. I remember that vividly. But not in this conversation."

I asked how the hour-plus meeting had concluded. "As I recall, I was sitting here"—he gestured—"he was behind his desk there. He walked around, shook my hand, put his left arm on my shoulder and may have walked [me] halfway to the door, and that was it."

Did Nixon say, "Good luck, Jerry"?

"Something like that. It was a very warm and friendly meeting. His composure was strong."

Personal sadness for Nixon tempered what Ford nevertheless admitted was an undeniable high: "I felt good. I didn't want the job, but it was gonna be mine. Honestly, Tom, I had absolute confidence I could do the job."

As Watergate's twentieth anniversary approached, several television documentaries of the scandal had aired. Ford hadn't seen any of them but was planning to buy them to absorb later. But he'd already gotten their gist: Dick Nixon was the villain-in-chief.

"From what I read about these documentaries, they are really highly critical of Nixon. What makes me mad, though, is I read John Dean is one of the principal people. I think he's a no-good son of a bitch. I really think he's a bad man. I knew him when he worked in the House. He was a self-seeking, ambitious smarty, and I didn't trust him then."

In our May 1994 interview, he had called Dean "the real skunk" of Watergate.

Today I asked him if he believed Richard Nixon was "a bad man." He vigorously rejected the characterization.

"Well, if you take his whole character, he had about a five to ten percent flaw in his character, and so ninety to ninety-five percent of his character was good, [but] every once in a while for unexplainable reasons the bad part of the character would take over.

"I think he had strong convictions and that would overcome his good character traits. You know, that happens. Some of us have a temper; some of us have more temper than others, and every once in a while we'll fly off the handle. I think in this case the bad would overcome the good, and it was just too bad."

Ford had observed him angry at times, but never the Evil Nixon captured on some of the White House tapes:

"I never saw it to that extent. I know he had bitter feelings about certain elements—some in the press, some of his political opponents.

But I never heard him go off as strongly as the tapes indicate, or the Haldeman diaries."

As the interview wound down, I wondered if he'd written a fuller exposition of those epic days that was locked in a drawer to be released in a hundred years or so. Not my style, he demurred: he'd told all to the ghostwriter of his memoirs and his former aide Jim Cannon for a biography published the year before.

"As far as I know, they laid out everything."

It was apparent that he hadn't spent all morning rehashing the events that had fundamentally altered his life, and the nation's.

"I mean, that's gone," he concluded. "The game's over. I took [that attitude] right before we left the White House. I have a new life; I enjoy the new challenge, and we've been lucky. We've survived. Some family problems, like Mrs. Ford's bout with alcoholism and addiction. But because we looked forward instead of backwards, whatever the problems, we think they've been solved—and we couldn't be happier."

The two presidents whose lives and careers were seismically altered by Watergate were utter polar opposites. One was a terminal neurotic, consumed by demons, prone to compiling enemies lists, ill at ease in social settings; the other was gregarious, forgiving, everyone's friend, and a bit naïve.

"It was a straight protocol relationship," an old friend who talked with Ford about Nixon dozens of times said recently. "Nixon had no social ease. They were far too different beings to be close. In thirty years, Ford never got near him."

A former senior assistant likes to point out, moreover, that in vetting his travel itineraries in retirement, Ford routinely asked aides to build downtime into his schedules to visit whatever old friend happened to live in the neighborhood. Nixon was never one of those old friends he asked to see.

Yet Ford always considered himself a close Nixon friend, one of the few. They went way back; the Quaker from Whittier, California, was elected to the House in 1946, two years before Ford won a seat from Grand Rapids, Michigan. A few months after Ford's arrival in the spring of 1949, they were among the fifteen members who founded the Chowder and Marching Society, a Republican social group.

"Dick Nixon and I were longtime close friends," he said. "I mean, for years. I knew him intimately from January of 1949. I campaigned for him, he campaigned for me. We were very close—as close as anybody could get to Nixon—because of our relationship with the Chowder and Marching Society.

"I think now as I did then, that in the area of foreign policy, he was as good if not better than any president I've known. [But] he had a character flaw: where even when he made a mistake and knew it, he would not admit it. Why? That I've never known, Tom. It was a stubbornness, self-righteousness that was just a damn shame."

Watergate, he added, was the prime example of Nixon "not acting forthrightly as he should."

"He also could be enamored with certain people; John Connally was one."

The silver-haired Texan was everything Nixon wasn't—debonair, self-assured, smooth-talking, and socially well adjusted. Nixon was so mesmerized that he planned to dump Ford as vice president in 1976 and replace him with the former Texas governor. That was fine with him, Ford told Nixon; he'd promised Betty he'd retire in 1976 and move home to Grand Rapids.

"In 1971, John Connally talked him into wage and price controls, which was a disaster and which everybody else in the Nixon administration opposed. Connally had a certain effect on Nixon that I never understood, though certainly I think John Connally was a very attractive, able guy, but he certainly had a big impact on Nixon."

In his memoirs, Ford says he got a thank-you phone call from Nixon about ten days after the pardon. He told me that in their annual birthday calls he and his predecessor had never mentioned the pardon in the seventeen years since that brief phone chat. He didn't seem perturbed by what some might conclude was a colossal lack of gratitude on Nixon's part; perhaps the less said about an awkward and controversial act, the better. In fact, Ford confided that the two presidents had confidentially agreed they should avoid appearing together to avoid fueling speculation that the pardon had been part of a precooked deal between the two.

"I call him on his birthday, he reciprocates on mine. When Betty or Pat are ill, we exchange phone calls," Ford volunteered.

Occasionally they *did* appear together; at Ronald Reagan's request, they and Jimmy Carter represented the new president at the 1981 funeral of Egyptian president Anwar Sadat. They joined Carter and George H.W. Bush at the dedication of the Reagan Library in 1991. And over the objections of some aides, President Ford had visited an ailing Nixon in a Long Beach hospital in October 1974 when he almost died from an attack of phlebitis.

But by design, they never got together privately, even long into retirement.

In fact, Ford's aides routinely monitored guest lists at events their boss would be attending to guard against the embarrassment to both presidents and their host if Nixon and Ford were to appear at the same function.

"It's a good relationship, but we obviously don't think it's a good idea for us to be together," he conceded.

The same was true, he acknowledged, for his other predecessor, Vice President Spiro T. Agnew. But Ford always gave Nixon a partial pass for lying to him because of their long association and because he felt sorry for the first president forced to resign. Neither mitigating sentiment applied to Agnew, the obscure governor of Maryland when tapped by Nixon in 1968 as his running mate.

The 39th vice president had fled Washington in disgrace after a plea bargain with federal prosecutors spared him criminal corruption indictments in exchange for his resignation. The Fords and the Agnews both lived in the desert, about five miles apart. I wondered if they'd ever gotten together.

"In the fourteen years we've been here in Palm Springs or the desert, I've run into him three times—twice at a party at Barbara and Frank Sinatra's; we're friends of Sinatra. I ran into him once in a golf locker room; we exchanged cordial chitchat. Betty has run into Judy [Agnew] several times at the shopping center. We just have nothing in common.

"I barely knew Agnew. I campaigned for him once when he was running for governor. I was totally surprised when Nixon picked him. I never had any warm personal relations with him."

But that wasn't the real reason Agnew was *persona non grata* with his successor.

Ford recalled that in 1973, when press stories about alleged cash kickbacks to Agnew in exchange for state contracts started appearing, Nixon superlobbyist Bryce Harlow dropped by Ford's leadership office in the Capitol and asked to arrange a meeting with House Speaker Carl Albert and Majority Leader Tip O'Neill to plead Agnew's case.

"As a courtesy to the vice president and particularly Bryce, a dear friend, I said yes." But Ford wanted to know: "Is there any truth to these allegations?"

"I was assured by Agnew there was nothing out of the ordinary; he hadn't done any more in Maryland politics than had been done by others for years."

Ford said Agnew had thanked him for his support and that he should feel comfortable continuing to defend him, since he hadn't done anything wrong despite all those nasty rumors.

"There's no question that he lied to me when I asked him about the transactions. I can't help but remember it now and remember it at the time."

Did Agnew ever try to make amends later?

"Never!" he said with a flash of irritation. "I don't think I ever saw him except [at] those two or three social events. We had absolutely nothing in common."

Except, perhaps, that they'd both been lied to by Richard Nixon and hung out to dry.

I didn't spend much time discussing the pardon with Ford, because I had strong reason to believe he wouldn't go beyond his adamant there-was-no-deal public declarations. In fact, CBS's Phil Jones had done an embargoed interview with Ford a few weeks earlier and had reported that he had once again vehemently rejected suspicions of a deal.

So I asked whether there was any truth to the rumors that he pardoned Nixon in part because he thought his former House colleague was becoming a basket case while waiting to learn if he'd be indicted.

"Subjectively, it probably was a factor. I was hearing that he was terribly distraught. I don't know whether you could call it irrational, [but] he was despondent, had an unhealthy state of mind. I heard that." He didn't remember if anyone had told him Nixon was sounding suicidal; he repeated that the word filtering back from California was that Nixon was exhibiting "general despondency, distressed attitude."

Asked about skeptics who will always believe there had to have been a deal, Ford said emphatically:

"Well, my reaction to that is my own firm knowledge and conviction there wasn't one. And I've done my utmost, including a personal appearance before a House subcommittee of the Judiciary Committee, where I was interrogated by about twenty members of the House. As I understand it, that was the first time a sitting president had gone up to the Congress since Abraham Lincoln [to testify]. So nobody could ever say I tried to hide something; if anything, I became more forthright than anybody might, or I had to be. I took an oath on Capitol Hill; I don't know how I could have been any more forthright."

Over the years, he'd become even more entrenched in his belief that he'd done the right thing—for Nixon and the country.

"I got lots of suggestions after the fact: Well, why didn't you wait until he was indicted? Why didn't you wait until he was convicted? Why didn't you wait until after the appeals? You know, I strongly felt the quicker I made the decision, the quicker that issue would get off the [political] agenda.

"It was a personal decision, and the suggestion for it didn't come from anybody. It was my own feeling then, just as strongly today: I have no reservations at all. I do feel strongly it was the right thing for the country, and whatever political consequences for me, I accepted.

"It's encouraging to find a better understanding today of the pardoning of Nixon than in the emotional period of 1974. You know, I was condemned, criticized, editorialized [but] I never wavered. I thought then as I do now it was the right thing, and it's becoming more evident among the public generally that it was the right thing to do."

Ford had been even more emphatic in a 1994 interview, on the twentieth anniversary of the resignation, when reflecting on his inner feelings during Nixon's funeral:

"I was very pleased that the press overwhelmingly talked about the good things he has done rather than the tragedy of Watergate. That really made me feel good, Tom. I was pleased that the ceremony went off so well. Clinton was there, the four other presidents, the atmosphere was very, very good.

"Subjectively, I said to myself, 'If I hadn't pardoned him, would this have taken place?' I happen to believe it would have been very unlikely. No question, Tom: he would have been indicted. The probability is he would have been convicted. It would have been a long, tortuous appeal. The odds are he would have gone to jail. If that scenario had taken place, the country would have lost the benefit of his continuing statesmanship in foreign policy. I feel very strongly on that now—and the pardon eliminated all of that [downside]. When I did it, I couldn't foresee all that, but in reflection at that funeral, again subjectively, I did feel it."

I asked him at that 1994 interview if history would give Nixon the same sort of pass the press had extended to him in the collective funeral coverage.

"The odds are it won't. Think of twenty years ago today."

He elaborated on that point in 1998: "History's not gonna treat him very well. He's getting better treatment today than I think historians will give him."

Almost three years before Nixon's death, Ford remained ambivalent about his flawed friend, and harsher about his handling of the cover-up:

"I'm pleased he's been able to resurrect his reputation," Ford mused in 1991. "I'm pleased he's becoming more acceptable, because in the area of foreign policy, his views can be beneficial.

"What is discouraging after all this process of getting back in a favorable light, these [Oval Office] tapes come out and they portray the darker side. It undercuts every upward step at rehabilitation."

Three years later, after Nixon's death, he was even more ambivalent.

"I flew out to the funeral on a private plane," he remembered. "I had about five hours to think about our lifetime of experiences. We had some great, enjoyable time together. I couldn't help but be sad about how ill-advised and just plain stupid he was in the way he handled the cover-up. In reflection, Tom, it's incomprehensible.

"He had a terrific loyalty to people. He was not good at firing anybody. Here [were] John Mitchell and the others who had knowledge— he just couldn't face up to biting the bullet. It's too bad; the whole thing could have been ended with an admission: 'These people knew [about] it, I can't tolerate it, they gotta go.' "

He told me the last time they'd talked was on January 8 [1994], the day before Nixon's birthday and fifteen weeks before his death. "We had a nice chat," Ford remembered. "He was very grateful that Betty and I had been to Pat's funeral and that I had gone to the twentieth anniversary of his first inauguration. We went up on January 20 [1993]; that's the last time I saw him—when I spoke and introduced him up there [in New York after his wife's death]. That was a lonely, lonely period."

———

I ended that first interview in 1991 by asking how he hoped history would remember him. He was predictably modest in offering his legacy:

"That I was a dedicated, hardworking, honest person who served constructively in Congress and in the White House."

# SIX

# The Reagans

THREE DAYS AFTER Ronald Reagan died at his home in Beverly Hills, Gerald and Betty Ford joined millions of their fellow Americans in mourning the country's heartfelt loss.

"He and I became very good friends," Ford told CNN's Larry King from his Beaver Creek home on the evening of June 8, 2004. "Let me be very forthright: I think Ronald Reagan was a first-class president, and I treasured my relationship and association with him."

Baloney.

Ford added that he and Reagan had seen each other "on occasion" and that he had visited Reagan in the latter's Beverly Hills office when Reagan's illness was well advanced.

"He barely recognized me. . . . I tried to bring things up that would refresh his memory, but he was not the Ronald Reagan that I admired and felt was a very good friend."

As Vice President Dick Cheney once famously said in a totally different context to CNN's Wolf Blitzer, that's also hogwash.

Perhaps I'm being grossly unfair; maybe it was more pure Jerry Ford, always striving to say something nice whenever he could, cushioning his zingers, not to mention adhering to the time-honored tradition of never speaking ill of the deceased.

The truth is, however, that that sort of lofty adulation of the 40th president wasn't what he expressed in private throughout their strained relationship. In fact, a politician with a reputation for never holding grudges harbored such uncharacteristic bitterness against Reagan that he never really softened his disdain until November 5, 1994—almost two decades after their nasty 1976 primary tussle.

That was the day Reagan announced to the nation he'd come down with the crippling Alzheimer's disease that eventually killed him a decade later.

Not long after Reagan's dramatic open letter to his fellow citizens, a shaken Ford told me the day he heard about that "terrible announcement" was one of the worst of his life.

Thereafter, Ford scrupulously modulated his animus, changing his tone—but not his tune.

For the next dozen years, in deference to the Alzheimer's, he never uttered a derisive word about Reagan to me.

Nonetheless, he neither liked nor respected the former Hollywood actor. He considered Reagan a superficial, disengaged, intellectually lazy showman who didn't do his homework and clung to a naïve, unrealistic, and essentially dangerous worldview.

No doubt there was a large measure of envy at play, a classic showhorse-versus-workhorse situation. Ford both admired and envied Reagan's undisputed skills as a communicator. "He had a helluva flair," he conceded in one of our interviews.

Yet to his dying day, Ford blamed Reagan for his 1976 loss to Jimmy Carter. In his public comments over the years, he usually listed Reagan's pro forma campaigning on his behalf as one of several factors in his defeat, along with the Nixon pardon and lousy economic indicators. "His lack of campaigning was one of three or four reasons that resulted in my loss to Carter," he told me in 1991.

But that was discreet window dressing: if Reagan hadn't looked at his shoes through the fall of 1976, Ford was convinced, he would have won four more years. He never forgave Reagan for dooming his dreams of being an elected president.

After their ferocious primary combat, he didn't want Reagan on his ticket in the fall of 1976 and was vehemently uninterested in being on the ticket with him four years later. He was so opposed to the idea of being the Gipper's running mate that he engineered a list of demands he knew were so sweeping that Reagan would be compelled to say no— much to Ford's relief.

Ford's feelings hardly mellowed in retirement. A few months before his death, he told author Lou Cannon, who interviewed him for a Princeton University Library oral history project on former secretary of state James A. Baker III, "It's not his [Reagan's] nature to help someone else. He believed in winning on his own."

He emphatically told me, moreover, that Reagan should have graciously stepped aside in 1980 so he could run against Jimmy Carter again and was monumentally irked when he didn't.

After 1976, the emotional chasm was simply too massive between the two. To Ford's thinking, Reagan had committed an even worse transgression than breaking his celebrated Eleventh Commandment: Thou shalt not speak ill of fellow Republicans.

Ford had his own version of that commandment: Thou shalt always help fellow Republicans, or at the very least do them no harm. By that standard, Reagan had committed the unpardonable and unforgivable.

He also thought Nancy Reagan was the hidden hand behind her husband's bad behavior, particularly his electorally lethal benign neglect toward Ford in the 1976 general election.

"She had a tremendous impact on his decision. She was very bitter, and I think she had a checkrein on him," he told me in 1991.

Ford felt far less kindly toward Nancy than toward her husband, who he always suspected was at heart a decent guy, if unduly malleable—particularly by his wife.

The truth is that until the Alzheimer's changed everything by injecting a humanitarian imperative into the relationship, neither Ford could abide Nancy—especially after they found out that she sometimes mocked Jerry Ford as "the unelected president."

When word reached Rancho Mirage in the 1980s, moreover, that the First Lady was also dumping on her husband's once-removed predecessor for profiteering from his White House service—something she later pushed her own beloved Ronnie into emulating, in spades—the breach was seemingly irreparable.

As Ford's biographer and former senior aide James Cannon observed at a 2006 Washington seminar, there was a simple explanation for why Ford and Carter, once bitter political enemies, befriended each other after their presidencies: "There was a bond because they both felt they had been defeated by Reagan."

It's easy to understand Ford's quiet rage toward Reagan in the early years of his retirement. Not long after he'd become a private citizen, for example, the Reagan camp asked him to cosign a fundraising appeal with his 1976 nemesis. The consummate party man didn't agonize over that decision. "They needed a putty knife to get him off the ceiling," as one of Ford's men remembered the moment.

Another early telltale sign of his true feelings: I asked him in a 1978 *Newsweek* interview if Reagan's nomination by the Republicans would hand the 1980 election to Carter.

"I don't want to get into that," he sidestepped. As lawyers say, asked and answered.

At a 1979 Washington Press Club dinner, he administered another thinly veiled shot at Reagan while bashing Carter: "Neither government by nostalgia nor government by ideological reflex will meet America's needs any better than government by inexperience has."

Three days after he decided against challenging Reagan in the 1980 Republican primaries, I had a brief conversation with Ford in his

Rancho Mirage office in which he said—with a notable lack of enthusiasm—that he'd support Reagan as the nominee of his party.

Afterward, I filed these observations to my bosses in New York:

Based on a deep background* conversation with Ford, I think we can say without fear of contradiction that Jerry Ford intends to support the party's nominee with far more diligence and grace than Ronald Reagan non-campaigned for him in 1976. It is very clear that he has more of a problem with Carter as president than Reagan.

But we are also safe in saying that Ford isn't going to stump for Reagan just for the hell of it. He remains deeply resentful of Reagan, still angry at his hand-sitting last time, still personally offended of Reagan's demagoguery on the Panama Canal issue, still believing in his soul that Reagan simply can't win against Jimmy Carter.

And because of all that, he isn't going to kill himself for Reagan simply because that's what the party would like for him to do. This time, it's going to cost Reagan something.

As Ford himself said at one point in last week's strategy session in Washington, "I can support the man—and I will. But he'll pay a price."

Another clue to his Reagan mindset: In 1984, Ford was telling me about how, on the basis of a private conversation with the president, he thought Reagan had belatedly experienced a pragmatic conversion about the need to expand relationships with the People's Republic of China. I asked him why he was so sure that Reagan had been weaned from his pro-Taiwan fixation.

---

*In the conventions of journalism, "deep background" means a reporter can use information he's learned but can't identify the source and can't put any of the information in quotations. The fact that Ford insisted on that ground rule was another index of his unhappiness over Reagan. He didn't want to be quoted saying anything nice about Reagan.

"Well, he listened," Ford said, emitting a big laugh. "You know, that's a first stage."

Ford always subordinated his dislike for Reagan to his fervent belief that even he was preferable to four more years of Jimmy Carter. At the height of his Reagan pique, for instance, the consummate party man could still say things like this, at an October 1980 Republican rally:

"Whatever course this campaign takes and whomever our party chooses as its presidential candidate, I will go anywhere, do anything in my power, and work with all my strength to elect a Republican president and Republican Congress in 1980. Carter must go!"

Even so, in our first off-the-record interview, fifteen years after his first unpleasant experience with the former California governor, Ford was still angry with Reagan's behavior in the 1976 elections.

"Well, that preconvention campaign was not helpful in the runoff," he told me. "You know, we thought, number one, I deserved an opportunity to run [unchallenged]. I did not deserve to have Republican opposition that took an awful lot of our time and our money, and it gave the opposition some reasons to make political points. I think it also— no question about it—delayed the kind of foreign policy decisions with the Soviet Union that we couldn't consummate."

Ford took pains to point out that Reagan was going through the motions in his minuscule stumping in the general election. "Whenever he campaigned—and he didn't campaign much—it was for senatorial and congressional candidates," he remembered.

When reminded that by contrast he himself had campaigned extensively for Reagan, he quickly concurred: "I campaigned for him in '80 and '84, sure did."

"Did he ever acknowledge your contributions?"

"Not very affirmatively."

So why had Ford buried the hatchet, at least for public consumption?

"Well, it's not my nature to go around knifing people. It isn't worth it. My philosophy has always been: You're in a ball game; you lose it, you've got some more games down the road; work toward those, forget about the past. It doesn't do any good to [brood].

"Totally off the record, he was not what I would [call] a technically competent president. You know, his knowledge of the budget, his knowledge of foreign policy—it was not up to the standards of either Democrat or Republican presidents. But he had a helluva flair. He could sell himself probably better than any president since FDR and maybe JFK. So I praise his assets, but I have reservations about his technical ability."

Despite his deficiencies, Ford conceded, "he was a helluva lot better than any of the Democratic alternatives."

Without a doubt, Ford was damning Reagan with faint praise.

"In terms of his ability, it doesn't sound like he's on your Top Ten list."

"No, I agree. That doesn't mean he wasn't effective."

Even so, Ford was appalled by Reagan's detached, disengaged style of governing, and thought it hurt the image of the office.

"No question about it. I've talked to several foreign leaders who were shocked at his lack of detailed information. On the other hand, they agreed with me: from the point of view of PR image, he was terrific."

Another plank in Ford's bill of particulars: Ford deeply resented Reagan's opposition to his participation in the 1975 Helsinki conference, which he always believed set in motion the democracy movement in Eastern Europe that finally reunified Germany and brought freedom to the Soviet satellites. He likewise thought Reagan's opposition to a Panama Canal treaty was shortsighted and narrow-minded.

"We believed there were people in the Pentagon giving Reagan information about our negotiations with the Soviet Union and our activities in Helsinki, rumors that could be exaggerated—and they were, by Reagan and his people."

In addition, he charged, "there were hidden faces over there in the bowels of the Pentagon and other departments who knew we were negotiating to try and get a Panama Canal treaty, and of course Reagan felt very strongly opposed to it. There were leaks to Reagan about [how] we were selling out the Panama Canal."

He also zapped Reagan for the controversial speaking deal where he was paid $2 million for a couple of speeches in Japan, overreaching behavior he believed rewrote the standards for an appearance of impropriety.

"Reagan started out with a very unfortunate arrangement with the Japanese trip, and he's done some others I think are on the borderline," he complained.

Even though he didn't accuse Reagan entirely for his 1976 loss to Jimmy Carter, it was apparent Ford laid most of the blame at Reagan's feet.

He also faulted Reagan for ignoring Ford's clear wishes by letting aides to the Republican front-runner gin up the ill-advised notion of putting Ford on the ticket with Reagan in 1980. Earlier, Reagan had floated the idea with him privately; Ford had rejected it summarily, and was annoyed when it resurfaced before the July convention.

"I did not go to that convention in 1980 in Detroit with the desire to be on the ticket," he contended. "I told Reagan in June when he came to my office—he first broached the possibility then. I said, 'Forget it, I don't want to be on the ticket; I can be more helpful to you *not* on the ticket. I will campaign for you.'

"I was totally surprised when an hour or two after Betty and I got to Detroit that Ron and Nancy asked to come to my suite. I was dumbfounded when he suggested that I be on the ticket. I said, 'I thought that was settled.' But he made a special plea and said would I reconsider? I said, 'Well, I'll do it in deference to your request, but I feel I have to know certain things in writing what my role would be if I were vice president.' "

Ford was mainly going through the motions out of courtesy. As he told one of those pushing the idea, "I don't think it will work, but he is the nominee, and we probably owe it to him to talk about it."

When a negotiating committee of Ford and Reagan agents couldn't come up with a workable formula for the extraordinary grant of vice presidential authority he was demanding, "we mutually broke it off," Ford said.

"George Bush was always my candidate for vice president. In fact, Betty and I went to Detroit with the hope that we could be helpful to him. But Reagan screwed it all up by getting me involved."

On the flight back to Colorado, Ford essentially admitted that he'd consciously scuttled the deal by raising the bar impossibly high. "Well," he mused to an aide, "we had a pretty good convention. I gave a pretty good speech, and I got Bush as vice president."

After that 1991 interview, I scribbled some quick observations to myself in my rental car before leaving Sand Dune Road. Here's what I wrote:

> Ford really doesn't like Reagan. Early on he singles out Reagan for dumping on the Helsinki Accords without my prompting him; complains that Reagan sat on his hands in the fall of 1976 . . . blames Nancy . . . offended by Reagan's lack of substance; resents his PR effectiveness . . . thinks his post-presidential buckraking cheapened the presidency (also made Ford's conduct look more in balance than excess).

Two years later, in our March 1993 interview, I wanted to see if he'd mellowed at all about Reagan, so I asked about the state of their relationship. He didn't have to parse his reply. "In the case of Reagan, because we're both in California, we see each other occasionally at social events, but we make no effort to really get together. Off the record, we have really very little in common, Tom."

I couldn't resist leading the witness a bit.

"Well, I think you've got a long memory, too."

Ford let loose with a hearty, prolonged chuckle, but didn't say a word, before smilingly moving on to the state of his relationship with

Jimmy Carter. As a *Chicago Tribune* reporter once said in nailing Ford after a similar nonanswer at a press conference, "Mr. President, I didn't hear a no."

From there we rehashed his decision to opt out of a 1980 primary challenge to Reagan. He surprised me with his riff on how Reagan, who'd been plotting his own candidacy since losing to Ford in 1976, should have stepped aside for him:

"I knew I could beat Jimmy Carter; I wasn't sure Ronald Reagan could. I would have liked to run if I could have run without a bitter Reagan-Ford preconvention battle. But for Ronald Reagan and me to get into another head-to-head confrontation, I was not prepared to do that."

"So the only way was if he had been graceful and would have bowed out?" I asked.

"Yeah, and he was not gonna do that. I would have— I've never liked to raise money, and it would have required a lot of money-raising. It would have meant a lot of time on the road, and truthfully Betty had just gotten started on her own recovery, and I didn't want to jeopardize that recovery. So it was a combination of personal as well as family reasons."

Curiously, Ford said he never considered sending an emissary to Reagan feeling him out about stepping aside; he was convinced, according to several former aides, that Reagan was so hell-bent on running that broaching the subject was a colossal waste of time.

So in Ford's version of reality, he refused to do to Reagan in 1980 what Reagan had done to him in 1976, with such disastrous effects for the Republican Party and Ford personally.

But he was absolutely convinced that had he run he could have made history as a latter-day Grover Cleveland, the only president elected to nonconsecutive terms.

"You would have beaten Jimmy Carter?"

"No question about it."

The Reagan relationship bumped along, correct at best. In 1986, Ford complained loudly that Reagan, whose military buildup is central to his legacy, was distorting his predecessor's contributions to national defense. Ford let it be known to the White House that he was tired of hearing Reagan talk as though the B-1 bomber, MX missile, and Trident nuclear missile submarine programs magically sprang to life in the Reagan administration, not the Ford years. Finally Reagan was forced to concede the point and apologized to Ford and Jimmy Carter, who'd also gone public with his irritation.

Everything changed forever in the fall of 1994, with Reagan's terminal illness.

"The day of the terrible announcement, we called and both of us talked to Nancy," he said in our 1995 interview. "That's sad. Betty has talked to Nancy several times since, and the report is not encouraging.

"He doesn't recognize people anymore, and Mrs. Reagan told Betty that he gets tired very easily and that she's trying to find somebody who will be an around-the-clock nurse for him. Sad. Because we called right away the minute we heard about it, we got within the week a nice letter from him. So he was still able that soon [after being diagnosed] to respond, but from what I hear now, it's a different situation. Too bad."

In talking about Nancy, Ford interjected another reference to the long-standing enmity between the Fords and the Reagans, which he stressed was now, out of simple human compassion, consigned to the past tense.

"Both Betty and I have great sympathy for her because from everything we hear, from her, from others, it's a terrible burden. So we're very sympathetic to her"—he couldn't resist chuckling as he truthfully admitted—"which isn't what we've ordinarily been. But in this tragedy she has our full sympathy and support."

I asked him if Reagan's sobering plight had dissolved some of the old animosities.

"I would think so, yeah, although recently we never had any of the tensions that were built up in the [1976] preconvention period. I mean, time heals a lot of that. This tragedy— You never think about '76 [anymore]."

In February 2000 he confided that Reagan's health was deteriorating steadily:

"I hear that it's taken a turn for the worse, Tom. I've heard that Maureen made a very startling confession that it was bad. Made it public somewhere. They can hang on [physically], you know. His [general] health is good. Physiologically I'm told he's doing all right, but then I keep reading about these wonder surgeries or medication that is supposed to be helpful, but if they were workable, gosh, why wouldn't they take advantage of it? Just be grateful we don't have to deal with it. Oh God, yes.

"I have not talked to Nancy for maybe three or four months. Betty talks to Nancy every three or four weeks. The net result is that he's deteriorating. Now, how much I don't know. I come to the conclusion he's becoming more difficult, with his physical [and] mental problems getting worse. It's too bad."

Five months later, he told me that he'd visited his onetime adversary and had been deeply shaken.

"I went to see Reagan in Los Angeles eighteen months ago, in Century City. He didn't recognize me at all. I must have mentioned a dozen things he and I were involved in—our campaigns, the Sadat funeral trip, et cetera. None of them registered."

I asked him what Reagan had talked about.

"Nothing, really. I did most of the talking. I spent all of my time trying to create recognition, but nothing worked. It was very, very sad."

# SEVEN

# The Clintons

A T FORD'S FUNERAL, two of the three surviving former presidents joined George W. Bush in memorializing Gerald Ford's life and public service. There's a simple reason why Bill Clinton was the only ex-president who didn't speak at any of the ceremonies: Ford himself wanted it that way.

He once entertained Bill and Hillary Clinton at his Colorado mountain retreat, and found the new president just as charming and charismatic as advertised. Like his view of Ronald Reagan's showmanship, he admired, if somewhat grudgingly, the 42nd president's undisputed political agility. Not long after their 1993 socializing, in fact, Ford told me that he'd telephoned old Republican friends and party leaders with a blunt warning: This new president shouldn't be underestimated as just another slick politician.

"This guy can sell three-day-old ice," he confided with a mix of envy and disdain. "He's that good."

At the same time, he was even more complimentary about Clinton's gifts in a conversation with a close associate: "I get confused by him. I don't know what's at his core. I don't know what's most important to him. But this guy is the best politician I've ever seen."

He compared Clinton favorably to John F. Kennedy, another charismatic politician. For some reason, he didn't refer to the 35th president as Jack, using his formal name instead.

"John was great, but all John had was the press. He was still an elitist; he didn't like the rope line. This guy loves the rope line—and the rope line loves him."

Yet he always believed Bill Clinton had disgraced the office by trysting with a young intern on the job as well as, in his view, obstructing justice and lying under oath and to his family, his staff, his Democratic supporters, and the American people.

As then vice president George H. W. Bush once told Ronald Reagan in an entirely different context, "There are standards." In Ford's righteously Middle American view of good and ill, Clinton's wobbly personal standards were enough to veto what would have no doubt been an elegant and heartfelt eulogy.

Even so, at the critical juncture of Bill Clinton's troubled second term, Ford had actually been willing to reach across the political aisle and offer Clinton some desperately needed bipartisan impeachment help. They could never agree to the terms. Ford wanted more contrition and admission of guilt than Clinton was willing to concede, so what would have been a remarkable deal between two Odd Couple presidents died.

He hadn't known Clinton before his election, but that changed in the summer of 1993, when Jerry and Betty invited them to their Colorado home and hung with them for three days.

"His daughter Chelsea likes to dance," Ford recalled in May 1994. Four years ago, the Vail Valley Foundation brought the Bolshoi Academy to Vail to set up a school for young American ballet students. They were there six weeks, and it's developed so that Vail is the center of summer ballet in the country. It's a great add-on to Vail's winter skiing.

"So the White House learned about it and they asked could Chelsea come out and get some [ballet] exposure. Well, the minute I heard that, I called Clinton. I said, 'We'd love to have you; Ambassador Firestone's home next door is available to you and the family. I hope you'll come.'

"He said, 'Well, I can't tell for sure.' Well, then the Pope was [coming to] Colorado. Clinton then called and said, 'When we're in Colorado for His Holiness, we could come up for two or three days.' So they came up. We played golf two days with Jack Nicklaus, and we had dinner three times. We got to know him quite well."

What had he learned about the new president, other than the fact, as Ford grumped to friends, that he cheated at golf?

"Well, he's a nicer person than I thought. I think he's a nice person. He's very persuasive. He's a helluva PR guy. He's a typical Chautauqua salesman who moves in, seduces everybody, and then starts to compromise his position based on the pressures that he gets politically and otherwise.

"He doesn't think it's wrong; he enjoys the process. I don't worry about that domestically, Tom. But I am very sincerely concerned about his handling of foreign policy. He's got a mediocre team and I don't think he likes foreign policy. In fact, when I see him come to the podium to talk about a foreign policy issue, he is uncertain, he doesn't look comfortable, he doesn't project strength, and that worries me.

"Look at North Korea, where he now is gonna buy them off with half a billion dollars' worth of aid. Certainly Haiti is a disaster; Somalia. I think you've got to decouple trade from human rights in China. And the handling of Japan is anything but successful."

He repeated that "he's a helluva salesman." It wasn't clear if he thought Clinton's evangelism was sincere or merely an act.

"I think he thinks he's sincere. I'll give him the benefit of the doubt. On domestic policy, I think he's sincere."

And effective, Ford added. He predicted that Clinton had to be favored for reelection in 1996.

"He'll be very hard to beat. I do not think the Republicans can win challenging him on domestic policy. He's very articulate, he's a helluva salesman, and on the assumption that the economy is okay, Republicans will have a tough time in '96 unless—and I think this is the key—he could have a foreign policy crisis, and his track record to date is terrible. If we have a crisis, the American people will reflect on the incompetence and they'll say, 'We can't gamble with this man for another four years.' "

As an American first and a partisan Republican second, he hoped that contingency didn't happen, and assumed Clinton would then breeze to a second term.

I asked if he agreed with many of his Republican pals back in Washington that the press was giving Clinton a pass on his personal life.

"There's no doubt they've treated him differently than they treated others. Whether you call that a free ride or not, it's hard to tell. Certainly, on domestic policy they haven't been antagonistic, and I understand that. Seventy-five percent of them ideologically agree with him, and subjectively they can't be mean to somebody they inwardly have a camaraderie with. I mean, that's human nature. And he is a nice guy, and he is a salesman.

"In foreign policy, the press is beginning to be worried and their objectivity is beginning to come to the surface. Anthony Lewis in the *New York Times* has been giving him hell in Bosnia for six months, with good reason. The facts are there.

"He's got a mediocre staff. You know, Warren Christopher's a very nice person, but he looks like a dried-up prune and he talks like somebody who should be a good number-two but has no role in the global atmosphere of foreign policy. And with all deference to [Deputy Secretary of State] Strobe Talbott, your former compatriot in the journalism profession . . ." Ford laughed derisively.

I followed up my earlier question about media coverage of Clinton's personal baggage.

"I don't see how in conscience the press can ignore some of it. Now, if I were in your boots, I would not like to write it, because I do have a certain feeling about privacy and I also know, Tom, there are damn few Americans, including myself, who don't have some skeleton in your closet.

"The difference is: lots of people make one mistake, but they learn and they don't repeat it. Everything you see about him is a pattern."

I was curious whether he'd picked up any evidence of Clinton's flirtatious side in their socializing at Beaver Creek.

"Turn that off," he commanded, pointing to my recorder.

"I'll tell you one thing: he didn't miss one good-looking skirt at any of the social occasions. He's got a wandering eye, I'll tell you that. Betty had the same impression; he isn't very subtle about his interest."

D espite his personal distaste for Bill Clinton's behavior, Ford never thought Clinton had committed an impeachable offense. He also believed, regrettably, that fellow Republicans were pursuing impeachment mainly for partisan political gain and that even if the president *had* perpetrated a high crime or misdemeanor as defined by the Constitution, the votes to remove him from office weren't there in the Senate anyway.

In early May 1998, with independent counsel Kenneth Starr's investigation of Bill Clinton's financial and alleged romantic entanglements in its fourth year, I interviewed Ford at his office in Rancho Mirage and asked, "Is any of this impeachable?"

"I don't think it is and I hope it isn't," he answered. "If they have a clear-cut case, it's no different in many respects from Nixon. But it's not clear yet, and I just don't like the country going through that kind of a traumatic experience [again]."

I asked him what Clinton should do to avoid being impeached.

"A lot depends on what the truth is. Obviously, Starr thinks he's got enough evidence to prove *something*. To take all this time and make all this effort and end up with zero, I can't believe he would go ahead [otherwise]. He can be surmising something with a lot of credibility, but that's different from proving the truth in the House Committee on Judiciary or the House, even the public. I think the public, despite some of their poll surveys, thinks something's going on."

Ford enjoyed a reputation for having sound political instincts, so I asked what his gut was telling him about the allegations Clinton had been fooling around with intern Monica Lewinsky.

"I don't want to believe it's true, but the cumulative evidence leads you to that conclusion," he said, remembering his experience while entertaining the Clintons at Beaver Creek. He and Betty had compared notes after one dinner party and were both struck at how aggressively Clinton had engaged several attractive women, even with his wife in the room.

"He's got his eyes wandering all the time," Ford recalled—not the first time he'd made that point to me. "He's attractive and he's persuasive, obviously."

Ford scoffed at Clinton's assertion that Secret Service agents he didn't want to talk to Starr were covered by executive privilege protections, like senior White House aides.

"His claim of executive privilege can't hold up in court. Executive privilege is not written into the Constitution. That's fractured legal theory." But he agreed that Clinton could drag out a ruling for at least a year "unless the Supreme Court takes the initiative and calls it up and takes quick action." That was Clinton's game, Ford thought: stall for time.

Since he was in the House then, I wondered how Clinton might fare if he went on television the way Vice President Nixon did in 1952 and made a "Checkers" speech of his own.

"It would solve a lot of problems, but I don't think that's his nature. He believes everything he says. Under any circumstances, at any time, and he's sincere about that. He just has a very facile mind." He chuckled at that.

I asked Ford if anyone had urged him to use his moral authority as a former president to talk about the institutional damage he believed Clinton was doing to the presidency.

"Nobody's come to me. It's not my style to interject myself, and as a result I've said absolutely nothing. Jimmy Carter hasn't done it, I don't intend to do it, Ronald Reagan can't, and George Bush to my knowledge has not. I think it's wise for the three of us, and Ron Reagan if he were able, to just stay totally out of it. It's a damn shame; it's undercutting the image of the presidency."

Actually, he didn't quite "just stay totally out of it." Five months later, on October 4, 1998, as Republicans ratcheted up their demands for Clinton's forced removal from office, Ford floated an idea for avoiding impeachment in an article in the *New York Times.* He skewered Clinton for having "broken faith with those who elected him . . . forced to take refuge in legalistic evasions" and "glossy deceit."

Yet to avoid a messy impeachment trial without letting Clinton off the hook, Ford also proposed a novel twist to the upcoming 1999 State of the Union speech: instead of reciting the usual laundry list of policy items, Clinton should appear in the well of the House and accept a verbal rebuke from legislators.

"By his appearance the President would accept full responsibility for his actions, as well as for his subsequent efforts to delay or impede the investigation of them," Ford wrote. "No spinning, no semantics, no evasiveness or blaming others for his plight.

"Let all this be done without partisan exploitation or mean-spiritedness. Let it be dignified, honest and, above all, cleansing. The result, I believe, would be the first moment of majesty in an otherwise squalid year."

Plainly, Ford was trying to avoid a constitutional mess and also lend a hand to a fellow president, but he was also motivated by an intense desire to save his beloved party from itself. He believed his fellow Republicans were so consumed by their animus for Bill Clinton, and Hillary, that they couldn't do the right thing for the country and, in the process, their own partisan political interests. He conceived of the op-ed as a road map for collective sanity, especially for his Republican brethren.

The House ignored his creative suggestion and impeached Clinton anyway, on December 19, 1998. So he tried again, collaborating with Jimmy Carter on a second op-ed. Writing in the *Times* two days after the House vote, the former presidents argued against Clinton's conviction and ouster from office by the Senate. Instead, they proposed a bipartisan senatorial resolution of censure:

> President Clinton would have to accept rebuke while acknowledging his wrongdoing and the very real harm he has caused. The Congressional resolution should contain language stipulating that the President's acceptance of these findings—including a public acknowledgment that he did not tell the truth under oath—cannot be used in any future criminal trial to which he may be subject. It may even be possible for the special prosecutor publicly to forgo the option of bringing such charges against the President when Mr. Clinton leaves office.

Ironically, Ford was precisely recycling his rationale for the Nixon pardon twenty-four years earlier. Without some remedy to bring the impeachment crisis to a swift conclusion, the country would almost surely be embroiled in bitter partisan strife for months, probably years. A censure, he was arguing, would eliminate the need for a Senate trial that would "only exacerbate the jagged divisions that are tearing our national fabric." The censure option, he was convinced, was the only route to avoid another Watergate orgy of recriminations and national gridlock.

After his knees were replaced and skiing became but a melancholy memory, Ford settled into a predictable lifestyle routine: the desert in the winter, the mountains in the summer. So when by coincidence

I was invited to make a speech in Beaver Creek in late January 1999, I was certain he wouldn't be there. I was wrong.

"You're in luck," Ford's chief of staff Penny Circle told me just before Christmas. "They'll be there for the World Cup."

The World Alpine Skiing Championships were being staged in Vail, and Ford had always been passionate about the sport. One of his fondest memories was a ski trip to Vermont with his drop-dead-gorgeous model girlfriend Phyllis Brown in 1940. Their junket landed them on the cover of *Look* magazine.

In typical fashion, when Ford learned that my wife and three-year-old son had come along with me, he invited the three of us over to chat. We arrived at the Fords' elegant Elk Track Court chalet at 2:45 P.M. on January 31, the Sunday of Super Bowl XXXIII between the Denver Broncos and the Atlanta Falcons.

It was a clear, cold, sunny day in the mountains. Ford greeted us at the front door and for the first and last time in my experience, took the elevator to the second floor, where Betty was waiting. "I've torn a ligament in my ankle," he grumbled, "and I don't know how I did it."

Just as in Rancho Mirage, Ford and I had always met in his study, on the south side of the staircase. This was my first exposure to their living room, an airy, inviting space with large picture windows that overlooked the town center of Beaver Creek below. From the sofas, we could see the chairlifts busily shuttling skiers up the slopes.

"We're still using the Christmas napkins," Betty said, laughing as their chef passed around a plate of cookies and took drink orders.

Communal chitchat quickly gave way to some triage: Mrs. Ford and my wife, Melanie, adjourned to another part of the living room and launched into girl stuff: decorators, cancer therapies, the perils of conception. My son, Andrew, occupied himself with playing with Happy, the Fords' frisky cocker spaniel.

It was ostensibly a social occasion, so Ford and I kept on with small talk. He was tickled that Andrew had been enrolled in the Beaver Creek toddlers' ski school and was becoming a "Mini-Mouse," ruing that skiing had been the first of his athletic passions to go because of his gimpy football knees.

Politicians being politicians and reporters being inquisitive pot-stirrers, the discussion predictably turned to Bill Clinton's impeachment, which the House of Representatives had voted six weeks earlier.

"Well, have I told you about my conversation with Clinton?" he wondered.

If my notebook had been out, I'd have dropped it.

He began a riveting narrative by telling me that during the previous fall, not long after his October op-ed appeared, Bob Strauss had called him in Rancho Mirage. The White House had commissioned Strauss to ask Ford if he'd be willing to testify on Clinton's behalf before the House Judiciary Committee. Strauss said that if he'd agree, Bill Clinton was willing to let Ford be the *only* witness to vouch for him at the committee hearing. Unspoken was the clever rationale for the extraordinary proposal: How could rabid House Republicans ignore the wise counsel of one of their most famous alumni?

"I told Bob there was just no way," Ford recalled. "I mean, can you imagine me, a longtime House Republican, testifying for Bill Clinton before a Republican House?"

Admittedly, the legendary Texas pol was the perfect choice for making the initial approach. He and Ford were old friends, throwbacks to the long-dead era when civility was still de rigueur in the Washington political process. They'd always been friendly, but Ford's admiration for Strauss had been enhanced by remarks the Democratic warhorse had made at the March 1975 dinner of the Gridiron Club, the capital's most prestigious journalists' organization.

"President Ford, our friends here in the press consistently write, 'Jerry Ford is a good man, *but . . .*'" he said, catching Ford's eye. "Mr. President, let me say to you that you are not 'a good man but.' You are a 'good man *and*.' And as chairman of the Democratic Party, let me say you are what this country needed."

Ford was so touched by that generosity of spirit from the political opposition that he wrote Strauss a glowing letter the next day. "It has always been my experience that political competition can be tough without being unpleasant and vigorous without becoming vicious," he said. "Thank you for going the extra mile the other night."

Their camaraderie, however, wasn't enough to change Ford's mind about fronting for Clinton. Strauss said he'd pass the thanks-but-no-thanks message back to the White House, and Ford assumed that was the end of it.

But not long after the full House impeached Clinton just before Christmas, Ford got a call from Charles Ruff, the White House counsel. Ruff praised the second op-ed piece Ford had written with Carter and wondered if there was anything more Ford might be willing to do to help a fellow president out.

"I told Ruff the only way I would do anything else is if Clinton admitted he'd lied under oath."

Ruff replied, "He will never do that, Mr. President."

"Well, if the president will admit perjury I will do more," Ford said. "You talk to him."

Ruff said again that Clinton wouldn't agree to that.

In that case, Ford countered, there was no way he could go beyond his op-ed. Having failed to get an admission of guilt from Nixon a quarter-century earlier, he wasn't about to make the same mistake again, especially with a Democratic president.

That still wasn't the end of it.

"A little later, Clinton called me; we have a Jerry-Bill relationship. He said he really needed my help and wanted to know if I could help," Ford recalled.

He offered Clinton the same deal he'd proposed to Ruff.

"Bill, I think you have to admit that you lied. If you do that, I think that will help—and I'll help you. If you'll admit perjury, I'll do more."

"I won't do that," Ford quoted Clinton as responding. "I *can't* do that."

The 38th president reminded the 42nd president, just as he'd previously told Ruff, that his op-ed censure proposal, which Clinton had lauded, included the same condition—Clinton had to admit his guilt as part of the deal. Clinton again demurred, but repeated that he could really use Ford's gravitas as a voice of reason with Republicans.

"They wanted me to give up my position," Ford said. "There was just no way."

Neither president was budging.

"Well, Bill," Ford said, "this conversation must end." After a few perfunctory pleasantries, it did.

Precisely what Ford was prepared to do to help Clinton was never broached between the two, because, as Ford remembered, "we never got past the crucial question" of Clinton meeting Ford's conditions.

Ford thought Clinton had been unduly stubborn and said he was amazed at his lack of contrition. "It's a character flaw," he told me. He predicted that Clinton nevertheless would beat conviction by the Senate but would be censured, with strong support from Democratic senators. He was wrong. As he'd feared, Clinton bloodlust blinded Republicans from taking a censure deal, which he was sure Clinton would have accepted. Twelve days after our conversation, the Senate acquitted Clinton—and there was no censure. Afterward, White House aides reported that Clinton was gleefully telling friends he'd beaten the rap.

At some point, our spouses wrapped up their sidebar talk to rejoin the three guys—and burst out laughing. Ford and I had been so engrossed in our Clinton dialogue we hadn't noticed that Andrew had sampled every cookie, taking a bite from each before placing it back on the plate.

That prompted a conversation about food. I said I was glad to see that the Left Bank, the fancy French restaurant where Ford liked to break the chef's heart by ordering liver and onions, was going strong at creekside in downtown Vail. It was still his favorite, Ford said.

When my wife said I had a cast-iron stomach, Betty interjected, "He'll pay for that later. Jerry was like that, too. He could eat anything. Now he can't."

Ford echoed his wife: "I can't sleep if I eat too much spicy food."

"I'm eighty-five," he mused. "It's time to put my feet up."

Back to impeachment: Ford told Betty that we'd been talking about Clinton's troubles.

"Betty and I have talked about this a lot. He's sick—he's got an addiction. He needs treatment. He's sick."

The former First Lady, whose Betty Ford Center has turned around tens of thousands of lives, joined in.

"You know, there's treatment for that kind of addiction. A lot of men have gone through the treatment with a lot of success. But he won't do it, because he's in denial."

Our chat was winding down. He mentioned that he was having more of his letters appraised and confessed to being a hopeless pack rat. "That comes from my mother. She saved everything about me; football clippings, everything."

He wondered why his party was having its 2000 convention in Philadelphia, sixty years after he'd stumped for Wendell Willkie outside another Philly convention.

"I can't figure out why the Republicans picked Philadelphia for the convention," he said. "It doesn't do anything for them politically, and Philadelphia doesn't have much going for it."

Finally we took the elevator downstairs, and Ford walked us out. On the front steps, he returned to his Clinton head-shaking theme without any prompting.

"I don't understand why any of his cabinet hasn't resigned. How can they keep working for him after he lied to them?"

On a human level, he was more concerned about what he believed was Clinton's denial—something he himself had witnessed with Betty for years until she faced up to her alcohol and medicinal dependencies.

"I'm convinced that Clinton has a sexual addiction," he repeated. "He needs to get help—for his sake. He's already damaged his presidency beyond repair."

Ford knew next to nothing about Bill and Hillary Clinton before the 1992 election. The only thing he said to me about the new president before he met him was during an uncharacteristic swipe at the press in 1993: "The media helped Clinton get elected."

But he always considered Hillary the one who got away; paraphrasing Marlon Brando, she coulda been a Republican. In fact, Ford thought Hillary, a product of the Illinois suburbs, had started out as a country-club Republican, much like himself.

He even had the visual evidence to prove it. On the last night of the Clintons' three-day visit to Beaver Creek in 1993, "she brought this photograph: Hillary Rodham standing between Mel Laird and me," he recalled. "She was a summer intern for Mel Laird when he was in the House; this was 1963, '64. And in the picture are Mel Laird, Hillary Clinton, Jerry Ford, Charlie Goodell, Al Quie. She was a Republican! Now she got converted to a liberal Democrat up at Smith College or wherever she went [Wellesley, actually]."

"Her mother took it off the wall and sent it to her, and she gave it to me. I sent it to my library."

It was a gracious gesture by the new First Lady, and Ford loved to regale associates with his Hillary-the-Republican tale. But he and Hillary were polar opposites ideologically, and he wasn't sure she would be a particularly appealing candidate if she ever ran for the White House.

But those first few encounters in the mountains convinced him she had the emotional toughness for the job:

"I learned this: she's stronger and tougher than he is," he told me in 1994. "When she takes a point, you're gonna have to be damn sure you're well informed, because she won't compromise as quickly or as easily as he. She's very bright, she's strong, and I think he defers to her. When she gets her dander up, she ain't gonna roll over."

In July 2000, Ford told me Hillary's race for the New York Senate seat being vacated by Daniel Patrick Moynihan, which he thought she'd win easily, was a calculated stepping-stone in her ultimate quest to become the first female president.

"They've been very nice to us, the Clintons," he admitted, "but I think there's a feeling in the country that she's only running for senator from New York so she can be a candidate for president, and [people] resent that. They think [a Senate race] is an expedient for her own [presidential] ambitions. Now, there's no question she's a very, very ambitious gal. Truth is, I think she is doing it [to run for president], but that's a handicap to her."

Even so, he continued, "The Republicans will make a mistake if they think she is gonna be a pushover. She is a tough, knowledgeable, articulate lady. On the other hand, her toughness in the political arena may not be a big asset. She obviously wants to stay in the political spotlight."

By 2002, he was certain Hillary had already decided to make a presidential bid:

"I'll make this prediction, as long as this is off the record. I'll *gar*-antee [*sic*] you, either in 2004 or 2008, Hillary Rodham Clinton will be a candidate for president. [And] I wouldn't rule out Hillary in 2004, I really wouldn't."

Asked if Hillary would be formidable, he replied that her nomination by the Democrats was a foregone conclusion: "Hillary is gonna be on the ticket in '04 or '08, one or the other, and you can write that down."

Why was he so sure Hillary was running?

"Because she has unlimited ambition. When you look at her record, she's a bona fide liberal with unlimited ambition.

"You look at her track record. She went to Arkansas and married Clinton because she saw in him a way to get national recognition 'cause she thought from the beginning he would be a candidate for president and would get to be president. There's nothing in her track record, Tom, which shows any [inclination] to stay in the background."

But he thought she'd have trouble getting elected because of all the political and personal baggage she'd be toting.

"It depends on the public sentiment in the years out [at the time]. Of course, she's very vulnerable—she was the mastermind of that terrible health care program which she tried to sell. So that would always be a liability for her."

Ford interjected that Laura Bush was a more popular and appealing national figure than Hillary Clinton, then segued into his long-standing belief that the political deck remained stacked against women candidates for the Oval Office.

"I don't think the country is ready for a lady president," he ventured. "I guess I've told you before how I think it's gonna happen." In fact, he hadn't.

"Both parties or one of the parties will nominate a male for president and a female for vice president. The ticket will get elected. The president will die in office. The lady becomes president automatically, and once that happens the dam is broken. And from then on, us men are gonna be number-two."

Had he ever ruminated about who that first trailblazing female president might be? "Haven't given it a bit of thought, Tom." Plainly, however, he didn't think America's first Madam President would be Hillary Rodham Clinton.


On August 13, 1999, Ford received the Presidential Medal of Freedom from Bill Clinton at White House ceremonies. "President Ford represents what is best in public service, and what is best about America," Clinton said in praising his appreciative predecessor.

"He made a helluva nice statement for me," Ford said in a 2000 interview. "I couldn't ask for a more complimentary comment. It was damn nice of him to be there and sit for an hour and a half and listen to all that stuff others said."

As those comments suggest, like every member of the most exclusive boys' club in the land, Ford was always somewhat ambivalent about passing judgment on fellow initiates.

"We have a good relationship," he told me in 1997, remembering that he and Betty had gone up on the stage after the 1996 Clinton-Dole debate in San Diego. After seeing Ford give Hillary a big bear hug, Clinton bounded across the stage to schmooze with his predecessor.

"I think you have to believe that people who have been in the Oval Office—it's a very small group and there's almost a historical camaraderie, which is healthy in my opinion. Having been there, you don't want to be hypercritical.

"When I'm asked at a press conference what I think of President Clinton, I give a very simple answer that ends the interrogation: 'I voted for Bush, and I voted for Dole.' Period. That's it. I don't go beyond that."

"But you'd help him if he asked?"

"Oh, of course. I helped him on the chemical treaty. I really went to bat for NAFTA. And I told Secretary [of State Madeleine] Albright when she was in Grand Rapids I hope the president would push hard on getting fast-track authority and the sooner the better, because I felt it was important to expand NAFTA into Chile and into other Latin American countries."

As an old Korea hand, Ford also applauded Clinton for having the good sense, in his obviously biased view, to reach out to him to discuss the troubled peninsula.

"I talked to him at length on the telephone," he told me in 1995. "He has had the NSC come out three times to make sure I was fully informed and kept abreast of everything. I'm grateful, because I'm one of the few politicians around who was there when Kim Il Sung started the war. I'm the only person around who flew over there and went to the signing of the Panmunjom Armistice. So I have a background [on Korea] that few people in public life have today. Clinton understood that, and I appreciated that he took it seriously."

Their relationship was sufficiently friendly that after Clinton hurt his right knee in 1997 while visiting golfer Greg Norman in Florida, Ford called to commiserate. "I told him I knew a little bit about knee injuries, and the main thing he had to do was what the doctors prescribe about rehabilitation." Clinton had probably paid little attention to the advice, since "he was still in considerable pain," Ford recalled.

Even so, Ford thought Clinton an unreconstructed liberal whose celebrated "triangulation" strategy was simply an expedient—and successful—device to capture the political middle.

"The truth is, Clinton only modified his political philosophy after the Republicans won [the House] in '94," Ford said in a 1998 interview. "He's only been a moderate Democrat since that election. But if you have a change in the control of the House [in 1998], you'll see a reversion to the basic Clinton liberalism."

Even before his stunning 1999 soliloquy on Clinton's roving-eye tendencies, Ford had difficulty keeping his straight-arrow disdain for Clinton's personal life bottled up in our conversations.

In a 1997 interview, for example, Ford brought up the sensational case of Lieutenant Kelly Flinn of the Air Force, a female B-52 pilot who'd just been cashiered from the military on allegations of adultery.

"Betty and I were watching *60 Minutes* last week and saw the story about this poor little Air Force girl," he remembered. "I turned to Betty and said, 'What about the commander in chief?'"

Given Clinton's history of peccadilloes, Flinn's punishment seemed grossly unfair to Ford. "Nobody's made that point yet: Why is *she* being penalized?"

In a 1998 interview, moreover, Ford said, "The president's got an addiction, and it affects his judgment."

Two years later, with Clinton free of impeachment and in his last year as president, Ford offered this valedictory: "He'll always have a blemish on the grounds of character, but on the other hand, you have to admit he's a hardworking, articulate, bright person who has done his darnedest to build up an image. But you can't erase character problems."

His most exhaustive dissertation on the subject of Clinton's "addiction" came on March 29, 2002, a Good Friday, in Rancho Mirage.

Out of nowhere in our wide-ranging sit-down, Ford the pol morphed into Ford the gossip.

"Let me ask you something," he said. "Is Clinton loyal to his sweet wife in his travels around the world?"

I passed on some of the Washington and New York whispers that have dogged the Clintons since Little Rock, and asked what he'd heard.

"I don't hear much," he admitted, but he knew what he thought, and he repeated what he'd told me in 1999.

"He's got a sex sickness; I mean that."

That reminded him of an old friend with the same roving-eye problem who was getting married—again.

"We just got a wedding invitation. [Name deleted] has that same problem [as Clinton]—except he marries them," Ford said, emitting a hearty laugh.

He agreed with me that Clinton's personal life, real or imagined, was a potential political time bomb.

"Oh, I agree on that. He's very skillful in handling it so far except for the Monica Lewinsky and the [Gennifer] Flowers matter, but he's his own worst enemy. But he's so slick he gets away with it."

Predictably, he also was scornful of Clinton's eleventh-hour pardons—except for one: Dan Rostenkowski.

In all his ex-White House years, Ford's single pardon letter had been for his old House pal Rostenkowski, once the powerful Democratic chairman of the Ways and Means Committee.

"Danny's problem was he played precisely under the rules of the city of Chicago. Now, those aren't the same rules that any other place in the country lives by, but in Chicago they were totally legal, and Danny got a screwing, and I was pleased that Clinton granted it."

"There was a lot of [pardon] skulduggery, a lot of it. I think the Marc Rich action was unconscionable. There's this case out here in L.A. where the old man was a big donor and he got all the politicians out here to write letters to grant the pardon."

By his reckoning, handing out political pardons while heading out the door confirmed Ford's views of Clinton's ethical shortcomings.

"The truth is, Tom, he's a very talented guy, but he has no convictions—none whatsoever."

Given such broadsides, Ford would surely have squirmed a bit had he known that Bill and Hillary Clinton rearranged their schedules to arrive in Washington a day early to pay their private respects to Betty before the funeral. He would have been genuinely touched, but probably not enough to recant anything—even though, ironically, their views on how to conduct a former presidency were simpatico.

"I haven't talked to Bill Clinton since he left the White House," he said in that Good Friday interview. "He's all over the world making a lot of bucks. He's in demand, and I understand he won't speak for less than a hundred thousand."

# EIGHT

# Carter, 41, and 43

A T GERALD FORD's burial service in Grand Rapids, Jimmy Carter began and ended his eulogy with the same dramatic first sentence from his own inaugural in 1977: "For myself and for my nation, I want to thank my predecessor for all he has done to heal our land."

At the finish, Carter struggled to maintain his composure in his grief for someone he considered a good friend, and whose friendship was firmly reciprocated, as Ford would have described it.

That unexpected rapprochement with an old political foe had journeyed a long distance, having its genesis in their bitter 1976 slugfest. Even five years later, on the very occasion where both Ford and Carter would always agree their enmity finally ceased, Ford was reminded why sometimes it was exceedingly hard to like the 39th president.

It happened on their trip to Cairo in the fall of 1981. Ford, Carter, and Nixon were traveling together on a government jet as Reagan's emissaries to the funeral of Egyptian president Anwar Sadat, who had been assassinated by Arab militants.

On one of that trip's long legs, an Air Force steward asked the three sort-of amigos to pose for a picture with the flight attendants. Nixon, never known for his warm bedside manner, had no problem with that. Predictably, Ford also agreed without murmur.

"How long will it take?" Carter wanted to know.

The steward assured him it would just be a couple of minutes.

Carter agreed, but said he needed it to be quick.

A few minutes after the historic photo op, Ford couldn't resist confiding to another member of the delegation, "You know, that just goes to show you can't make chicken salad out of chicken shit."

That was probably one of the worst things he'd ever said about a political adversary, no doubt reflecting lingering animosity from 1976. Significantly, it came amidst a series of casual conversations on the plane that began the process of consigning their differences to the ancient-history folder.

A few days after he returned to California, I talked with Ford via telephone about the better vibes with Carter.

"After several meals we had together, I felt there was a warmth that really hadn't existed [before], and I felt very good about it."

Ford said that at the outset of the trip, he'd suggested to Nixon and Carter that to avoid confusion they should refer to one another as Jimmy, Dick, and Jerry. The icebreaking continued over several meals they had together in the VIP cabin of *Air Force One*.

They talked about some of the nasty things each had said about the other in the 1976 campaign and decided to consign those to an inactive memory bin.

"I guess we figured we were gonna be in a plane together forty hours, more or less, and in order to be pleasant [chuckles], it was a good idea to just wipe the slate clean, which we did."

They spent a lot of time discussing presidential libraries, the newest former president picking his predecessor's brain about how to raise money and put together a staff. The exchanges were more comfortable than Ford had expected.

"There was more warmth than I had seen previously. We were always friendly on a professional basis, but we found in talking about a number of non–issue-oriented matters that we had an understanding of one another."

The social dynamics between Nixon and Carter, however, were another matter, according to Ford.

"I made a bigger effort to get along with them than they made to get along with each other," Ford said. "Maybe that's my nature. On the other hand, on a professional level, I thought both of them tried to be discreetly polite—but they're just such different personalities."

He laughed heartily when I reinforced that point by confiding that a few days before, a senior Reagan aide had told me, "Carter's so strange he makes Nixon look normal."

Even so, Ford was pleased with the trip and thought it sent a powerful positive signal to the rest of the world.

"This was a very wholesome trip from my perspective. The fact that the three of us made that effort with our historical background was a big plus for the country. If the occasion arises, we ought to do it again. The impression over there was tremendous."

Considering the way Carter and Ford had trashed each other in 1976, some aides to both men doubted the bad blood would ever dissipate. Throughout the fall campaign, Ford had repeatedly disparaged Carter—particularly after the challenger had, in Ford's estimation, deliberately distorted Ford's record.

He poked fun at Carter's height and his smile, and didn't like what he termed Carter's commercializing his religion for political purposes. Aides also heard him say several times that he considered Carter unfit for the job and, despite his earnestness, lacking in principle.

"Teddy Roosevelt said, 'Speak softly and carry a big stick,' " Ford liked to thunder when assailing his opponent's defense views. "Jimmy Carter says, 'Speak loudly and carry a flyswatter.' "

(At one torchlight rally at the end of a long day and after a couple of martinis, it took Ford three tries to nail the punch line. "Speak softly and carry a flyswasher . . . flyspotter . . . flyswatter.")

Some of that vitriol was the inevitable byproduct of a bitter contest that Ford had once thought was hopeless. He'd roared back so dramatically, however, that he could taste the victory that then slipped away in the final days. As his fortunes improved, Ford never mellowed. In the final weeks, I was told repeatedly that this most mild-mannered of presidents simply couldn't abide his challenger.

After the fateful second debate in San Francisco, Ford was seething after Carter claimed that Henry Kissinger was the real president and that Ford couldn't cite a single accomplishment of his administration. Some of his top counselors said Ford's pique with Carter's stinging accusations rattled him so badly that it was a major factor in his blowing the Eastern European question later in that debate.

In a chilling wind at the Grand Rapids Airport waiting for Ford to return to Washington on Election Day, I was told by one of his closest aides, "Jimmy Carter is probably one of the few people in the world he genuinely dislikes."

The devastating loss made Ford's dyspepsia even worse. He couldn't believe he'd been beaten by a peanut farmer. When Carter came calling during the transition, Ford was gracious, but his lack of warmth was transparent. He was still seething when he left for California on January 20, 1977.

Ford recognized that the code of conduct had changed when he became a former president. He resolved to be more circumspect about his disdain, at least for a decent interval, but for years biting his tongue about Carter was always exceedingly hard work.

"The facts are we do have some differences and there's no use to paper them over," he told me in 1977. "I don't agree with the energy program. I don't agree with the proposals to rescue the Social Security program."

Not to mention Carter's human rights crusade:

"It's important for 215 million Americans and 260 million Soviets not to have a nuclear holocaust. Those are pretty important human rights, too. I don't want a campaign of human rights to destroy the chances of a SALT II agreement."

He complained that Carter embraced a double standard on the issue. "He can't ignore it vis-à-vis Cuba and Vietnam, and insist upon it with our Latin American friends."

As the 1978 midterm elections came around, Ford wasn't feeling any kindlier to Carter. In an August *Newsweek* interview, however, he told me that Republicans who thought Carter was an easy mark for 1980 were "being very naïve. Presidents can and do come back," he said, citing his own resurgence in 1976. Then he used golfing terminology to skewer Carter's performance.

"He's hit a few out of bounds, had a number of double bogeys, quite a few bogeys, a few pars and not many birdies. His constant flip-flopping is his fundamental difficulty. The inconsistencies and uncertainties worry people. One day he's here and the next day he's there. It's a pragmatic approach that has no ideological consistency."

Carter remained Ford's favorite punching bag. His belief that Carter was a national disaster kept him flirting with the notion of running again in 1980 long after most of his counselors concluded it was a foolhardy idea. Once he decided against opting in, he ratcheted up his rhetoric as he stumped the country for Republican candidates.

On October 15, 1980, his thirty-second wedding anniversary, Ford was campaigning for Reagan in California. As usual, he delivered his stock blistering denunciation of his successor:

"I have thought back over my 1976 campaign warnings that Mr. Carter was given to wobbling, weaseling, and waffling on issues all over the lot. That he was all promise and no promise. That he was ill-equipped and woefully innocent about Washington and the real world.

"I am sorry I said those things. I was much, much too kind.

"His economic program has been a disaster; his energy policies have been misguided and ineffective. His foreign policies have been contradictory, erratic, and dangerous."

And aside from refusing to second-guess Carter on his handling of the Iranian hostage crisis, Ford even took a rare swipe at a fellow member of The Club on a foreign policy issue.

"Mr. Carter has forfeited his immunity at home," Ford thundered. "We cannot permit him to create crises that threaten our very survival and then cry for unity and a moratorium on debate until this election is over."

In an interview the next day, he told me his fervent support for the Republican nominee was motivated less by any altruism toward Reagan than by his deep animus toward the man who had beaten him in 1976.

In my experience, Ford always tried to find something nice to say about even his political adversaries. "Most people are mostly good, most of the time," as he explained his half-full philosophy in 1999.

The best he could manage for Jimmy Carter in this conversation was to observe, "We don't have very much in common." Then he launched:

"I think he's the weakest president I've ever seen in my lifetime," Ford said. "And he's defending the poorest economic record of any incumbent president since the Depression."

The thought of Carter's being reelected was literally too horrible for Ford to contemplate. "God help us," he said quietly. "I really mean that."

He didn't stop there, accusing Carter, National Security Adviser Zbigniew Brzezinski, and Secretary of Defense Harold Brown of willfully distorting his record on national defense.

"There are a couple of things that really irritate me," he complained. "The president himself, Brzezinski, and more recently Harold Brown—so it had to come straight from the White House—say that in the last eight years of Republican administrations, defense spending was reduced. That is a distortion, and a deliberate distortion, of the truth.

"In all of those eight years, there was a Democratic Congress. We proposed in my budget increases in defense spending, and on each occasion except the last one, the Democratic Congress reduced the defense spending of the Republican president.

"Now, that's the truth," he said, spitting out his scorn. "And for Mr. Carter, Mr. Brzezinski, and now Harold Brown to repeat that untruth really galls me."

He was also extremely irked that Carter was trumpeting his alleged hikes in military spending. "A significant part of that is caused by Carter inflation," Ford argued. "The cost of living has gone up, for crude oil, for food, for everything. Now, to take that inflation and say that it has helped the Defense Department is an inaccurate distortion that really burns me up. That really gets me, because as you know I've always been proud of my advocacy of the Defense Department in the Congress, as vice president, and as president."

I provoked a quick morality tale by making what I thought a seemingly benign reference to Carter's much-ballyhooed government reorganization proposal, which Ford considered just another pointless, sleight-of-hand gimmick often favored by liberals to camouflage their big-spending schemes. He dismissed the idea with a clever little story about a purported conversation between Herbert Hoover and his predecessor, Calvin Coolidge, who was a legendary tightwad.

"Former president Coolidge and President Hoover were discussing what was going to happen to the horses assigned to the White House. Hoover said somewhat proudly that he'd had them transferred from the White House to Fort Myer. Coolidge said, 'Who feeds them?' That's very applicable to the Carter reorganization plan. The government still picks up the tab."

After Ford and Carter's icebreaking talks during the Sadat funeral trip, the pace of détente accelerated. The vehicle was Carter's trouble with getting his presidential library off the ground. While Ford had made staffers available to discuss the problem, in time Carter approached Ford directly for help. Having left office as an unpopular and more or less failed president, Carter was having trouble raising the millions of dollars in private funds needed to build his library.

Not knowing how his onetime foe would react, Carter asked a favor: Would Ford be willing to come to Atlanta and participate in a symposium to help raise some interest—and more to the point, cash—for the Carter Center?

"I told him I agreed on one condition," Ford told me in 1982. "That he would come to an event in Grand Rapids or Ann Arbor for my museum or library."

Carter accepted, triggering a Jimmy-Jerry tag-team match extending over several years.

These back-scratching appearances didn't convert them into friends, but the relationship was notably friendlier. They began staying in regular contact, talking on the phone, and exchanging birthday greetings.

Their contacts were sufficiently public that some of Ford's closest political allies grumbled that he was spending altogether too much time with Carter—not unlike similar complaints from Bush 41 partisans today that he hangs around Bill Clinton too much. Ford brushed off the complaints.

Beyond their shared practical interest in presidential libraries, another unifying bond was at play. Both ex-presidents had strong reasons not to like Ronald Reagan, which helped cement their ties even though neither one would ever admit it publicly.

To one old Ford friend, the calculation was simple: "Once you did something for his library or museum, you were a friend for life."

Perhaps, but Ford blew hot and cold with Carter. Even at their friendliest, they were never ideological soulmates. And Ford took a dim view of what he considered Carter's meddling in foreign affairs, behaving like a shadow secretary of state in places like Haiti, the Balkans, and the Korean peninsula.

"He came to my museum and library, I went down to Atlanta, but we have not done as much lately," he noted in 1991. "He's gone off on these tangents overseas, and frankly, I think he's doing too much of it. He's well intentioned, Tom, but it's just not my interest. I like him as a person. We're friendly. But I think our activities have diverged."

He could be considerably less delicate with close friends. "Well, you know Jimmy," he commiserated with one of them once after one Carter extracurricular diplomatic venture. "He can be a real pain in the ass, but we get along."

In 1995 he told me that President Clinton was furious with Carter for involving himself in efforts to ease tensions between North and South Korea:

"I thought he interjected himself in the North Korean negotiations unwisely. I told President Clinton that. The White House was very upset, I can tell you that. Personally, his effort in Bosnia was well intentioned, but that whole thing's fallen apart. Now he has volunteered, is anxious to get into the baseball negotiations.

"I think he's well intentioned. He wants to do something that enhances his postpresidential reputation. I don't question his motives, but I think he's so zealous about it he undercuts his credibility."

Trying to exorcise a failed presidency? I speculated.

"That's the net result of it. He hasn't gotten very good reviews on his poetry. I've read a few; I had a hard time. I don't think it's Robert Frost." He laughed.

Two years later, however, in May of 1997, he was mellower about Carter: "It's warmed up, it's gotten more intimate, and Betty and Rosalynn have become, I would say, close. . . . It's healthy for the institution."

They were an odd couple, to be sure: a short, wonkish engineer and a tall, gregarious jock. But in time they managed to bridge their ideological gulf and end up, unexpectedly, genuine friends. The fact that both had once been, in the celebrated description of a *Time* reporter about another president, the "highest source in the land," has a way of doing that.

Having endured his own grand funk for a while after losing to Jimmy Carter, Ford knew something about the postpresidential blues. So when he heard that George H.W. Bush was in a bit of a tailspin after his defeat by Bill Clinton, Ford took it upon himself to stage a friendly intervention.

"I've had a lot of contact with George since he left office," he told me in 1993, "because I wanted him to know that there was life after the White House."

Apparently, 41 hadn't seen that memo, so Ford had decided to engage in a little life-goes-on pep talk.

"I'd heard he was down in the dumps. Two or three people called me and told me that; he wasn't gonna do this, he wasn't gonna become active in various organizations. I said, 'George, the quicker you get active, the easier and better it is.' So I tried to urge him to become active in a variety of organizations, because he's relatively young, he's healthy. He ought to do more than just relax in Houston.

"When I asked him, 'Are you down in the dumps?' he was very upbeat. He said, 'Those stories aren't true. Don't believe that: I'm in good health, mentally, physically.'

"I said, 'Well, I'm glad to hear that'—but it had come from two or three people who thought they knew. But when I confronted him, he said, 'That's a lot of crap,' so I assumed it was."

On the other hand, I interjected, Barbara Bush has been asking friends to invite her husband to lunch because he was climbing the walls.

"These are the kinds of rumors I heard, but when I called him and"—he chuckled—"talked to him directly, he totally denied it."

Did that sound like a bit of denial? I wondered.

"Could be." He smiled knowingly.

That led him to reflect on how he came around to picking Nelson Rockefeller as his vice president in 1974, even though the conventional wisdom favored the elder Bush.

"Who was the gentleman that was such a lovable, wonderful adviser to presidents? My memory fails—little, short fellow."

"Bryce Harlow," the legendary presidential counselor with strong ties to Capitol Hill.

"When I was trying to pick the vice president, I had Bryce, sort of behind the scenes, take charge, and he made a chart—who favored Rockefeller, who favored Bush, who favored Reagan."

In his memoirs, Ford wrote that former congressman and United Nations ambassador George H.W. Bush topped Harlow's chart; Rocky came in a weak fifth. Ford didn't care.

"I said, 'Bryce, I need somebody like Rockefeller on the ticket, somebody that has a different ideological view, is more liberal than I, who's had state experience.' Bush had none. Reagan had only limited. Rockefeller had had Washington experience. Rockefeller had had three or four terms as governor, and I said, 'I'm gonna exercise my own judgment and this is who I'm gonna recommend.' "

Bush was the also-ran again two years later, but in Ford's telling, Bush was cheerfully willing to give up a shot at being vice president four years before he was tapped to run the Central Intelligence Agency.

"I wanted to appoint him head of the CIA, because there was a vacancy there. And the Democrats said, 'Oh, you can't do that. We'll never approve him because that means he'll be your candidate for vice president [in 1976].' So I called George 41 into the Oval Office and I said, 'George, you have to make a choice. You can be CIA director, but you'll have to make a public commitment you won't go on the ticket in '76. If you don't make that commitment, the Democrats won't approve you as CIA director.' I said, 'It's up to you, I'll play it either way, George.'

President Nixon and Vice President Ford in the Oval Office, August 8, 1974, at the meeting in which Nixon informed Ford he was resigning. *(Courtesy Richard Nixon Presidential Library)*

The next day, Nixon walks to his helicopter, accompanied by Pat Nixon, Gerald Ford, and Betty Ford, to return to California. *(Courtesy Richard Nixon Presidential Library)*

September 8, 1974, the bombshell announcement on live national television: a "full, free, and absolute pardon" for Richard Nixon. *(Courtesy Gerald R. Ford Presidential Library)*

Playfully avoiding a question about Vietnam from CBS News' Phil Jones, Ford runs to his plane, April 1, 1975. *(Courtesy Gerald R. Ford Presidential Library)*

While on the campaign trail with the president in Peoria, Illinois, during the primaries, Tom DeFrank is lured out of his hotel room with the promise of a scoop, only to return to . . . a roommate. The prank was engineered by *New York Times* reporter Jim Naughton, with the blessing of Ford and his deputy chief of staff Dick Cheney. *(*Newsweek *photo by Susan T. McElhinney)*

Ford and Reagan emerge grim-faced from Reagan's hotel suite at the 1976 Republican convention. Their deal was that the winner of the nomination would go to the loser's suite as a courtesy. Ford always blamed Reagan's lack of support for his loss that year. *(Courtesy Gerald R. Ford Presidential Library)*

The cover of *Newsweek*—if Ford had beaten Jimmy Carter in 1976. (Newsweek *photo by Wally McNamee)*

Ford with his family in the Oval Office, just before his concession speech.
*(Courtesy Gerald R. Ford Presidential Library)*

In late November, *Newsweek* reported that Ford was taking his defeat very hard, in an article known around the West Wing as "The Sulking Story." Dick Growald of UPI drew this cartoon on *Air Force One* stationery. *(DeFrank collection)*

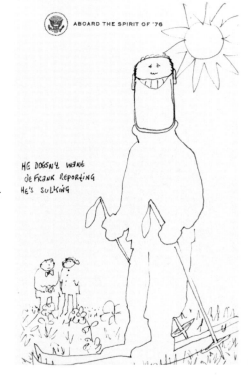

ABOARD THE SPIRIT OF '76

HE DOESN'T WANT
de FRANK REPORTING
HE'S SULKING

January 20, 1977: the handpicked Auld Lang Syne pool flying Ford home to California. Left to right: Dick Growald (UPI), Phil Jones (CBS), Tom DeFrank, Ford, and Maggie Hunter *(New York Times)*. *(David Hume Kennerly photograph courtesy Gerald R. Ford Presidential Library)*

Jimmy Carter, Gerald Ford, and Richard Nixon in the Capitol on January 15, 1978, for the memorial service for Hubert Humphrey. *(Courtesy Jimmy Carter Library)*

A favorite activity in retirement, playing golf, here with President Clinton. Their dramatic phone conversation during Clinton's impeachment process is revealed in this book for the first time. *(AP/Wide World)*

President Clinton awards Ford the Presidential Medal of Freedom, August 11, 1999, while Hillary Clinton looks on. Ford thought Hillary would make a strong presidential contender. *(Courtesy William J. Clinton Presidential Library)*

President George W. Bush visits the extremely frail Ford at home on April 23, 2006, and emerges tenderly holding Ford's hand. "Boy, this dying's hard work," Ford told a friend the year before. *(White House photograph by Eric Draper)*

ASSOCIATION OF
AMERICAN EDITORIAL CARTOONISTS

PARKER HOUSE · BOSTON, MASSACHUSETTS
MAY 25, 1974

On November 14, 2006, the author paid his last visit to the bedridden former president, bringing with him a memento, the program from a meeting of editorial cartoonists in 1974. It showed Ford in his Michigan football uniform, the jersey bearing the number 76 for the upcoming election. Ford studied it intently. "I used to play football" was all he said. *(DeFrank collection)*

Presidents, First Ladies, and thousands of other mourners crowded Washington's National Cathedral for Ford's funeral on January 2, 2007. *(AP/Wide World)*

[A day or two later he said,] 'I'll take the CIA job.' Well, with that commitment, his name never came up in '76."

Given their long professional association, Ford had high regard for the elder Bush, and vice versa. As president, Bush ordered secure telephones installed in Ford's California and Colorado offices. They consulted frequently, particularly on foreign policy matters. While he thought Bush was less strong on domestic affairs, Ford especially liked Bush's handling of the Gulf War in 1991.

"I'm very proud of what he's done in meeting several crises," he told me later that year. "The Persian Gulf crisis was extremely well handled. You know, he had three choices. He could have done nothing when Saddam Hussein invaded Kuwait. If he *had* done nothing, there's no doubt in my mind that Saddam Hussein would have moved into Saudi Arabia, into the Arab Emirates, into Bahrain, into Qatar—might have gone as far as Oman. That would have been catastrophic. He had another choice—he could have done just the diplomatic, but you and I know the track record of the UN between Harry Truman's day and then was poor, very bad. So the third option, which was the right one, was to combine military and diplomatic, and I think it was a tremendous success.

"They made one miscalculation: I do not think they foresaw the Kurdish problem to the degree that it developed. On the other hand, after it developed over four or five days, they corrected it and they came out of it in good shape.

"Lots of argument: didn't Bush stop too soon? You go back and read all the press before he decided to stop. Most of the press *wanted* him to stop. Of course, they forget that [now]."

Because of Desert Storm, Ford thought Bush was in strong shape for reelection in 1992, with one caveat: "His only worry [is] will this economic recovery continue? If we should have a double-dip recession, that would be a hangover into 1992, and that could have very tough political ramifications. I don't see that happening." Neither did President George H. W. Bush.

Ford never developed much of a relationship with George W. Bush, though he had a generally favorable view of him. But in our February 2000 chat, he worried about Bush's prospects against former vice president Al Gore. John McCain, he thought, would be stronger against Gore:

"Six months ago, I thought [Gore] would be a dull, uninspiring loser candidate for the Democrats. Today my opinion is he's gonna be tough to beat. He's improved as a debater, and of course I remember how he devastated Jack Kemp. We haven't heard much from Kemp since Gore whitewashed him.

"Now, as Gore has gotten better, I have noticed in his contacts with [former Senator Bill] Bradley, he's got a mean streak in him which is becoming more and more evident when he's under pressure, and that is unattractive. Nevertheless, he's gonna be formidable.

"As of today, he would make George W. look bad. I'm talking about the debates. And I think as of today it would be close, but Gore would beat George W. head-to-head.

"Now, as of today I think McCain would be a better candidate against Gore. He looks stronger, he *is* stronger. Gore-McCain would be a race that I think McCain could win. He's a good contrast to Gore."

In Ford's estimation, McCain had more gravitas versus Gore, especially because of his military service and Vietnam prisoner-of-war hero's status. "You know, he had a helluva military record."

In sharp contrast to Bush, he added: "Bush has that air reserve [Texas National Guard] record; of course, Gore's war record in Vietnam ain't much, either."

"George W. is not a good contrast to Gore as of today. He doesn't look tough enough, and I must say bringing in his dad and mother was a tactical error."

He was referring to a celebrated incident at a rally just before the New Hampshire primary where Bush's father told an audience, "This boy, this son of ours, is not going to let you down. He is going to go all the way and serve with great honor all the way."

That prompted snickers at the Clinton White House, where aides started referring to the candidate as Boy George, and quiet ridicule from fellow Republicans and the media.

"To say 'my boy'—God almighty, that was terrible. I think that's very unwise; he's got to win it on his own. Now, I think he's doing better; he's handling himself in the debates and his public speaking—he's doing a hundred percent better than a month ago, but he's got to get tougher and more articulate.

"I think once he gets toughened up and more knowledgeable and more articulate, he could be a good candidate. But he's got to do that in the next month, because Michigan is not encouraging."

How did he think the Republicans could beat Gore?

"You've got to attack him, I think legitimately, on his fundraising excesses—the Buddhist temple deal—he's got a lousy track record. And he's got a record of switching, the abortion issue being one, the tobacco issue. He's pretty flexible on whatever is politically expedient, and I think you have to tie him to the Clinton problem. You don't do it brutally, you do it subtly. He can't shake that tie-in."


For a guy who liked reporters and had a grown-up tolerance of their essential if frequently nettlesome role in the democratic process, Ford also worried that Bush might have been unduly influenced by the anger toward the media by his mother and his father, who once admitted publicly, "I hate them."

"A week ago in San Diego, I had a half hour with Barbara Bush in a holding room," Ford said in 2000. "Boy, is she bitter about the press. If George W. loses, she's gonna pop off about the press, and I'm sure it's a reflection of George Senior's attitude toward the press."

The Bush press-bashing didn't abate, even after their boy became president.

"He and Barbara were staying over at the Annenbergs'," Ford said in 2002. "He had a speech, and we were over there for dinner, and we played nine holes of golf. We rode together on the golf cart, but we didn't spend much time talking about his son. I sat next to Barbara at dinner. She obviously is very proud of George W.," he said, chuckling. "She gets very upset with the press. Boy, she's not very subtle with her attitude vis-à-vis the press."

After Bush was elected, Ford thought that the crucible of the September 11 attacks turned him into a leader overnight.

"I think he's done very well," he observed in 2002. "He was a little uncertain until 9/11, but since 9/11 he's catapulted to the forefront, and has changed a great deal of public support and public favor [his way]."

Those comments, of course, were made well before the Iraq War began falling apart.

# NINE

# Staying in the Game

HE'D DEALT WITH five vice presidents, been one himself, and picked another, so Jerry Ford felt he knew something about America's second-highest office. Even after three years of on-the-job training, he didn't believe Dan Quayle was up to the task.

It wasn't entirely the fault of the former Indiana senator, in Ford's somewhat sympathetic analysis.

"He's a lot nicer guy and he's a lot more qualified than you in the press make out," he complained to me in 1991. "I think he's gotten an overcritical press. He wasn't my candidate; I was for Alan Simpson and I talked to Bush about it. But, Tom, I think it's true there are people in public who for one reason or another, justified or unjustified, get the wrong image and they'll never change it.

"Dan Quayle is one of those. The good Lord could anoint him, and there's no way he's going to change that image."

"So what do you do about that?" I asked.

"Well, if the economy's good and there's no other reason for George

Bush to lose, Quayle will be on the ticket. But if they find the economy's bad or some other incident arises where they don't think they're going to win, they'll find another candidate."

Asked if Quayle was presidential timber, he laughed, then delivered one of his trademark cushioned zingers: "Well, let me put it on a comparative basis: Dick Cheney would be much better."

By early 1992, Ford grew increasingly restless with Bush's prospects. The economy *wasn't* good, and he feared Bush seemed out of touch with the mood of the country. Moreover, he'd decided that Quayle's persona as an amiable chucklehead couldn't be repaired, at least in time for the November elections. He concluded that if Bush was really serious about improving his reelection chances, it was time to replace Quayle.

As a historical proposition, Ford believed that Quayle was easily expendable. "Up until recently, vice presidents didn't have a guaranteed retention on the job. Roosevelt got rid of [Henry] Wallace." Bush's political survival was infinitely more important, Ford thought, than a running mate who had become a national laugh track.

"Prior to our convention in Houston," he remembered in 1993, "I became very concerned that the campaign was really dead in the water and that it needed some good, strong change, and I called Stu Spencer; he and I talked about it. He said, 'Well, you may have to go directly to the president.'"

Spencer was the legendary California political consultant who'd successfully managed Ronald Reagan's first campaign for governor. He'd stayed close to the Reagans but defected to Ford in 1976, helping devise the strategy that beat Reagan by a hair in a bitter Republican primary contest. Nancy Reagan vowed eternal revenge, but welcomed him back into the fold in 1980 and 1984; winning was even more important to her than settling scores. The two political junkies lived a few miles apart in the desert and had always stayed in touch, on the phone and the golf course.

Ford had seen this movie before; he'd dumped Nelson Rockefeller from the 1976 ticket, and spent the rest of his life being irritated at himself for it. But Ford had naïvely convinced himself that Rocky had approached him, which made it easier for Ford to go along with political advisers who thought dumping a liberal Yankee Brahmin was Ford's best chance to beat Jimmy Carter.

"We agreed that if it were to be done, Quayle had to take the initiative and go into the Oval Office as Rockefeller did and say, 'It's more important that you be elected than I be on the ticket.' So I called Jim Baker and I said to Jim Baker, 'You've gotta do something, you aren't gonna win if you just run a regular campaign. You've got to get a new spark.'"

James Baker, Ford's delegate hunter and later campaign manager in 1976, by now had been dragooned to resign as secretary of state to help run the campaign out of the White House. He gave Ford the same advice he'd heard from Spencer: best to call George yourself. He placed the call; Bush rang Ford back from *Air Force One.*

"So I called the president and I said exactly what I told you before: 'George, the campaign is dead in the water. You could lose unless there's some new spark. The one that I think would change the atmosphere politically would be to have Dan Quayle himself, on his own initiative, walk into the Oval Office and offer to step aside.'"

That little it's-my-idea minuet was the key, Ford told Bush. "It would not work if Bush called him in; it had to be unilateral action on the part of Quayle."

(There was talk, Ford recalled, of sending an emissary to Quayle with a loaded pistol to leave on the nightstand, but apparently nobody ever approached the VP.)

Bush's "body language" over the phone left Ford with the distinct impression he wasn't buying. In the fall of 1987, *Newsweek* had famously suggested on its cover that Bush was a wimp. ("Fighting the Wimp Factor," the headline had blared.) Five years later, he remained terminally touchy about the perception. He was still being hammered for caving on his promise to the 1988 Republican convention, "Read my lips—no new taxes."

As Ford remembered in 1993, a few months after his phone chat with Bush, "the president's reaction was, well, he didn't like to change his mind and he didn't think Quayle was as big a problem as some of us thought, and he doubted if he would respond by having something like that happen." In other words, Read my lips—no new veep.

He recalled Bush saying, "You know, I changed my mind on taxes and this looks like I'm too willing to change my mind on major issues."

It was also telling to Ford that Bush didn't ask him who might make sense to replace Quayle. Ford would have told him Dick Cheney or Jack Kemp, with his former chief of staff the clear preference, but it never got to that.

"He knew the problem, but it did not appear to me that he was probably gonna do it."

In fact, Baker and Spencer were part of a senior cabal of Bush aides who wanted Quayle dumped. A strategy memo prepared by one of Baker's closest aides in the summer of 1992 had in fact recommended the veep be replaced by Colin Powell. The plotters had hoped that Ford's backchannel counsel would lend credibility to their putsch plans, but Bush thought he'd come off as a real wimp for caving.

"I think the press would murder me if I do this," Bush told several of the plotters.

So Quayle survived, at least until the fall election, when he and Bush were both sent packing. Ford always believed Bush might have won if his counsel had been heeded.

The Dump Dan offensive was one of Ford's more ambitious political gambits after leaving Washington. Throughout his retirement years, however, in ways large and small, on the record and in the shadows, he worked assiduously to keep himself in the game.

Exploiting his cachet as a former president and his network of hundreds of political movers and shakers, he did favors for friends and charities, sometimes approaching the current incumbent himself to call in a chit. He doled out political advice to aspiring candidates, advised presidents on foreign policy, and sought to influence the political debate through thousands of speeches and scores of interviews.

Until he started slowing down in his seventies, he probably campaigned more during national elections than anyone except the actual candidates themselves.

In 1980, for instance, between Labor Day and the November 4 election, Ford was on the road fifty-three of sixty days, logging sixty thousand air miles and visiting thirty states. He made ten appearances for the Reagan-Bush ticket and also campaigned for twenty-nine congressional candidates, fourteen U.S. Senate hopefuls, and four gubernatorial candidates. Even by his usual travel credentials, he outdid himself that fall.

He liked to point out afterward that he did far more for Ronald Reagan that fall than Reagan had done for him in 1976, and always believed that his indefatigable stumping had helped Reagan win several states in what turned out to be a landslide anyway.

Despite another heavy round of campaigning by Ford, his party wasn't so fortunate in 1992—and he wasn't bashful about assessing blame in a postmortem during our May 1993 interview.

He didn't want to dump on his dear friend and fellow Michigander Bob Teeter, but he made clear that he thought Teeter was a far more capable pollster than campaign chairman. He left little doubt that the candidate himself shared much of the blame for blowing the election.

"Bob is a good pollster, but he isn't necessarily a good political strategist. He can get whatever the answers are out there in the field, but there's a big difference between getting information and then utilizing."

"[Also they] were not alert to the economic problems quickly enough. After the euphoria of Desert Storm, they didn't realize that the gut political issue was still going to be the economy. As industries started to have trouble, as areas in the country began to have economic problems, they were not on the ball. If they had jumped right in and said we don't like the economic picture, we think something oughta be done about it, I want you to know I'm gonna be out there trying to change the economic environment—if they'd done that, they would have stolen Clinton's biggest asset. But for some reason they never recognized that was the major issue until it was too late. They didn't have any comprehension that their basic issue was not gonna be the great success of Desert Storm but the failure of the economy."

He gave Jim Baker a pass from criticism that he'd been a reluctant warrior, that he'd been going through the motions after Bush yanked him back from the State Department to help steer a losing reelection effort.

"I couldn't help but note [his invisibility], but I have no reason to know why. I think he reluctantly left State, where I think he did a fine job, and regrettably from his point of view he got into the campaign before there was much he could do about it.

"I think he had some people around him who didn't do the best job for him. [Chief of Staff Sam] Skinner; thank God his tenure was so short."

As the 1996 election cycle approached, Ford was pessimistic about Republican prospects for toppling Bill Clinton even though his ethical and political difficulties offered an opening.

"Moving his Little Rock staff almost intact to the White House was a terrible mistake," Ford said in early 1995. "They weren't up to the job, and I think the evidence is very convincing.

"Number two, he ran as a new, moderate, middle-of-the-road Democrat and that was totally destroyed as an image when his major legislative program was a revolutionary health care bill. I don't want seven politicians deciding what's medically necessary; I want my doctor to do that.

"Number three, I don't get into the character issue; it speaks for itself. There's been so much about his various actions, or lack of responsible action, the American people hear it and finally they begin to wonder.

"I do think the Republicans can win, but they've gotta find the candidate, and I don't see any candidate today in the forefront." In no particular order and with no particular enthusiasm, he mentioned Bob Dole, Phil Gramm ("he just looks too sour"), Lamar Alexander, Dan Quayle ("he has a hard time convincing people he's believable"), Arlen Specter ("he's not going anyplace"), Jack Kemp ("too bad about Jack but somehow the train's going by"), and Pete Wilson.

"The best president would be Bob Dole, now that Cheney's out of the picture, but I don't know whether Bob can get elected. I think if he goes all out he can get the nomination. Gingrich makes him look good; that's a hard way to get your image, but Bob looks more and more like a statesman because of Gingrich. But he's had for a long time the image of a gut fighter. I happen to think he had that role because that's what he had to do. But that's the way a lot of people think. It's too bad."

Given a field he plainly viewed as unappetizing, Ford offered up his dream candidate:

"Betty and I heard Colin Powell speak here a month ago. He spoke at a fundraiser for the University of California–Riverside. He made as fine an oration as I've heard—talked about foreign policy, military policy; on substance he was damn good. He has really learned how to make a speech.

"The Walter Annenbergs were there; Walter was ecstatic. I don't know what Powell's gonna do, but if he were to jump into the political arena as a Republican, I think he could get the nomination—certainly the vice presidential, if not the presidential, and he in my view would beat Clinton easily."

Absent Powell's star power and given the dwarflike Republican alternatives, Clinton would probably survive, Ford glumly mused.

"Primarily it's because we haven't found a candidate. The target is great but you gotta have an arrow that can hit it," he joked.

He was proven right in 1996, when Clinton was reelected despite his scandal baggage. With an open seat in the Oval Office for 2000, Ford was more optimistic about his party's chances when he analyzed the electoral landscape in 1998:

"The Republicans are preparing to learn from the mistakes the Democrats made when they ran Mondale, Dukakis, and McGovern. All three represented the liberal element in the Democrat Party, and they lost. The Democrats learned in the case of Clinton that at least superficially they had a middle-of-the-road Democrat, and they won. Now, there are other reasons why Clinton won, but at least he portrayed himself as a moderate. If the Republicans run an extreme hard-right candidate, they can't win the election in 2000. That knocks out [Steve] Forbes and [Pat] Buchanan.

"My impression of Bush is that he's moderated his views, more so than his dad did. So he's a possibility. I don't want to pick one, but they ought to have learned you can't have an extremist. The Democrats couldn't win with one on the left, we can't win with one on the right."

He thought Vice President Al Gore was a bad bet for the Democrats—more liberal than Clinton, and far less politically adroit.

"He's such a bore," Ford said. "When I went to Congress in 1949, his father was a firebrand—a hellfire-and-damnation Southern liberal from Tennessee—and his father was a helluva speaker. He would compare favorably with Ev Dirksen in his day. In contrast to his son; God, I can't sit there and listen to him. He pontificates. Oh, God, he's awful. His father was an interesting person to listen to. Can you imagine anybody, knowing that his tax return was going to be public information, spending $365 [$363, for charitable contributions]—that doesn't wash."

Ford was a lifelong Cold Warrior who believed in détente and dialogue but also shared Ronald Reagan's trust-but-verify skepticism toward the Russians.

"I strongly think we should not put all our eggs in the Yeltsin basket," he told me in 1996. "We have a tendency to get euphoric over some Russian leaders. I remember we thought [Mikhail] Gorbachev was the answer. He's now irrelevant. It's dangerous to think of [Boris

Yeltsin] as the long-term solution to the Soviet-Russian republics problem. When you look at the implications of Chechnya, all of those republics are potential spin-offs, and if that happens you'll never have a rebuilding of the old Soviet-Russian Empire.

"It's a tough job he's got, but I don't think we can assume he's gonna be the person for the next five years. If he had fewer personal weaknesses, maybe. But somebody that erratic, with all those personal unreliable characteristics—boy, that's a weak reed to put our faith in.

"I told President Clinton that we're dealing with a bunch of thugs—don't trust them."

In 2002, despite the U.S. invasion that toppled the Taliban and installed a pro-Western government, Ford was sounding nervous about the future of Afghanistan.

"Boy, that Afghanistan problem is a lot more complicated now," he said. "These warlords are making it difficult for Karzai, and whether they would work with him if and when we pull out is a big question."

Asked if the United States would have military forces in Afghanistan for a very long time, he said he thought so. "And instead of it getting [to be] a lesser commitment, I think it's gonna be more."

"You're not becoming in your old age a little bit of an isolationist?" I asked.

"No, I have not said we shouldn't do these things. But I'm saying if you do, you've got to build up your military so they're not stretched too thinly. I've never criticized the commitment to Yemen, to the Philippines, to Kosovo. My concern is you're trying to do more with fewer forces, and you can't do that. That's not good military policy."

For the most part, Ford didn't offer unsolicited advice to his Oval Office successors. Occasionally, however, he wasn't above proselytizing a president, particularly on foreign affairs. In the case of Bill Clinton, whom he considered a weak foreign policy leader, there were at least two Ford tutorials.

In our May 1994 interview, he patted himself on the back for single-handedly persuading Clinton to pay attention to the North American Free Trade Agreement treaty, which was then languishing in Congress.

"There was one real benefit out of them coming to Beaver Creek and Vail [in 1993]," he contended. "Up until that point, Tom, President Clinton cared less about NAFTA. He wasn't interested. I spent most of my time with him promoting NAFTA, urging him to take action, to get going, to get a bunch of former presidents together at the White House so we could show solidarity. I honestly can claim full credit for getting him off dead center on NAFTA.

"Now, once he got interested, he did a damn good job. He twisted arms, he browbeat Democrats, and he put on a good event in the East Room with Carter, Bush, and myself." Once again he said, "You know, he's a helluva salesman."

In 1994, Ford read that Jimmy Carter was planning to travel to North Korea to interject himself into delicate negotiations between the Clinton administration and North Korean dictator Kim Il Sung. He was afraid Clinton might pay undue attention to Carter, whom Ford, despite their friendship, thought meddled too much in foreign policy.

"So I called Clinton," Ford said in August 1994. "He was flying, and he called me back. I'll tell you what I told him. I said, 'Bill, I'm telling you this because I know about it. I'm telling you that Kim Il Sung is a bad man.' I was in Congress on June 25, 1950, when he invaded South Korea, so you know he's an aggressor. Number two, I was in 1953 and 1954 chairman of the Army panel on appropriations—that was the last time Republicans had control of the House—and after we adjourned in 1953, I flew over to Korea with Secretary [of State John Foster] Dulles and Secretary of the Army Bob Stevens, and I was there at Panmunjom when they signed the peace treaty.

"You've got to understand how this peace treaty came about. The negotiations had gone on for about a year between the North Koreans and Americans, and during the campaign of 1952, Ike said, 'I will go to Korea.' Well, the minute he said that, the presidential election was over, and Ike beat [Adlai] Stevenson badly. After he got sworn in, these negotiations were still dragging on and on, and Ike went to South Korea. When he came back, he did two things: Number one, he said unless these negotiations are consummated we will use whatever weapons necessary, or something to that effect, which was the inference of nuclear weapons. And number two, he moved an Army division from Japan to Korea to let the North Koreans know that we were prepared to accelerate the war.

"And you know who was the [commander] of that division? [Vietnam commander William] Westmoreland. That's where I first met Westy, because after the peace treaty signing, Westy took me all along the whole range of the dividing line in a helicopter.

"Well, anyhow, the day after the treaty was signed, I flew up to the dividing line, DMZ, with Bob Stevens and [General] Max Taylor, and I saw the first prisoners of war come over the mountain in Chinese trucks, and I saw them being processed.

"I said 'Bill, Kim Il Sung started this war, he thought he could get away with it. Harry Truman did the right thing to take him on, and I supported Truman right from the beginning. Secondly, the way it ended was Ike said if you don't settle this thing, the war's gonna expand. He understands power, and you should act accordingly.'

"He was very nice. He said, 'Well, I think that's my policy.' He then sent the number-two or -three man at NSC, a young fella, out here to see me. He gave me this step-by-step evolution of their policy. When he got through, I gave him what I told you. Of course, he wasn't around, he didn't know any of that history. He went back and he obviously wrote an excellent letter for Clinton to sign thanking me for calling him and giving him historical information that he hadn't heard and reassuring me that their policy was gonna continue to be firm, hard-line.

"I hope he's right, but trouble is, somebody's gonna talk to him after I talk to him, and it scares me he's gonna go soft. They're negotiating; they could be giving away the store. I hope not, and I was told they wouldn't—but his reputation is not one of consistency."

In 1998, I asked Ford if he'd spoken with Clinton lately. As a matter of fact, he had—and not about foreign policy.

"I had a strange thing happen. I had one conversation with him this calendar year. Walter Annenberg came over to see me three months ago, maybe, here at the office. Betty and I have developed a good friendship with the Annenbergs. They asked me to speak at his ninetieth birthday dinner along with three or four others, and we had them for dinner for Betty's birthday. He came over to see me; he was mad. He had written Clinton about a tax proposal he felt strongly about. It was not a major, universal tax issue, but it had some implication to charity giving. It had gone to the president personally, and two or three months had passed, and no answer; no contact. He was very upset. I had a sudden inspiration [chuckles]: Well, why don't I call Clinton and ask him why?

"So Walter was sitting there," he said, pointing to my seat. "I told Penny to call President Clinton; I wanted to talk to him. And so, by golly, he got on the phone. Right then; right here. It took about a minute. I said, 'Mr. President, I've got a friend of yours who's got a complaint. Walter Annenberg's sitting here and he wrote you a letter and you haven't answered it and he wants to know why. I'll put Walter on [big laugh] and you two discuss it.'

"Well, surprisingly, he knew about the letter. I couldn't believe that."

At this point, our interview was momentarily suspended by a phone call from Betty.

"I've gotta get our family dog in. Are you in a hurry?"

After tending to his chores, he continued:

"They had a little conversation. I don't know whether he then wrote Walter, but I just assumed it was [a case of] screwed-up office management." Annenberg's problem ultimately went away.

More often than not, Ford's string-pulling was centered on Capitol Hill instead of the White House. That wasn't surprising, since he had scores of pals there, many of them in powerful positions and willing to intercede for an old colleague and friend.

"Now let me bring up a thing that happened in the last ten days," he said in 1992, during our second off-the-record conversation. "Several months ago, the IRS issued a tentative order based on a previous law that money that's paid by—we'll say Chrysler out here for the Bob Hope Chrysler Golf Classic—was income to the Classic. Well, that affects all these charity events all over the country, including football bowl games where some corporations are some of the sponsors.

"Well, the Eisenhower Medical Center, that gets about a million dollars a year from the Bob Hope Classic, came to see me and said, 'My gosh, what can we do? This will devastate us.' I called Danny Rostenkowski, with a fellow from the medical center sitting right here, and I said, 'Danny, what the hell's going on here? Do you know anything about this?' He said, 'I know a lot about this; I think the IRS is going to back off because there's an awful lot of pressure all over the country. Let me look into it.'

"Two days later, I got a full explanation and a personal letter from Danny saying in his opinion the matter is settled.

"The point I'm making is I still have some people in the Congress, where I can be helpful, influential, and constructive. That's perfectly legitimate. It's a good case. I think the IRS was wrong to dredge up an old law to try and do what they did."

I n 1998, four years into Newt Gingrich's Republican revolution, Ford reflected on the changes in his beloved House of Representatives. He wasn't thrilled with what he saw happening in the legislative branch. Still worse from his perspective, much of the damage had been inflicted by his own.

"Congress has changed. Fundamentally it's the same institution, but generationally it's different. I'm not sure it would offer the same satisfaction or thrill of being there. You know, when I came there I, like many others at that time, we were relatively young, we were inspired by the opportunity. It was a great, great opportunity to serve. I'm sure many of those things are still true today, but there's a lack of civility that bothers me.

"When I and a bunch of other World War II veterans came, Democrats as well as Republicans, there was a hierarchy of old-timers around that added something. So you had this interesting mixture of new blood that were inspired to come for all the good reasons, and then you had some old-timers who had survived and were stable and good. I don't see that today. Sam Rayburn was a great speaker [of the House], and my best mentor was Earl Michener. He had come in with Sam Rayburn, but was beaten in 1932 in the debacle, but came back in '34.

"He was my guiding counselor; he was most helpful. He said, 'You can either be one of two kinds of members: you can sit on the floor and learn how to be a parliamentarian, how to be a speaker, how to conduct yourself, or you can be a committee member. But if you're going to be a committee member, don't try to be superficially knowledgeable about a lot; be the best expert on an important issue, so that when you go to the floor of the House to discuss something, people know you know more about that subject than any of them do.'

"You know, Tom, the House was my home. I loved it, and still love it, but I'm worried about it."

Asked how the decline could be fixed, he admitted, "I don't have an answer for that, unfortunately. I think the speaker has a big impact, and Newt Gingrich got off on the wrong foot. The best speakers are those who conform to the role of speaker of the House, not speaker for the majority. Now he's changed and moving in the right direction. What he ought to do is keep himself up above the fray and let [Majority Leader Richard] Armey carry the ball on the floor of the House. I'm not sure he has full faith in Armey; he just doesn't measure up to a strong majority leader, that's his problem.

"Speaking of Republicans in the House, I've watched with interest on what's happened to the revolt against Gingrich. Two problems—and I know something about revolts [having been elected minority leader when Young Turks ran him against Charles Halleck in 1965]: Number one, you can't beat an incumbent with four candidates. You have to have one unified opponent to the incumbent. You get four, you spread the effort, there aren't enough votes. Number two, you should never challenge an incumbent party leader in the middle of a session. You should do it after an election or before—at the time the parties organize—so you're focusing on that issue.

"That's what we did: we all agreed I would be the candidate: [Mel] Laird and [Charles] Goodell and [Don] Rumsfeld and [Al] Quie wouldn't be competing candidates, and they'd all vote for me. And we did it after the 1964 debacle when the Republicans were organizing [the new Congress], so that the only issue was whether you wanted new leadership or not. It wasn't all involved in who's gonna be for tax cuts or who's gonna be for this or that.

"The members that orchestrated the effort against Gingrich hadn't been around the House long enough. They just hadn't understood how those kind of things work. It was screwed up, and it ended up a failure. I'm not saying they should or shouldn't have done it; I'm just telling them why they didn't win."


Ford and Alan Greenspan were longtime friends, dating from when the chairman of the Federal Reserve Board had been chairman of President Ford's Council of Economic Advisers. When Ford heard via his Washington grapevine that Greenspan was being shut out of the first Bush White House, he seized on a target of opportunity to do some high-level power-brokering.

"About two months ago, in December, John Sununu came down to see me," Ford recalled in 1992. "They were out here for something and he drove down here on his own, no publicity, and spent an hour or two with me. It was when he made his decision to leave [as White House chief of staff]. He asked my advice. I said I was worried that there isn't better rapport between Bush and Alan Greenspan. I said that in my case I had a superb relationship with Arthur Burns. We had been friends a long, long, long time. I enjoyed his company and admired him.

"Arthur used to drop by the Oval Office unannounced about every ten days, two weeks maybe, and we would chat informally for about a half hour. I would tell him what we were trying to do, and you know we had a tough economic problem, and Arthur would tell me what he thought the Fed would do, and we tried to make sure that we weren't going in opposite directions. That relationship paid big dividends.

"I said, 'John, I don't think that's happening [with Greenspan],' and he said, 'That's true.' I said, 'Why can't you get the president to invite Alan to come in and sit down and talk?' I had seen Alan at the White House when Betty was there to get the Medal of Freedom. Although Alan didn't ask me to do it, he reminisced about how nice it was when Arthur Burns and I were there. I know Alan didn't feel he had ever been invited. Now, why he wasn't, I don't know. I think that's [finally] happening now. If I could accomplish that one thing, that would be more important than any speech or any criticism or any praise. If George and Alan are doing that, it will pay big dividends."

Over the years, academics and reporters frequently asked Ford how the country could harness the collective institutional wisdom of retired presidents. He consistently opposed the notion as well intentioned but woolly-headed.

"There should not be a formal organization or process," he emphasized in 1992. "There have been proposals to have a Former President's Council with a staff. That would be totally unnecessary and, I believe, counterproductive. The truth is, a president has unlimited access to a former president, and a former president has unlimited access to a president. When Carter was there, I could call right from here and get him. He could call me. That was true of Reagan; that's true of Bush. It would be totally unnecessary and just another bureaucracy to have a Council of Former Presidents. Each president knows where his predecessors are; he knows where their influence is, what their views are. If he wants help, all he has to do is call 'em on the telephone."

Historically, it's rare that a former president turns down a plea for help from a successor, even one from the other political party.

"Reagan sent me to Oman to represent him in the fifteenth anniversary of the sultan's accession," Ford pointed out. "Nixon had a unique situation with the Chinese, and sending him there under those circumstances was a very, very good idea."

"If a president wants my advice, there's an open line," he echoed in 1993. "To try and get five former presidents to sit down periodically and come up with specific advice would be an action in futility. If you start having a Council of Former Presidents, then you get another damn bureaucracy and God knows how much that would cost. It's just one of those academic exercises in trying to fix the world without any dealing with reality."

# TEN

# *Personalities*

J ERRY FORD WAS a mild-mannered soul for the most part. Like any politician, however, he had strong feelings about some of his contemporaries, especially Ronald Reagan. But in all our conversations, stretching across thirty-three years, nobody prompted more genuine vitriol from Ford than his father.

Eighty-nine years after his mother fled from Omaha to Grand Rapids with her infant son Leslie King, Ford still had never mellowed toward his real father.

"I make a speech on occasion that says, Isn't this a wonderful country?" he mused in 2002. "A person can come from a broken home and become president of the United States. And then I tell them about my mother, who when I was two months old took me by a taxi across the state line in Nebraska because she was being physically and otherwise abused by my real father. And then she went to Grand Rapids two years later, married my stepfather, who turned out to be a wonderful, wonderful person.

"The divorce trial of my mother was a big news story in Omaha back in those days. People think I just came from Grand Rapids. Well, I had a tough time getting there. If my mother had stayed, my whole life would have been totally different.

"My father was a bad man. In the divorce case, the court ordered him to pay twenty-five dollars a month to my mother for my support. He never paid a nickel. His father, who was a very successful business-man in Omaha and Wyoming, paid it, and when he died, my own fa-ther never paid a nickel. And so my stepfather raised me really, financially and otherwise, and of course my stepfather had a tough time during the Depression—very tough. One of his businesses went bank-rupt. So when I went to Michigan in the fall of 1931, the tuition was a hundred dollars for a year. Well, my principal in high school was a great Michigan supporter, and he wanted me to go to Michigan so I could play football there. South High had a school bookstore, and prin-cipal Arthur Krause established the bookstore scholarship and gave me a hundred dollars. That's how I got my tuition.

"Well, when I got to Michigan they didn't have football scholarships in those days; they didn't exist. But the Michigan coach got me a job working at the university hospital, where I waited on tables at the in-terns' dining room and cleaned up the nurses' cafeteria after lunch, for which I was paid fifty cents an hour, and I earned enough every day to buy my meals.

"I lived in the third floor of a rooming house with another fella; we paid four dollars a week. Then I joined the Deke [Delta Kappa Epsilon] fraternity and I got a job washing dishes there, and then eventually my senior year I became house manager. But anyhow, in my junior year, during the depths of the Depression, my stepfather couldn't send me a penny, because they had three other sons younger than I. And he had this small paint company that was right on the edge of bankruptcy. I didn't get any money—except I would go to the university hospital and give blood every two months, for which I would get paid twenty-five dollars. I was desperate. I wrote my real father asking for six hundred dollars. I never got an answer. Never!

"Well, after things got better and I was back practicing law [in Grand Rapids], I said to my mother, 'Your husband and my father must have been an evil man.' Because he inherited all his own father's money and property when [my] grandfather died. And one day I was talking to a friend of mine, a lawyer in Detroit, and I told him about all this accumulated unpaid child support, and he said, 'Well, why don't we start a lawsuit?'

"He was a young, struggling lawyer that wanted to get a case, so he pulled all the facts and the money and it came to about five thousand dollars. So he filed the lawsuit in Omaha, and the court somehow found out that my real father was in Omaha, although he now lived permanently in Wyoming. And they nabbed him [big laugh] and put him in jail until he paid this four or five thousand dollars.

"In desperation, my father called me. He said, 'Get your mother off my back.' I said, 'That's her business, it's her money, it's not mine.' And that was it: I never did anything, and he finally paid up."

For altogether different reasons, Ford similarly had no use for film-maker Oliver Stone, whose movie on the Kennedy assassination, in Ford's opinion, had distorted the truth and impugned the work of the Warren Commission. As the last surviving member of the commission, Ford felt strongly that Stone's movie was artistically and historically ir-responsible.

"I signed the report," he recalled in 1992. "I've never changed my opinion. I feel as strongly today, Tom, on the two basic fundamental issues. Number one, Lee Harvey Oswald was the assassin. Number two, the commission found no evidence of a conspiracy, foreign or domestic.

"I should add a footnote: The staff, in its draft of the report, said there *was* no conspiracy, foreign or domestic. The members of the commission unanimously changed it to say the commission *found* no evidence of a conspiracy. Now, the question is raised: Has there been any new, credible evidence since 1963? In my opinion, absolutely not.

"I don't understand how Oliver Stone latched on to the weakest conspiratorial theory with Jim Garrison. The Garrison theory is totally discredited. It bothers me that a commercial, moneymaking movie can be believed by so many people. Even Stone says it's not a documentary. I guess my only solace is they're still raising questions about the assassination of Abraham Lincoln 130-some years ago. So I guess conspiracies can be raised by anybody, and those that raise them seldom have an answer. I've looked at it again, I've studied it, restudied it. Truth is, I'm more convinced than ever."

Had he seen the movie?

"No, I've read the text. Let me tell you something off the record. Betty and I were in Hawaii at a big YPO, Young Presidents [Organization] meeting. Walter Cronkite was there with his wife and we were on a program together. We were both asked about the Stone movie, because Stone uses him and his interview with Kennedy as a basis for the thesis that Kennedy was about to change his mind on Vietnam, which is bullshit. That—well, let me finish this. Walter Cronkite is very, very upset with Stone using shots from that interview without getting his permission, and he's equally upset with CBS for authorizing it without getting his approval. And the truth is, he's contemplating at least going to see lawyers, about suing.

"I've read the script; I don't want to see the movie, because I would be so upset with the damage it does. You know, to allege that Lyndon Johnson and the seven of us on the Warren Commission are a part of a conspiracy is ridiculous. None of us wanted to serve on the commission, but Lyndon, in his arm-twisting way, in effect told us it was our patriotic duty. I remember on Monday night, after the assassination, I was home. I got a call from the White House: the president wanted to talk to me.

"He said, 'I want you to serve on this commission.' I said, 'Mr. President, I've got a full-time job in the Congress, important committees, all this and that.' He just brushed that aside and said, 'This is critical, you gotta do it,' and so forth.

"I'm bothered by a commercial movie, which is biased and filled with half-truths, [that] can be believed by so many. It is *not* a documentary. I really get upset with it. If I went to the movie I wouldn't sleep at night I would be so upset."

(In a 2003 interview, Ford told historian Douglas Brinkley that he in fact had seen the "ridiculous" film, but totally by accident. He was on an American Airlines flight from New York to Los Angeles, and the movie was the featured entertainment. So he watched, but not happily.)

Enough time has passed, he added, that it's time to release the entire commission report, which still hasn't happened fifteen years after he recommended full disclosure in our conversation.

"The time has come to do it, but you have to be forewarned: there are some stories that'll come out that were never verified that could be harmful to some people." He wouldn't be more specific about who they were: "I'll just say some people that are known. You know how that happens—somebody investigates, somebody asks questions, and they make a statement. They're never verified, it's rumor, et cetera. That's gonna happen, and that's too bad."

"I am a total devoted person to the [commission's] conclusions. But seventy-five percent of the people don't believe the Warren Commission anymore. It just makes me sad and unhappy. I was talking to somebody the other day in the movie business. I said, why don't you do a documentary? Her answer was it wouldn't sell. In the *New York Times* last Sunday, nonfiction bestsellers, Mark Lane's book, *Plausible Denial,* was in the top five. In the paperback bestsellers, three of the first five were books that criticized the Warren Commission. The public is being overwhelmed with these irresponsibilities.

"The trouble with the movie, experts tell me, is, eighty percent of the people who go to movies are between the ages of sixteen and twenty-four. None of those were alive when JFK was killed. So they're getting a totally distorted story about that tragedy."

Including one of his sons. "He came out of the movie and said, 'Now I understand.' I said, 'Sit down.' The son of one of my agents did the same thing. It's frightening."

Our conversations weren't solely about politics or his career. We sometimes veered off into contemporary topics as well. In 1995, for example, I asked him about the infamous O. J. Simpson murder trial, where the former football star was later acquitted of killing his ex-wife and her friend.

He asked me to turn off the tape recorder and put away my notebook. That was a rarity; when he asked me to turn off the machine, he usually let me keep taking notes. Not this time. As soon as I got back to my car, I pulled out my notebook and wrote this memo to myself:

He didn't want to say on the tape that there was no doubt in his mind that O.J. was guilty, that he'd done it. But he thought he was going to get off because "all you need is one juror," and he thought it was going to be a hung jury.

He told this story that he said, "I hope you completely forget it." He said he had many friends who were friends of O.J.'s, and they had all told him years and years and years before this had happened, that O.J. had a really dark side, that there was a flaw in his character. He told me a story that about two years ago he and Mrs. Ford were at a concert here with Frank Sinatra for the Sinatra golf tournament and O.J. was sitting two places away from the Fords with a beautiful white woman not his wife, and that O.J. spent the whole time pawing her and had his hand up her dress. You could see how offensive Ford thought this was. He just kept saying, "It was really offensive." He said, "Betty and I aren't prudes, but I was even embarrassed to tell my wife to look at this. Of course I did, but it was still embarrassing."

In that same interview, Ford showed me a letter he'd gotten from Jordan's King Hussein, his first state dinner guest in 1974, about the Arab-Israeli peace treaty. That reminded him that he'd been a lifelong pack rat.

"You know, the original of this letter would be pretty valuable, don't you think? My mother was an incredible collector, and she taught me to hang on to everything. I have kept over the years all my letters from presidents and important people. About two years ago, I had Sotheby's appraise them; I just wanted to see how much they were worth."

He was shocked to learn that he was sitting on $365,000 worth of letters, later reappraised upward to $400,000.

"Do you know the most valuable letter I have?" he said, chuckling at the recollection of a moment I would have thought he'd prefer to forget.

"It's a letter I got from Sara Jane Moore saying she didn't regret trying to kill me," he divulged, laughing uproariously.

Moore tried to shoot him as he emerged from a side entrance of San Francisco's storied St. Francis Hotel on September 22, 1975, the second assassination attempt on him in California within seventeen days.

He said that Sotheby's had appraised the letter at $9,000.

"I couldn't believe it," he recalled. "That's more valuable than my letters from Nixon during Watergate, or anything else."

He showed me the letter, dated December 30, 1975. The operative line: "Although part of me regrets not being successful in this task, I am very thankful I did not kill another human being." That caused another big chuckle.

(Signed "Sally Moore," the letter also notes, "May I apologize for the pencil and paper. No disrespect is intended; it is all we are allowed at county jail.")

"You know, I'm not going to live forever; you've gotta start thinking about what you want to do with stuff like this. What I think we're gonna do is give some to the children and then we're gonna give the rest to the foundation, and they'll probably end up at the library at Ann Arbor."

As his mirth over the Moore letter suggests, Ford was in good spirits—except for his bum left shoulder. He said he was desperately trying to avoid surgery, because that would mean six weeks in a sling and six months without swinging a golf club. Almost as bad, as a southpaw he wouldn't be able to write for six weeks.

"I'm just too old to be an invalid for six months at this point in my life," he grumbled.

In 2002, I asked him about some private buzz in Bush circles that Dick Cheney had served his original purpose—getting George W. Bush elected by reassuring moderate and independent voters that Cheney's gravitas compensated for Bush's relative inexperience—and could now be replaced as vice president if necessary. Ford bristled at the notion:

"It would be wrong politically and substantively. Dick Cheney's got a support group out there in the country that I think feels that Cheney was a big asset [in 2000] and would be an asset in the future."

I asked him to compare Rumsfeld and Cheney, his two chiefs of staff.

"In many ways, very similar. Both were very well organized, both were able to speak up and tell me what they thought. Very loyal, both hardworking. They both ran the White House very effectively and the way I wanted it. So it's pretty hard for me to pick any differences."

On reflection, he thought of one: "I would say Don is a little more sensitive to criticism than Cheney. Cheney laughs about it; he may resent it, but he doesn't show it."

He made it clear in a 1995 interview that he wasn't enamored of H. Ross Perot, the billionaire Texan who'd run for president in 1992.

"I don't know what he'll end up doing, but he's going to be mischievous at best. Anybody with that much ego who wants that much power with that much money you can't discount. I think he's disgraceful. I've never seen him do anything constructive. My friends in Michigan can tell you horror stories about his days on the General Motors board. I can tell you stories from people who dealt with him politically, so I see nothing constructive in what he's done—except make a helluva lot of money. The worst thing for him to do is get into Republican primaries, because he would really be a time bomb politically. He's gonna be in the political arena directly or indirectly, and it will be no good for the country in my opinion."

House Speaker Newt Gingrich fared a bit better in that same interview, but Ford's praise was faint. Mr. Congeniality didn't much care for Gingrich's scorched-earth tactics.

"Obviously, he is very smart," Ford allowed. "I wish he would moderate a little. I think at the moment he has a tough choice: the book deal and other things, primarily the book deal. Unquestionably he's slowed down the legislative process with the Contract with America. If that continues, he has to make a choice—is he gonna be stubborn about the book deal and jeopardize the Contract with America? If he gets to be stubborn about the book deal, it'll hurt him and it'll hurt the Republican image. I think he could make a ten-strike if he forgets the book deal. I'm more interested in making strong, effective progress on the Republican contract."

Before Betty Ford stole his heart in perpetuity, Gerald Ford's first great love was Phyllis Brown, whom he'd met when she was an eighteen-year-old student at Connecticut College for Women and Ford was at Yale Law School. They'd had a torrid romance that lasted nearly three years, but Phyllis, now a Powers model in New York, dumped him when he announced he was absolutely serious about returning to Grand Rapids after Yale.

"I talk to her on the phone about once every five years, or if I'm in Reno I call up. But I don't have her come to my hotel room," he said in 1997, giggling like the lovelorn young buck he once was. "I sit in the coffee bar, and we have a Coke.

"When I was courting her from 1939 to 1941, she was on most of the *Cosmopolitan* covers when Bradshaw Crandall was the artist, and we had a pretty deep romance. But when I got through law school, I made a very firm decision to go back to Michigan, and she was one of the top models in New York, so [Grand Rapids] wasn't a very good choice for her," he said with a chuckle.

"But you still remember her fondly, and vice versa?"

"Oh, yeah. I mean, only trouble is, she's been married at least three times, maybe four, so I don't think she ever would have been a very helpful wife for a politician. Very smart, very beautiful, very great—really a great gal. But she was a New York girl."

I asked if she'd ever shown up in Rancho Mirage or Beaver Creek—their ski weekend in Vermont made the cover of *Look* magazine in 1940—and he said no.

But there's a sequel to the story. A few years ago, Phyllis did turn up in the desert, unannounced, and asked if she could drop by for a quick hello with her old flame. Much to her chagrin, the answer was no.

They never spoke, but no doubt he was torn; his days with Phyllis were among his happiest memories. But Betty Ford, understandably, had never been high on the brassy babe. There was no way the straightest of arrows would have seen her without telling Betty, and after nearly sixty years of marital bliss, he wasn't about to risk hurting the uncontested love of his life, the woman he described a few weeks before his death as "the greatest of all my blessings."

# ELEVEN

# Lifestyles

AFTER SEVERAL DAYS of therapeutic golf with Arnold Palmer at Pebble Beach, the newly retired president flew back to Rancho Mirage at the end of January 1977 and started remapping the rest of his life.

"I thought that leaving the White House was terrible," he admitted to me in March of 1993. "I tried hard to stay. But that was a closed chapter, so I plunged right in."

That was a classic Jerry Ford understatement. For more than a third of a century, until he began to falter, he and Betty reveled in a comfortable, exhilarating lifestyle. To varying degrees, we talked about that in all our interviews.

As every writer understands, sometimes useful insights and vignettes that help illuminate a person's life don't fit neatly into a chapter.

What follows, then, are random human glimpses, including some of my favorite moments with Ford, that deserve a better home than the cutting-room floor.

In 1997, Ford unexpectedly broached the subject of marital infidelity, a contact sport he'd watched only from the sidelines.

"You know, Tom, next year will be fifty years, knock on wood, without any fooling around—unlike my friend Frank Gifford."

Pro football icon Gifford was all over the tabloids for having been caught in a fling with a former TWA flight attendant.

"I called Frank yesterday," he said, "just to say, 'Betty and I are thinking about you, you're in our thoughts and prayers and we hope everything works out.' We're going to see him in Beaver Creek in three weeks."

He felt bad for his old friend and worked hard not to be judgmental about the tryst, which he obviously believed was ill-advised. I told him what one of his closest political allies had once said: Jerry's the only guy I've ever worked for who never strayed.

"You have to think of the ten bad things that could happen to you from something like that and the one good thing," Ford philosophized, "and tell yourself the one good thing will get taken care of some other way."

In Rancho Mirage in 2000, I asked him, "When you go out, what do you do?" He responded with an eclectic dissertation on the Fords' social life.

"Last week we went to a fundraiser for our Episcopal church here. They have an annual dinner. The next night we went to a fundraiser for the McCallum Theatre, which is a local civic theater. We try to cut back on those, but we probably go to one or two of those a week, because I'm on the church vestry, I'm on the McCallum Theatre board. Then Betty's got a golf tournament here this week. All these LPGA girls stay over, thirty of them do, and play in the Betty Ford Center Tournament, and the Betty Ford Center makes about $300,000 because they charge the amateurs $2,000 to play. We have the sponsors for dinner, and they have a big dinner Monday night, but they raise enough to pay each of the pros $2,500. And then they net for the Center about $300,000. That keeps her busy. But it's good for her, and of course the Center does a helluva job."

(He'd been touting his wife's center since it opened. "Have you ever been over to the Betty Ford Center?" he asked in 1993. "In the first ten years, twenty-two thousand people went through, and their record is tremendous. She is a hands-on chairman, she works at it, and I support her. Sometimes they keep her so damn busy I get irritated, but nevertheless, it's for the good.")

"I haven't had a drink in twenty-two years, she hasn't had one in twenty-three years. And neither of us smoke anymore. I've got a few of 'em [his once-ubiquitous pipes] around here, but I never use 'em. She stopped drinking in 1978. I kept drinking for a year; then I got tired of drinking alone, so we drink [chuckle] tonic and lime at night."

He said his favorite dining-out spot in the desert was Jillian's. I teased him about ever having liver and onions there, as he was known to do at the Left Bank in Vail, his mountain favorite.

"No, whitefish. He has a delicious whitefish. I've shifted to more fish now."

He was also making other lifestyle adjustments:

"I've cut back to three corporate boards. I make one speech a month instead of three or four. I've been doing about four of the Peter Lowell events. This organization will rent a hall and they have speakers from eight in the morning until six at night, and I'm one of twelve or fourteen. They had Margaret Thatcher, they had me, they had Barbara Bush. I did one in San Diego, I'm gonna do one in Seattle, I'm gonna do one in Detroit. I do about four a year. Those are easy—you give the same speech. They have twelve to fourteen thousand people there. They provide a private plane, which makes it easier.

"I finally capitulated to my wife and children: I on occasion wear hearing aids. I don't wear 'em all the time, I don't have 'em on in the office here, but if I'm going out to a party I wear them. If I'm going to make a speech I wear them. But that's the only change in my physical condition."

At this point Ford was still swimming laps twice a day and trying for nine to twelve holes of golf three times a week, having finally stopped playing eighteen holes at a clip. "At going on eighty-seven, your legs get a little weary," he admitted. "If I play eighteen, boy, those legs are shot for a couple of days, so I enjoy nine holes. I'm what they call a nine-holer. The truth is, I'm playing better. I'm hitting the ball straighter; it doesn't go as far, but I won't wander all over the ballpark like I used to do."

Like all sane adult males, Ford started keeping closer track of his prostate health for telltale early warning signs of cancer. Unsurprisingly, his prostate-specific antigen (PSA) test scores had started creeping up as he aged.

"I'm gonna go to my urologist tomorrow," he volunteered in February 2000. "I have to watch my PSI, PSA. My old urologist retired; I've got a new one tomorrow. I'll be curious what my latest PSA says.

"You know, I learned something about prostate cancer. At my age, they say you're better off living with it than dying from it. So unless it [gets worse] . . ."

"Dying from the operation, perhaps?"

"Yeah, yeah. But I have no symptoms aside of getting up four times a night to go to the can."

"But that's a symptom of age."

"It is. Other than that, my hearing aids—I've finally capitulated. My eyesight is—now I have to have reading as well as distance glasses, but my eye doctor says other than that, my eyes are great.

"I'm lucky—I feel good, Betty feels good—although she, the back bothers her occasionally. But we're happy and healthy, considering eighty-seven and eighty-one—eighty-two, she'll be eighty-two in April."

I asked him if he was planning a blowout bash for his ninetieth birthday in 2003.

"I'm not counting on that far down the road yet," he said, laughing.

When I saw him in July, I reminded him he'd raised the prostate issue in February and asked how he'd fared with the plumbing doctor.

"Oh, yeah, I had a checkup just before I came up here, and—stable. I have a new urologist 'cause the fellow I've been with for fifteen years retired, and we got a new, young urologist, so he approached it from a totally fresh point of view. He had all the old records, of course, but he said things looked stable. In the month before I came up here, my general physician is so thorough—he had me take a CAT scan, a bone scan, a colonopathy [colonoscopy], MRI, something else—and I got an A-plus on all of them.

"Now, I must say this: my endurance isn't what it used to be, and my, oh, strength isn't what I used to be, but as far as the doctors are concerned, I'm fine."

Particularly considering that he would celebrate his eighty-seventh birthday in three days.

"I know it," he earnestly replied. "No, I'm damn lucky—Betty and I both are."

Apparently, his prostate numbers remained stable. In 2002, he told me about his latest checkup:

"I just went yesterday to my urologist, and my PSA was a little higher, but he said it's nothing to worry about. And he took the physical exam and said it had not enlarged, and he didn't urge anything except to come back in about six months, which is what I have been doing."

The general scrutiny level diminishes significantly once a president is out of office, but an ex-leader still has to cope with constraints as a formerly well-known person. "You're still in the public spotlight,

Tom, and you have to act accordingly," he said in 1992. "Not that I would ever do anything illegal or unethical anyhow, but you just have to be overly cautious."

Especially since, by his own choice, he was in the public eye more than most because of his herculean travel schedule.

"I've probably worked too hard," he mused. "I was supposed to re-tire, and when all these things came up—that's not retirement. But I'm healthy, so I guess it didn't do me any harm."

As an aside, he showed me the scar from his knee-replacement sur-gery, which had landed him in the hospital for eight days and required crutches for five weeks but was pronounced successful. "I have more flexibility than I do with the other one," he bragged.

The surgery wasn't enough, however, to get him back on the ski slopes.

"The doctor would shoot me if I did." He laughed. "To tell you the truth, I'm trying to convince Betty I don't want to take a [vacation] trip in the fall because I know I'm gonna get asked to campaign and I don't want to be in the Mediterranean when the White House says, 'Where's Ford? Won't he help us?' Because I think it's gonna be a close election."

By 1992, Ford was significantly pruning his political work. He'd campaigned for Bush in Grand Rapids and had stumped for just seven congressional hopefuls that fall. A decade before, he'd done at least forty events.

He was also down to four corporate boards, and had pared his speak-ing schedule from forty talks to twelve.

"I would say everything is cut back at least fifty percent," he said in 1993. "I'll be eighty in July, for Christ's sake."

As the 2002 midterm elections approached, Ford was fervently committed to staying off the campaign grind. "I'm gonna do minimal," he said. "I got a call from [former congressman] Bud Brown day before yesterday. His son is running for Congress in Ohio, and I said, 'Bud,

I'm just not getting involved.' He understood it. I got a letter from a congressman today, a Republican who must be nameless, who wanted my support and asked me to contribute $2,000 [chuckle]. My answer to him was, 'I don't contribute to candidates, I contribute to national committees and state committees.' I didn't even know who the hell he was. Been in Congress about six years."

Football Flashback: He reminisced in 1995 about ceremonies at a Michigan football game where his number 48 was retired. He was so thrilled by the honor that a picture of the festivities adorned the cover of the Ford Christmas card that year.

"It was a great occasion," he said nostalgically. "You know, they gave you the number in those days. The equipment manager threw you a jersey and that was your number. But that was the year—'48—that I started in politics."

Eventually, football and old age caught up with his shoulder. In 1995, it was giving him fits. He said that even though he'd be returning from two board meetings in New York, he was determined to play in the Bob Hope Desert Classic.

"It all depends on how my shoulder is . . . what really irritates me is this damn shoulder."

More than a decade into our off-the-record conversations, I'd never asked him about his controversial 1975 decision to deny federal loan guarantees to New York City. That seemingly flinty judgment prompted one of the more famous headlines in the history of my current employer, the New York *Daily News:* "Ford to City: Drop Dead."

By Ford's account, the headline should have read, "I Saved New York."

"The truth is," he told me in 2002, "by our firm position, New York City changed its irresponsible fiscal policy, where they were giving pay increases to employees and committing to pensions that were outrageous. They tightened their belts, and when they did that I [eventually] authorized the federal government to loan them money."

He never understood why New Yorkers thought he hated their city. Manhattan always held some of his fondest memories. When he was at Yale Law School, coaching football on the side, he remembered, "I had this very beautiful gal [Phyllis Brown] as a close-to-three-year romance. I used to drive down to New York most every weekend. We didn't have the interstate, but they had a pretty good highway and it took about two and a half, three hours. But as a result, I got acquainted with a lot of the things you do in New York—the theater, et cetera."

In retirement, Ford returned to the Big Apple several times a year for corporate board meetings, mixing work with Broadway plays. Two of his favorites: *The Lion King* and *The Producers.*

In 1997, I asked if there was anything about being a former president he didn't enjoy.

"No, we've learned to live with it, and the truth is I've been busy enough in other things that I think I handle it responsibly."

"You mean the celebrity and autograph-signing?"

"If you're gonna be a former president, that has to happen, and you might as well relax and enjoy it."

"Anything you can't do as president?"

"I fortunately have no hidden vices," he said. "I really don't feel hemmed in. Fortunately, I don't have any extramarital experiences," he added, laughing. "I mean, we've got fifty years of marriage a year from now, in October of '98."

There was one downside to his status, he admitted. As he aged, he wearied of autograph hounds. In February 2000 we talked briefly about the recent Super Bowl. "Well, I never go to those games, I watch 'em on TV," he said, although he could have seats for the asking. "Because if I go to the game, everybody wants to ask me a question or shake my hand. I want to watch the damn game."

"I get the feeling that you don't like to do autographs as much as you used to."

"I do it, but it's not with enthusiasm."

Ford had mentioned more than once over the years that he was an incurable pack rat. So in our February 2000 interview, I asked him about a story I'd heard a few years before that his compulsion was worse than advertised. I wanted to know if it was true that in his early years as a young congressman, every time he was invited to the White House he'd stuff his suit pockets with presidential matchbooks and take them back to his constituents. As he moved up the congressional ladder, he spent more time at the White House, under Republican and Democratic presidents, meaning more opportunities for matchbook-pilfering.

"Well"—he laughed, a bit sheepishly—"I always picked up a couple, starting with Truman. We kept them in the house, and I guess if we had guests, we would pass them out as little mementos."

Which explains why, one day at Camp David, when he spied a reporter cramming matchbooks into his sports jacket, he just smiled indulgently.

Ford was a resolutely old-fashioned guy, never much into newfangled gadgetry. Like computers. In 1998 I asked him if he'd gotten around to buying himself a personal computer yet.

"I don't have one," he replied, "but Betty and I talk about going over to the College of the Desert to get a beginner course, but we never get around to doing it."

Two years later, in a February 2000 conversation, I asked him, "Have you learned any new tricks? For instance, the one thing I never see in this office is a computer."

"Well, that's interesting," he responded. "Betty has one of these laptops over at the house, and she has become sort of an enthusiastic fanatic. She corresponds with people [chuckles], and she's tweaked my interest. So I'm thinking of getting one for my desk. I feel out of the circuit not knowing how to operate one. That's the only way I can learn; I can't learn using hers. I've got to have one, so the next time you come, I'll have one."

He was true to his word. During our Beaver Creek interview in July of that year, a laptop was prominently perched on the side of his office desk. I asked him how his computer skills were progressing.

"So far Betty's taught me to do the fundamentals," he said, pointing at the laptop. "We brought it up from California and we'll take it back when we go."

"You spend time on it every day?"

"I try to."

"What have you learned?"

"Well, I'm very preliminary. I've learned how to play solitaire and hearts. My next step is to learn how to write letters and receive them. Betty has her own computer, and she's good."

"This is a laptop, right?"

"Yes, it's a Microsoft. [!] I probably fool around with it about every other day. I have not mastered it, I can tell you that, but I've gotten so I enjoy it.

"I enjoy playing bridge on it because I'm an old bridge advocate and that's easy to do," he added.

Clearly, his computer immersion was still in its infancy. Where it always remained: he once agreed to do an online interview from a computer in his office. When the first question arrived, he mused about his answer for a moment. Then he started barking into the monitor. Suppressing a smile, an aide had to explain that he could just speak his answer in a normal tone of voice and she'd type it up and send it along via the magic of the Web.

# TWELVE

# March 2004

I N MARCH OF 2004, I flew to the desert for what would turn out to be the last interview where Ford was still seemingly at the peak of his intellectual faculties. I couldn't know that at the time, of course, particularly since by all outward signs he seemed totally unchanged from our previous encounters.

That interview was also the last that fit our standard pattern: an informal, scattershooting, around-the-world blend of politics, gossip, current events, historical flashbacks, and personal chitchat.

We sat down in the study of his office at 3:00 P.M. on a balmy Monday. Ford was dressed in his standard desert uniform: golf shirt, chinos, brown casual shoes.

He was less a former president this day than just a ninety-year-old guy musing about what anyone his age would have at the top of his agenda: the state of his health.

"I've had a couple of little interim setbacks. I was out playing golf on a hot day and stupidly got caught . . . and my doctors are doing their damnedest to balance out my blood pressure. It goes from too high to too low, so they've got me taking medication to balance it. When I stand up they want me to count to ten so I don't faint.

"I took a spill the other morning getting out of—well, not getting out of bed but getting dressed, and I was damn lucky. I fell into another piece of furniture, and, boy, I couldn't get up, couldn't get Betty. We finally did, and we had to get the agents over to untangle me. I thought, My God, supposing I was here alone."

"Well, but you're almost never alone, right?"

"That's true, thank God.

"I bruised a hand here, but I took some Celebrex and it went away. But other than those little incidents, it taught me a lesson: to be damn careful. I keep reading about people my age taking a spill and bringing bad results." Consequently, "at night when I get up to go to the john, I am extra cautious. I'm not in that big of a hurry."

After talking about it for years, Ford had finally decided to curtail his traveling, particularly to New York for his corporate board meetings.

"I'm still on the board of American Express and Citigroup as adviser. They kick you off when you're seventy-five or whatever it is. And I used to go to the board meetings up until last year. Finally, Betty and I talked it over; to go to New York from here is a three-day trip and I just decided those three-day trips, Tom, were just too tough. So I talked to Sandy Weill at Citigroup, Ken Chenault at American Express, and said, 'I'd like to stay on the board as an adviser; I have been for many years. I can't travel. Can I do it telephonically?' And they both agreed. And I did an American Express meeting for two and a half hours this morning telephonically, and I'll do a Citigroup board meeting next week sometime.

"I swim twice a day. I got up this morning at 7:30, took a swim, had breakfast, and then had my board meeting. And I'll swim this afternoon. I swim two laps in the morning, two laps at night. I used to do ten."

He was still golfing, but that passion had also been cut back and was steadily heading toward a fond memory, like skiing.

"I'm a nine-holer. In fact, if I play, I play three to six holes—just enough to loosen up and— I've got a couple of—well, we've got a group over at Vintage Golf Course here that at ten o'clock, if you want to play nine holes or less, drop by and you'll find one or more that'll be glad to play with you. So we call it the Nine-Holers. Up until last month I probably did it once every two weeks. But I haven't—for some reason I didn't have much ambition to play the last month or two."

There was another major change in his schedule; I'd heard he wouldn't be attending the 2004 Republican convention; the doctors didn't want to risk a repeat of 2000, where he'd suffered a stroke at the Philadelphia convention.

"I don't think so, Tom. I will be ninety-one and I will have been at how many of them? First one I went to was in Philadelphia in '76, wasn't it?"

"Didn't you go to the convention with Willkie—'We Want Willkie'—in 1940?"

Ford lit up at the memory of his Young Turk days. "Oh, yeah! My God! Yeah, that was also in Philadelphia. We were out there [outside]. 'We Want Willkie.' But then I had the years in the military where we didn't go [in 1944]. Didn't I read someplace that Herbert Hoover went to one when he was ninety?"

He might not be heading to New York, but his mind was very much engaged in election politics—specifically the matter of Bush's running mate. I wasn't prepared for what happened next: an admission that it might be best for President Bush if he dumped Dick Cheney, Bush's controversial and increasingly unpopular vice president.

In four short years, Cheney had gone from huge political asset to huge political liability. In 2000, his long service in the legislative and executive branches had reassured moderate and independent voters tired of the Clinton years but worried that Bush was too inexperienced to be president.

Now Cheney's muscular views on just about everything, but especially the Iraq War, had become a problem for Bush, according to many Republican leaders.

In fact, Ford volunteered, he'd gotten feelers from old friends on Capitol Hill and Republican political associates disgruntled with Cheney:

"I've had several people come to me about 'are they gonna make a change in the vice presidential selection,' and in effect suggesting that I should do something about it," he said, chuckling. "Which I'm *not* gonna do.

"But *totally* off the record, Dick has not been the asset I expected on the ticket. As you know, he's a great friend of mine, he did a great job for me, but he has not clicked, if that's the right word. God knows he works at it."

"So do you think he has become a liability for Bush?"

"Oh, he's not as big an asset as he should be. I put it on the affirmative."

"You're not the only person who thinks that. Some people say it's because he's just become—moved too far to the right. He's just not stayed in the middle like you—you know, kind of a middle-of-the-road conservative, that he's just kind of been too far out there."

"Well, when the problem of Saddam Hussein came up, they justified going to war on the basis of finding weapons of mass destruction. That was the wrong place to put the emphasis, Tom. They had plenty of good evidence that Saddam Hussein was a bad man and should be thrown out. There was no question they could prove that. Why they got hooked on the weapons of mass destruction is beyond my comprehension. I think it was a mistake to use that as the justification when they had all the evidence they needed—this bad individual. Do you have any idea why they did that?"

"They got into this mode where it was kind of we're smarter than you are," I replied. "We know better, and if you knew what we knew, you wouldn't question us, and just go leave us alone. I think September 11 just so traumatized Bush that he just—I was told Bush decided to attack Iraq a week after September 11."

"Hmmm."

"And the guy who told me that was [General] Tommy Franks. He told me that he got a call from Bush a week after September 11 saying, 'How quickly can you put together a plan to attack Iraq?' "

"Well," Ford responded, returning to his WMD theme, "they're still looking for those weapons, and they ain't gonna find them, or at least not sufficiently to justify . . . as cause to go to war."

As quickly as I could without being too obvious, I steered the conversation back to Cheney. Ford was telegraphing, in his let-them-down-easy style, that Bush might be better off getting himself a new running mate. Out of affection for his old chief of staff, however, he wouldn't be party to a cabal, as he had been in 1992 with Dan Quayle.

"A lot of people say to me, 'You've known Cheney a long time,' " I said. " 'Do you think he's changed?' And I go back and forth on whether I think he's changed. What do you think? Do you think he's the same guy [or] has he changed?"

"I don't have a lot of contact with him, but from my contacts, I don't think personality-wise he's changed. I don't think he's moved way over to the right; that's not my impression. I don't like his view on why they went to war, but I think he's still a good man, but that doesn't mean he's the best candidate for vice president."

"Well, do you think Bush should make a change?" I pressed.

"I have not talked to anybody [about] do I think they should get rid of him. I just say that other people are talking to me about making a change, but I have not promoted it myself. I'm apprehensive as to his help to the ticket."

"Who do you think would be a good [replacement] choice?"

Perhaps as a salve to his still-hurting conscience over dumping Nelson Rockefeller in 1975, Ford mentioned two New York politicians:

"Well, they all ask me that. How about Pataki? Good governor, a winner, would bring personality to the ticket. He won New York twice. What about Giuliani?"

"I think he would win New York," I answered, "but he is such a loose cannon, and he's pro-choice, you know. And he's not a team player. And the Bush people—look at what happened to Paul O'Neill—they just can't handle somebody who's not a total team player. So Giuliani would be good, but he's not their kind of person."

"No."

"He's got the dynamism, he's got the hero stuff, he would help a lot, but I just don't think that unless Dick has a health problem, I don't think Bush is gonna take him off the ticket."

"You're probably right," Ford concluded. "He's stubborn about those things."

I asked if he'd spoken to George W. Bush lately, and he said they'd just missed connections.

"We were supposed to go to dinner at Annenberg's last Saturday; he was here. But we had another commitment. I haven't talked to either Bush for probably a month. I don't believe in calling him to have a friendly chat. I want him to have something to ask me, and vice versa. We [recently] talked about problems in Iraq and Afghanistan in generalities, not into why they did and so forth. You could infer why they wanted to do it."

I wanted to know if he thought Iraq was still a political plus for Bush, but before answering he took a potshot at Richard Clarke, the former National Security Council counterterrorism expert who had been critical of the administration's war planning.

"Did you see that guy Clarke last night? He's a pain in the ass. He looks like an egotistical jackass—very pro-himself."

As for Iraq: "I think it's lost some of its appeal politically, but I don't think at this stage—at this stage, Tom—it is a terrible liability. If they got a break and got bin Laden, a lot of the apprehension would fade away. [The casualty rate is] over five hundred now. It becomes more difficult as time passes, just like in the case of Vietnam. When they started Vietnam, those early losses were not looked at as too bad. But as they got up to a thousand, it became more difficult.

"I'm asked often, does the president have a tougher job in the current circumstances than you had, or Reagan had, or Carter had? And my answer is yes. President Bush has a much more difficult job. When Reagan and Carter and I and Johnson were in office, it was a challenge between the Soviet Union and the United States, their allies and our allies. When we negotiated, we understood what the problems were. We knew that they had so much in weapons, we knew they knew how much we had in weapons. And it was a much more responsible negotiation, even though the weapons were scary. President Bush has to deal with a worldwide, multifaceted problem, and that makes it much more complicated, and I say much more dangerous.

"Considering the problems on his menu, I think he's doing fine, but he's got problems that are gonna make it difficult to win unless they get better. Fortunately, the economy seems to have turned around. In fact, the latest employment figures were very encouraging. But the war, gasoline prices, something like that could be a pain in the you-know-what."

I knew that Ford was a longtime deficit hawk, so I wondered what he thought about Bush's mushrooming budget shortfalls.

"I never saw the figures change so dramatically as they did, what, three years ago. Two or three surpluses to $300 billion deficit. It scares me, Tom. I'm amazed that the White House doesn't seem to worry about it."

I reminded him of what former secretary of the treasury Paul O'Neill, a longtime Ford favorite from his days in the budget office, had said in the book he'd collaborated on after being sacked. Cheney had told O'Neill that Ronald Reagan proved deficits don't matter. That prompted Ford to ask for a little gossip.

"I got a copy of Paul O'Neill's book with a nice letter from him. What's the story there? Did he just have an out with the president? I stayed out of the public press on it. He was a first-class bureaucrat. He was number two in OMB with me. I think it wasn't handled very well, whatever."

Turning to the fall elections, Ford predicted, "It's going to be a very close election, and I wouldn't gamble that Bush is gonna win. It's that tight, Tom. You got, what, six months, eight months, a lot can happen between now and then. My dear wife, who's a pretty well-read, knowledgeable person, she thinks it's gonna be a horse race."

Whom should John Kerry pick as his running mate? Ford hadn't given that too much thought, but did allow it was probably better that the Democratic number two should be somebody outside of Washington.

Parenthetically, I asked for a progress report on his attempts to become computer-literate. I knew what the answer would be.

"I've kinda given up on that, although my dear wife is our computer expert. Our kids and grandchildren, they're all in that and know all about it." Then he abruptly changed the subject to a happier topic:

"I want to tell you about some good news. It really is not a part of this interview. But you know, two years ago the University of Michigan established the Gerald R. Ford School of Public Policy. They wanted to build a new building for $32 million, and they wanted—the university put up $20 million, and I and my friends had to raise $12 million. Well, you just don't go out and raise $12 million with a few campaign speeches. I'm gonna give you some figures that will maybe shock you. Sandy Weill and his wife gave $4 million. Jay Van Andel gave a million, Max Fisher from Detroit gave a million. Paul O'Neill gave a million. Betty and I gave a million. Lee Annenberg gave $3 million. We are over the hump, and they're going to have a groundbreaking probably in November of this year. I never thought people, even though they were good friends, would step to the plate and do something like that. Brent Scowcroft gave $250,000."

His namesake school was so important to him that he'd already abandoned his new rule about flying east. "We get a private plane; both Betty and I will go."

"Especially if it's a football weekend, right?"

"Well, it just so happens Michigan's playing Northwestern," he said, laughing heartily.

Aside from relatively good health for a nonagenarian, he seemed unusually serene to me.

"When I see what my friends did for a project involving me, I can't help but feel serene or comfortable or whatever, because I never thought there would be this kind of response. In each case it was *their* initiative. Sandy and Joan [Weill's wife]— Of course, you know I've done very well with Citigroup, and he and I have had this wonderful friendship. But to have somebody come up and say here's four million dollars. Lee Annenberg—we've been a very good friend of hers since Walter died. For her, first there was a million, then she came up with another two. Sandy requested that his name be on the building, and the university agreed. Well, they should. It's gonna be the Sanford and Joan Weill Building at the Ford School of Public Policy."

He was also mellow about his four kids, all of whom seemed to have discovered their niches.

"Jack and his family were up at Beaver Creek last week, skiing. Steve still hasn't found a prospective bride. Susan and Vaden are down in Albuquerque, and Mike has one of his daughters getting married, and we're going to the wedding on October 15 down at Winston[-Salem]. Betty and I are taking it easy."

I'd heard Mrs. Ford hadn't been well.

"Well, you're right. I'm ninety and she's eighty-five; we can't complain. Married for fifty-five, going on fifty-six years."

Without discussing that fateful conversation where he'd sworn me to secrecy, we reminisced about his first trip to the desert as vice president at Easter 1974. I asked about the family of Leonard Firestone, his neighbor and dear friend, who owned the home where we were now sitting.

"Well, Leonard passed away. His wife at that time was never a good friend of ours. We disliked her. He had two previous wives that we knew; both died of cancer. We liked them very much. The third wife was very aggressive. Of course, one of his grandchildren was in TV. He was with ten women, or whatever it was."

"One of those reality shows?"

"Yeah. We thought Leonard would roll over in his grave."

Morbidly, that reminded me that I hadn't asked him what he'd heard about President Reagan's medical condition.

"Not good, no. Betty talks to Nancy; I have very limited conversations with her, but she's having a very difficult time. His health is obviously not getting better; it's tragic that he hangs on."

"Well, Tom, speaking of leaders—I've had the exposure to all of the recent world leaders during my life. The Chinese: Mao Tse-tung, Teng Hsiao-p'ing, Chou En-lai. Sadat, Rabin, Callaghan, Valéry Giscard [d'Estaing], Schmidt. What a blessing to have had that exposure and to have had that involvement. I was just lucky as the devil."

It had been a long trip from Omaha, I observed.

"It's a long way from Grand Rapids," he corrected me politely. Omaha was his birthplace; Grand Rapids would always be home, even in perpetuity.

"I've had several opportunities to write another book, but the truth is I'm too lazy at this age, at ninety. To write a really good book takes a lot of time."

Wrapping up our visit, we chatted randomly about old friends and acquaintances.

"I'll tell you who's a big asset to the president, and that's Laura. She was down here for an event down at Annenberg's, and we were invited. She is a very nice lady—articulate, attractive, well mannered. She just is classy. I know they're using her to raise money; she is an asset.

"Let me finish with another good-news thing. Dick Nixon and I were longtime close friends. I mean, for years. Every time he wrote a book, he gave me a copy with an inscription. Dear Jerry, whatever, whatever. The other night we were at dinner with some guy who was connected with one of the New York book companies. I don't know whether you'd call it a publishing company, but he's knowledgeable about books. And I don't know whether you know it or not, but every Sunday in the *New York Times* they have a book review, and there's a company that publishes the value of books on the back page. Well, I had Shelli, one of my secretaries, check with this company and this friend that I had learned, because I've got eight of Nixon's books here, and all of them have an inscription. Dear Jerry, something, something, something. I said to Shelli, find out what they're worth. They came back and said a minimum of $7,500. So if you've got any book that Nixon autographed, inscribed, don't throw 'em away. I'm gonna give two each to the children. I'm torn between keeping them intact or giving them to the children, and I've finally decided it would be nicer to have the children have them."

That gave me an opening to steer him back to Nixon and his efforts at rehabilitation, a subject we'd broached many times.

"Oh, I think he's gradually being enhanced. His downfall was Haldeman and Ehrlichman and Colson. They were a terrible disaster."

"Yeah, but they didn't lead him to tape conversations."

"They sort of got him in the wrong direction. He wasn't smart enough to detect their being a liability."

Had they played to his insecurities?

"Vanity—no question about that, Tom."

"Probably his paranoia," I interjected. "I always felt Nixon felt he had a lot of people out to get him."

"There's no doubt about that."

"But not you?"

A wistful tone crept into his voice, as though he was remembering days that had altered his life forever.

"No," he replied softly, adding that Nixon had never questioned his loyalty.

"No. Never. In fact, he trusted me implicitly."

Ford was never the world's greatest anecdotalist, but I was always scrounging around for a new tidbit from the Watergate era. So I asked if Nixon had ever given him a secret assignment that history didn't know about. He said no—then, no doubt trying to be helpful, embellished an interesting fact from his memoirs that I'd forgotten.

"I remember when Mel Laird called me and said, 'Would you take the vice presidency?' Betty and I were having a martini, and I said let me check with Betty, and we said, 'Tell him to go ahead.'

"He was torn between Reagan, Rockefeller, and Connally, and he couldn't get any of them confirmed; the conservatives wouldn't take Rockefeller, liberals wouldn't take Reagan, and Connally was in the milk scandal. So as a bad fourth choice, he picked me."

Did he think Nixon regretted it?

Typical Ford humility: "I hope not."

I asked him to flash back to that famous scene on the South Lawn of the White House, when he and Betty had walked the Nixons to their helicopter to begin the long journey to exile in San Clemente. I wanted to know what they'd said to each other as they shook hands at that epic moment of triumph and tragedy—triumph for democracy, tragedy for the Nixons.

"I think I said to him, 'Dick, I'm sorry about this. You did a good job.' It was a plus [comment]; I wanted to bolster his spirits."

What had Nixon said to his old Chowder and Marching Society comrade?

" 'Good luck, Jerry,' or something to that effect. There was no bitterness between him and me. None whatsoever. It was a sad day, though.

"Watergate, the war in Vietnam, the economy problems—we went through a helluva period."

# THIRTEEN

# Growing Old

REMARKABLY, and much to his surprise and delight, the juggernaut of old age didn't really catch up with Jerry Ford until he was nearly ninety.

"Some people age a lot in a uniform manner," Ford mentioned to an old friend in 2003, not long before becoming a nonagenarian. "Hell, I didn't age until three years ago. I like the way it was for me."

He'd remained physically vigorous well into his eighties, mainly because of a twice-a-day routine of swimming laps that he maintained religiously. He seemed to recover fully from his stroke at the 2000 Republican convention, but later admitted to friends that his energy had sagged and was never quite the same afterward.

Part of it was his therapy: he needed to take blood thinners because of the stroke, but sometimes the medication caused bleeding around the esophagus and caused erratic fluctuations in his blood pressure that caused brief bouts of dizziness.

He'd always seemed indestructible to me; whenever he'd say something about finally getting old, I'd remind him I'd been saying for years he'd outlive us all.

Nonetheless, I can remember clearly the day his mortality came crashing home to me.

It was June 3, 2002, at the conclusion of one of the annual reunion dinners for old acquaintances the Fords loved to host every summer back in Washington.

As Melanie and I exited the dining room, someone grabbed my arm. It was the former president.

"Tom, you haven't been out to see us for a while," he admonished. "You should come out."

I stammered my apologies, offering the usual Washington copouts: things are crazy at the office, busier than I expected, editors driving me insane, it's an election year, et cetera, ad nauseam.

"But I will, Mr. President. I'll do better; I promise."

"Okay, but you're overdue. Wait till we get to the mountains."

I didn't have the heart to remind him that we had spent ninety minutes together in Rancho Mirage only ten weeks earlier.

My wife grasped my arm and winced empathetically. She had been through this with her father before his death at eighty-nine, but Ford's memory lapse, not uncommon in people his age, shocked me. In the winter of 1999, during our Beaver Creek conversation, I'd noticed that he was having some trouble with his hearing. Now, by all outward appearances a seemingly hale eighty-eight, Ford had dramatically exhibited a clear sign of slippage.

In retrospect, I should have paid more attention to the last lines of the brief speech he'd given just before our encounter.

"I look forward to seeing you next year," he'd said, a standard line for him. Then he unexpectedly departed from the script.

"I *hope* to be around," he added, choking up.

As the audience camouflaged their concerns with hearty applause, the honoree recovered his composure, and his usual optimism. "I do hope to celebrate a ninetieth birthday, so we'll see you then."

He was true to his word, attending the next three reunions before infirmity grounded him.

These dinners were one of the more enduring traditions of the Fords' twilight years. Beginning in the summer of 1983, he and Betty would return to the capital on the first Monday in June. He'd hand out a couple of journalism awards named for him, make a speech at the National Press Club, take a few questions, meet with the trustees of his educational foundation, then host an alumni reunion dinner at the Capitol Hill Club, one of his old haunts from his days in the House.

Unless they were traveling or dead, the murderers' row of public servants that Ford had assembled in August 1974 always turned out in force: Henry Kissinger, Brent Scowcroft, Dick Cheney, Don Rumsfeld, Alan Greenspan, Bill Simon, Bill Coleman, Carla Hills, Paul O'Neill, and dozens more.

Including aging congressional cronies, former White House staffers, and a smattering of journalists, there were usually 150 to 200 guests on hand to trade insults and reminisce about some of the finest days of their lives.

One year, for instance, Cheney exploited his strategic advantage as toastmaster to needle Don Rumsfeld, his old mentor. "I look at Don now and I see the secretary of defense," Cheney deadpanned. "He looks at me and sees an assistant to Don Rumsfeld."

In 2004, he was at it again. "When you're around," he told Rumsfeld, "people start seeing me as a softie, all warm and fuzzy."

There was never any pressure to show up, but these gatherings were a command performance of sorts anyway, a vehicle to recall halcyon days of yore and say hello to the boss. A celebration of decency, one of his former cabinet officers once called them.

O'Neill, who was Ford's deputy budget director and a particular favorite of the Old Man, explained the emotional imperative this way one year: "Even if it's hard, you come to see President Ford because of the person he is and what he did for the country."

Indeed, it's hard to imagine any other president, no matter how successful, commanding the sort of affection to guarantee that sort of turnout for nearly a quarter-century.

For most of the guests, the dinner was their only glimpse of Ford all year, and he always looked surprisingly hearty and healthy as he circled the room like the seasoned, glad-handing pol he'd always been.

The irrepressible Bob Barrett, his first postpresidential chief of staff, parsed Ford's longevity this way at one of these gatherings: "He'll deliver my eulogy, and when my son goes, he'll [also speak and] say, 'I knew his father.'"

Despite his reputation as an accident-prone bumbler, Ford had always been a gifted athlete. After leaving the White House, he kept to a robust exercise routine. When skiing became impossible after his knees gave out and had to be replaced, he played tennis and golf regularly.

Early in the new century, however, Ford had been reduced to the status of occasional duffer. Except for a few holes of golf and his swimming, the athletic regimen he'd followed in retirement was now history.

At least he knew his limitations, announcing the end of the Jerry Ford Invitational three years before the last putt was holed.

"I'm not gonna be like my friend Bob Hope and be wheeled around my own golf tournament," he explained to an old friend.

In a 2002 interview, Ford reminded me that he was the last surviving member of the Warren Commission and the last original member of the Chowder and Marching Society, "so I guess being [still] around, you earn a little recognition.

"I don't hear as well, I don't see as well, I don't play as much golf, but I'm [knocks wood twice] lucky to be around."

He also noted that his corporate perks weren't as appetizing any longer.

"Last week, Citigroup had a quarterly board meeting, and they just left the day afterward, all the directors that wanted to go to Japan or China or someplace else, and I said no. We used to jump at a chance like that, but I just told Sandy [Weill] travel like that is just too tough, and he understood. Not being in your own bed—those things affect me now; they never used to."

I reminded him of the dozens of years when Ford was lucky to sleep in his own bed a hundred nights a year.

"That's right, and now I enjoy it."

After the 2002 alumni dinner in Washington, Ford vowed to a friend, "That's the last speech I'm giving. I can't do them anymore. It's become a burden."

True to form, he soldiered on, speaking a few times a year anyway, with diminishing verbal dexterity.

In November 2002, in a brief phone interview where we discussed presidential commissions, I asked how he was feeling.

"I feel pretty good, but you know, Tom, we're getting old." There was a touch of plaintiveness in his voice I'd never sensed before.

His constitution weakened further in May 2003. Ford was playing golf on a day when the desert thermometer reached 90 degrees. He suffered a major bout of dizziness and was rushed to the Eisenhower Medical Center. To prevent a recurrence, Ford thereafter had to wait a few seconds when standing up to give his blood pressure a chance to stabilize.

The 2003 dinner was held at the White House, with President Bush and Vice President Cheney hosting the festivities to commemorate his ninetieth birthday. Even that command performance was opposed by Ford's medics. "The doctors have been telling him he can't fly anymore since Philadelphia," one pal said at the time, referring to the stroke.

He resisted the air ban as long as he could. Many of his closest friends believe that having to give up his peripatetic travel habit was the biggest blow of all. Getting on a plane was like drawing breath, like mother's milk to him. He always said he was glad to finally stay home more, but none of us believed him. He was an incurable travel junkie; once he couldn't fly anymore, part of him died forever.

By 2004, he was still swimming laps and managing an occasional few holes of golf. But everything was getting harder, especially travel.

On a hot summer day that year, Ford was walking into the storied Willard Inter-Continental Hotel, where he usually stayed on his return visits to Washington. As he emerged from the revolving door he grabbed the arm of his companion and said: "Stand here for a minute." It was another dizzy spell, a byproduct of the 2000 stroke and his medicines.

Insiders knew there had been several more fainting spells that never got out.

The 2004 reunion dinner had been moved from its usual slot on the first Monday of June to August 9. That was to commemorate the thirtieth anniversary of Ford becoming president on August 9, 1974. On that Monday, Ford and Herbert Hoover became the only former presidents to live long enough to observe the three-decade milestone of their inaugurations.

To make it a truly memorable occasion for a guy who loved the House of Representatives so much that he often wore a congressional tie when he was vice president and president, the venue was moved to the old House chamber in the Capitol, the scene of so much epic history.

At the outset, it was apparent he wasn't doing well. He was an incurable mingler, coming early and staying late at these special events to meet and greet his friends. For the first time at one of these dinners, he and Betty were seated during the reception line this night.

Moreover, he looked awful; one of the Ford alumni remarked that he was so pale he appeared positively cadaverous.

When it came time to speak at the end of the evening, Ford needed help from Dick Cheney and Don Rumsfeld, his two chiefs of staff, just to make it to the podium.

They stayed by his side to make sure he didn't falter. He spoke seven minutes, and lost his place early on. He fumbled and stumbled, groping for words, and it seemed he wouldn't be able to finish. But he eventually righted himself, and his voice firmed up as he went along, to the relief of all.

As usual, his comments were short, to the point, and from the heart.

"History will judge our success," he reminded, "but no one can doubt our dedication."

He paid tribute to "parents who taught me that character and courage are inseparable," and his family. "I thank God every day," he said, "for Betty and the kids."

He signed off by thanking his guests for "sharing the past, savoring the present, and anticipating the future."

Afterward, he was extremely upset with himself. He told friends he'd let everyone down by what he quaintly called his "underperformance." He vowed that he'd given his last speech. It was just too hard now, and he didn't want to embarrass his friends, or himself, any longer.

More than one of the guests observed on the way out of the Capitol that if there was another dinner in 2005, there was no way it would be in Washington. That's exactly what happened.

But Ford did do another speech. In November of 2004, he attended groundbreaking ceremonies for the new public policy school named for him at his beloved University of Michigan. The day before, a Thursday, he addressed the Wolverine football team to help get them psyched for their Saturday game with Northwestern.

Ford was totally into the moment; he spoke without notes for about twenty-five minutes, calling on several star players by name and bidding them stand up as he summarized their strengths and weaknesses. Then he analyzed the entire season: best game, worst game, the works. It was a virtuoso performance by an aging but enthused jock, and the kids ate it up.

At the Ford school groundbreaking the next morning, he was a different, sadder study. All he had to do was say a few perfunctory words. He lost his place and couldn't find any words to ad-lib. The awkward pause ran on for about thirty seconds; finally, he mumbled a couple of thank-yous and sat down.

"That's when I first knew he was losing it," an old friend remembered, grimacing at the painful memory.

That same month, Ford didn't show at one of those institutional gatherings he considered especially important to attend: the dedication of Bill Clinton's presidential library in Little Rock. The weather had been so raw and wet that some of his friends later speculated he might not have survived had he been there.

Another ominous milestone was observed a month later. Ford had been flipping the switch on the Vail Village Christmas tree since the 1970s, but in a cruel emotional blow, the Ford clan celebrated Christmas 2004 in Rancho Mirage, not his beloved Beaver Creek. He never spent another holiday season in the mountains.

In January 2005, Ford tripped on the carpeting in his office study. Unable to break his fall, he slammed headfirst into the side of a door. He had neck injuries, needed several stitches, and was out of commission for weeks. News of his mishap never got out, but the family knew the accident had hastened his decline.

Somehow, improbably, he seemed to get stronger. "I thought this would be the year," Susan Ford confided to a friend, "but he's amazed all of us."

Not all, however. Somehow word leaked that he was frailer than advertised and might be finally in his terminal throes. Suddenly, television producers were calling Rancho Mirage to inquire politely if their telephone contact numbers for family members and Ford staffers were still accurate—just in case, mind you.

"I know why they're calling," one of the kids would later grimly recall.

He wasn't dying, but he was definitely faltering. For years, Ford had been telling me that flying east for the Washington summer reunion and board meetings in New York had extracted an ever-greater toll on him. By now he was doing his corporate work by conference call. As the 2005 reunion dinner date approached, he wasn't up to it. So for the first time, his foundation trustees decided to go west to honor the Old Man; the dinner would be held in Palm Desert.

It was a useful if imperfect behavioral test; having to spend real money to fly out and honor the Fords separated the hangers-on and wannabes—call-in friends, one Ford associate dubbed them—from those associates and former colleagues who genuinely cared about the guy.

"We'll follow you wherever we have to follow you," explained Marty Allen, the esteemed director of the Gerald R. Ford Foundation.

The dinner was at The Lodge, a favorite Ford hotel hangout with a stunning view of the Coachella Valley far below. Dapper in a navy blazer, Ford leaned on a cane and was noticeably frailer than he was at the previous dinner.

"Except for a couple of creaky knees, I'm doing okay," he told me in the receiving line, where he sat on a stool. "I'm slowing down a little, but I'm hanging in there."

Cheney was the emcee, mixing genial insults with memories of The Way We Were.

"Every day that I'm in the White House," he reminisced, "there's a sight or a memory that makes me think of President Ford."

After a dessert of his lifetime favorite, butter pecan ice cream, the Ford medal for public service went to Betty Ford for her work at the center named for her.

"Do I get a kiss?" he asked his spouse of fifty-six years.

He did, as well as another tribute: "He's been my ideal of the perfect mate," Betty cooed.

Then Ford thanked everyone for "a super, super job" at the White House.

"I know this will surprise many of you," he concluded. "The truth is, *I'm* Deep Throat." The audience roared at the reference to Woodward and Bernstein's secret Watergate source, whose identity had just been divulged as former FBI official Mark Felt.

The one-liner brought down the house, but couldn't totally mitigate the sober reality that Ford was failing.

As he himself told an old friend that year in supposed jest, "Boy, this dying's hard work."

B y year's end, the medical reports from Rancho Mirage weren't en-couraging. His stamina was waning, his speech halting, his ability to read diminishing. He could function normally for a half hour or so, then had to rest.

Motor skills were a growing problem: he was still signing the occa-sional autograph for special friends, but some of them arrived with mis-spelled names and words.

In February 2006, Phil Jones and his wife, Pat, paid Ford a visit in Rancho Mirage. They immediately noticed that the former president was having some difficulty with his language. He'd pause before an-swering even the simplest questions, and when he did answer after a few seconds' delay, the wrong words sometimes tumbled out.

Phil was legendary back in Washington for being a pugnacious ques-tioner; frequently Ford had tried to deflect a Jonesian barb by saying, "Now, Phil, we can disagree without being disagreeable."

It came out a bit differently this day. "Phil," he wanted to know, "who have you molested recently?"

Toward the end of their chat, Ford decided to autograph a copy of a book he'd recently read for our old *Air Force Two* seatmate. Unexpectedly, he labored with the inscription, and had particular dif-ficulty crafting a capital P. It came out looking like the J in Jerry, not the P in Phil.

Phil teasingly tried to lighten the awkwardness by suggesting that Ford write something throwaway like "A Ford, not a Lincoln," which he well knew was one of Ford's signature lines about himself.

It was a welcome respite from what had once been a rudimentary chore. Ford looked up from his penmanship struggle and grinned: "Pretty good line, wasn't it?"

Then he scribbled, "To my good friend Phil Jones—Ford, no [*sic*] a Lincoln." It may have been the last autograph he ever signed.

After the success of the California reunion, the regulars assumed the venue had been permanently changed and we'd all be invited to an encore dinner in Palm Desert in June 2006. Instead, the invitation noted that the dinner would revert to its historical norm and return to Washington—this time at the National Archives.

More worrisome, the chatty letter of invitation from Ford informed guests that "although Betty and I won't be physically present that evening, we will be with you in spirit through the magic of modern technology"—a videotaped message.

Many of us wondered what was up; we knew his doctors wouldn't let him fly, so his not being in Washington was understandable. But he'd had a grand time at the California bash; it had been a genuine tonic for an ailing patriarch. It made no sense to settle on a location that precluded the guest of honor from attending his own dinner. Betty had missed a couple over the years, but he'd never been a no-show before.

In due course the answer emerged: Jack Ford. The president's second son, a businessman from San Diego, had begun steadily insinuating himself into the operations of the Old Man's foundation, not for the better in the view of most Friends of Ford. Jack wanted the dinner in Washington—even if it meant cutting out the honoree, who also happened to be his father. The elder Ford really wanted to be there, but if it couldn't be in the desert, he knew there was no way.

"Jack is alienating all the trustees who loved the Old Man," one of the president's closest pals would later complain. "He's acting like he's entitled to everything his mother and father had."

"He really wants to come," said another irate family friend who heard it from Ford himself, "but the kids want it in D.C. They think it's easier to raise money there, and there were complaints from some people last year about having to go to California." Call-in friends, indeed.

So for the first time in twenty-four years, Jerry Ford was AWOL from an event he relished, and not by his own preference.

I remembered what Ford had told me years earlier, kidding-on-the-square: "Jack would like to be a $250,000-a-year park ranger when he grows up."

The Fords' absence cast the first-ever real pall on an alumni event that had always been just plain fun. It got worse when the videotaped message of Jerry and Betty was shown. They both looked terrible, programmed and pasty-faced as they read their greetings from cue cards. He was halting and feeble. "Oh my God," someone blurted out at a nearby table. It was a huge downer; the bonhomie of the dinner never recovered from that depressing visual. Ford himself was also very upset at the way he and his bride looked in the video. But Jack Ford had insisted they cut a tape instead of sending a written message.

In fairness, Ford was so frail by then that he might not have been up to attending that dinner even if it had been in the desert. At the predinner reception, a close Ford friend told Phil Jones that Jerry needed major cardiac surgery—a heart valve was defective and needed to be replaced—but the cardiologists had ruled it out because of his age.

Earlier that day, Jack Ford had presented me with the Ford Prize at the National Press Club. Four days later, a letter arrived from Rancho Mirage in the familiar cream-colored envelope. Ford was congratulating me on the award he'd sprung on me five weeks earlier during our final interview. It was a thoughtful letter, totally unobjectionable to the unobservant eye. In an alarmingly weak hand, it was signed "Gerald R. Ford."

It had been a very long time, decades for sure, since he'd sent me a missive ending with his formal signature. From the labored penmanship it was obvious it had taken considerable effort to sign his name at all. I was humbled by his generosity of spirit and saddened by its prophetic meaning: Jerry Ford was nearing the end.

# FOURTEEN

# Lunch with a Legend— May 11, 2006

E VEN BEFORE I saw him, I suspected this encounter would be different from our usual visits. I walked past the fruit-laden grapefruit tree in the front yard of his office complex woefully unprepared for how profoundly different it would be.

For more than thirty years, our meetings had followed established protocols. Jerry Ford was a politician of rare amiability. Long before the pomposity and pretension of Richard Nixon's White House praetorian guard had offended his Midwestern sensibilities, Ford had always been a study in courtliness and civility.

In the final hours of the ill-fated 1976 campaign, for example, his entourage arrived at a Marriott Inn in Cleveland. As he entered his ninth-floor room for a few hours of downtime, the president noticed he was booked into the Emperor Suite.

"I don't like that," he growled to an aide. A piece of cardboard was hastily taped over the nameplate with the suite's new name scrawled in felt-tip pen: "Jerry Ford's Room."

Similarly, he didn't like visitors to be ushered into the royal presence. He much preferred greeting them personally, particularly after his retirement.

Whenever I turned up for a visit, the routine never varied. Ford would bound from the study of his office to fetch me with a booming "Hello, Tom," then usher me inside the cozy den with a view of Thunderbird Country Club's fairways.

Penny Circle had warned me the plan would be different this time. "He wants to meet you at the house," she'd said a couple of days before.

That could only mean one thing: he was too frail to negotiate the thirty-yard walk from the house to the office.

Unfortunately, I was right. Ford wasn't even able to stand up as I entered the study of his home. He was seated in an easy chair, feet propped up on an ottoman. Fighting an infection and a nasty cough, he was sucking on a throat lozenge.

Ford was two months shy of his ninety-third and final birthday as we began a chat that lasted about forty-five minutes. He was wearing a golf shirt, khaki trousers, and brown soft-soled shoes. Except for his annual trip east for a Ford alumni dinner, I hadn't seen him in a jacket and tie for years. He once told a reporter, "You can come see me as long as I don't have to wear a tie."

I knew he'd be fragile; the year before, the alumni dinner had been moved from Washington to Palm Desert because he wasn't up to the flight. Still, he was frailer than I'd ever seen him.

The major difference was his voice: weak, grainy, almost childlike. My wife had often remarked that even as he aged he'd retained the robust voice of a much younger man. No longer.

Moreover, good old Jerry was in an unexpectedly foul mood, something I'd seen only twice before since our first interview in the fall of 1973. It wasn't just a hacking cough he couldn't suppress that caused his black demeanor. He was beyond feisty—he was ripped.

I opened with a totally benign inquiry—"How are you, Mr.

President?"—and walked squarely into the path of a runaway locomotive. Despite his genial reputation, Ford's closest comrades liked to say he was ninety-eight percent koala bear and two percent grizzly, and you never knew when his raging Michigander underbelly would surface and grab you by the throat. This was my day.

"My damn doctors won't let me go in the pool," he bellowed.

Penny gently reminded him of the white scrap of paper in his right hand.

"Oh, yes. I have good news for you; at least I think it's good news. You're getting the Ford award."

For nearly two decades, Ford's foundation has handed out an award for White House reporting. I'd never won. By total coincidence, the judges had reached their verdict an hour or so before I was supposed to see him. In classic I've-got-a-secret fashion, he'd decided to spring the news himself.

At what should have been a professionally satisfying moment, my mind inexplicably flashed back to 1976, to another sheet of paper—a telegram that read, "Congratulations. You've been selected as one of the questioners for the Presidential debate."

It was totally bogus, a hoax perpetrated by the merry prankster of the White House press corps, Jim Naughton of the *New York Times*. Naughton was legendary for stuff like that; he brokered the deal with Ford and Cheney to put that sheep in my room in Peoria, Illinois, and once wore a chicken head to a Ford press conference.

I thought to myself, Oh my God, thirty years later, Naughton strikes again. I couldn't help myself. I blurted out, "Mr. President, is this for real?"

He gave me one of those what-planet-do-you-live-on looks. "Of course it's for real," he said. "Why the hell do you think I'm telling you?"

I thus concluded with great relief it *was* for real, and told him that no award could ever mean more to me than one with Gerald R. Ford's name on it.

He'd always handed out the prize personally at the National Press

Club each June, but he couldn't cope with the travel any longer. (At his request, Dick Cheney filled in.) This was his gracious way of doing the honors anyway, and, given our long association, a special dollop of lagniappe for me.

Niceties concluded, Ford resumed his rant. A gifted athlete who swam laps twice a day well into his eighties had been beached, and he wasn't a happy ex-swimmer.

"They won't let me go in the pool and swim," he fumed. "Why? I'm ninety-two years old, and I think I'm in pretty good shape, too. I [only] go in and paddle back and forth at the shallow end. It's terrible.

"He's a very good doctor and he's very accommodating, but it worries me that I'm under these limitations. He's got me under a leash. I go over and I take all the health exams and I pass 'em with a hundred percent."

I smiled at his tangled phrasing but understood his irritation. A swimming ban was no small deprivation for him. He was religious about his routine; a Secret Service agent once told me his detail marveled that sometimes Ford would get back after midnight from a grueling trip and head straight for his lap pool. No more.

Something else was bugging him this day. Three weeks earlier, on April 23, he'd been visited by President Bush, who was in the desert tending to fundraising chores. Once again, Ford's irksome side surfaced.

He hadn't been thrilled to learn that Bush would be in the neighborhood but wasn't planning to drop by for a visit. "He didn't have any plans to meet me, and I said, 'Goddammit, I want to meet you.' Very fortunately, he came by, I thought for the usual routine five-minute meeting, but he stayed for an hour and ten minutes. I couldn't have been more pleased."

(The photos of the two presidents emerging from their chat are unusually poignant, with Bush tenderly holding Ford's hand.)

Helped along by our delayed-release ground rules, Ford had never been reluctant to talk about private conversations. When he didn't follow suit this time, I figured it was because he couldn't. His ability to elaborate on a topic was now marginal at best.

"We talked across the board; I can't give you the details, but he couldn't have been more accommodating. He was very pleasant; it was an excellent meeting, Tom."

They hadn't talked about Bush's dismal standing in the public opinion polls, but Ford was sure "he had to be observant of the situation." So he sympathized a bit: "I couldn't help but remind him that when I became president we had our full platter of problems [too]. We did our best and we came out in good shape."

Just a modest little pep rally between two of the five members of what a Republican political operative likes to call The Big Guys' Club.

He didn't answer directly when I asked if Bush could defy the lame-duck gravitational pull of the calendar and make something of his last two years in office. "It's gonna be tough, but he's working at it, I can tell you that. He's on the job all the time."

They hadn't mentioned the 2008 presidential campaign, he said, but the war in Iraq came in for plenty of discussion. Ford told the commander in chief something he'd mentioned to me two years before: he supported the invasion but felt Bush had done a poor job prepping the public for why it was important to U.S. national security interests. He repeated his criticism that Bush had erred badly by staking the war on Saddam's supposed chemical, biological, and nuclear programs.

"The truth is I disagreed with the [rationale] of the White House: I thought they made a mistake about weapons of mass destruction. There was plenty of reason to do what he did; Saddam Hussein was an evil person and there was justification to get rid of him," he observed, "but we shouldn't have put the basis on the weapons of mass destruction. That was a bad mistake, and I don't know who advised the White House on that."

Bush hadn't responded directly to Ford's critique, and Ford implied that Bush might be in denial: "I don't think he admits it," he said, "except that it's a fact."

Throughout his life, Ford was the classic glass-half-full politician. He seldom delivered a barb without some accompanying balm. "Anytime you have a war and you have to make an unpopular decision, the polls slip," he reminded me, no doubt remembering what happened to *his* polls after he pardoned Nixon. "I think that's just a fact of life."

Asked how he rated the job Bush was doing, Ford said, "I think he's handled himself respectably and I don't mean to be critical of him. It's important for him to win in Iraq."

When asked if the time had come to admit a colossal mistake and withdraw from Iraq, he was adamant. "No," he barked emphatically.

"We made a tough decision to get in and now we gotta find an answer. It's interesting—I don't have the impression the White House understood the conflict between Shiites and Sunnis, which complicated the whole invasion strategy. There is a very sophisticated part of the analysis; it's a very subtle distinction between Iraq as an enemy—you've got dual enemies."

But he preferred to talk about dual friends—Dick Cheney and Don Rumsfeld, his two White House chiefs of staff. Ford adored them both; he considered them surrogate sons and liked to brag that he'd raised them as political pups. He wasn't above wondering where the hell their heads were from time to time, but his affection was absolute. He was predictably defensive about the veep and secretary of defense.

"I'm not critical of old friends such as Cheney. I was surprised when he was selected, but as an old friend I was glad to see him selected. He's done well; I have a lot of faith in him and he hasn't disappointed me," he said, in contrast to what he said in 2004.

So why had Cheney become one of the most polarizing figures in American politics, with anemic poll ratings and a reputation as a latter-day Darth Vader? Part of that was Iraq, he said, and part was his style.

"Dick's a classy guy"—he smiled—"but he's not an electrified orator. He makes a good speech, but it doesn't stimulate a lot of good reaction. Dick Cheney is a classy guy, and it bothers me that he's having trouble."*

We had to stop when Ford was racked by a prolonged coughing spell. "Carol"—he called for his therapist/nurse—"could I have another Ricola?" His infirmities were embarrassing him now; "I really apologize, I'm sorry," he said.

As the interview played out, Ford lost his train of thought at times. He had several memory lapses. Once he said that Don Rumsfeld had helped him write an op-ed piece; he meant historian Richard Norton Smith, a longtime friend and collaborator. He also groped for words, as if he was having difficulty processing his thoughts. He was more conversant than I'd expected, but still diminished. He spoke in halting sound bites instead of paragraphs; he knew what he wanted to say but couldn't manage to say it for more than a sentence or two.

He was still lucid for the most part, but labored to process his answers. His analysis and commentary weren't as crisp as in our last interview. There was no question his mental faculties were now in full decline. I predicted to myself a couple of times that this would be our last interview no matter how long he lived.

It was an interesting interview, but more awkward, and I suspect difficult, even painful for him, than any of our previous encounters.

I wondered if Rumsfeld had asked him to write his recent op-ed column hammering the six generals and admirals who'd urged he be cashiered for botching the Iraq policy. Ford shot me a dagger of disbelief.

"Rummy didn't have to ask me. I thought it was terrible the way these generals were critical of his operations as secretary of defense. I thought that was irresponsible. After all, they did run the war, and then to be Johnny-come-latelies—that's poor responsibility. That [article]

---

*When I passed along Ford's comment to the vice president two weeks after his old boss's funeral, Cheney laughed and couldn't resist saying, "Look who's talking." Ford was such a middling thespian that he himself regularly made fun of his oratory. Ford couldn't tell a joke but enjoyed a good one. He would have loved being needled by Cheney, whose affection for Ford is unassailable.

was totally on my own. I think Rumsfeld is doing a good job under the circumstances. I don't go around being a second-guesser. He's doing the best he can under very difficult circumstances."

He was starting to wear down, so I steered him toward the 2008 elections. He answered with a query of his own.

"Let me ask you: Do you think John McCain is gonna be the nominee? What kind of a guy is he?"

I told him McCain was the front-runner but that his political enemies were already dusting off an attack line that George W. Bush's partisans had peddled against McCain in the 2000 primaries: that his years of captivity and torture in North Vietnam had affected his emotional stability.

"I think it's unfortunate if that is his temperament—that's a bad characteristic for a person to be president." But he was emphatic about dismissing the rap: "I don't agree with that assumption."

His Republican favorite was still Rudy Giuliani. "I think Giuliani is an electrifying guy. He's a great speaker. He's had a good record of winning in New York City, and he can be tough."

Ever the political junkie, the House minority leader who used to travel 250 days a year boosting Republicans said he was relishing a head-to-head confrontation between Hillary Clinton and Rudy. For years he'd been telling me Hillary was consumed by ambition, was intent on running in 2004 or 2008, and that despite her political baggage—and her husband's—would make "a darned good candidate."

"That would be a great contest between Hillary and Giuliani." He wasn't sure who'd win—it would depend on what else was happening in the country—but he thought Giuliani had the edge.

I asked about Bush's domestic surveillance program, something I'd heard Ford had turned down flat when somebody floated a similar program in his administration. He tried to be understanding, but it was obvious he wasn't buying the need for it.

"It may be a necessary evil. I don't think it's a terrible transgression as far as being an operation of the White House, [but] I would never do it. It surprises me they worry that they think they *have* to do it. I was dumbfounded when I heard they were. I didn't think it was necessary. Where does he get his advice?"

Vice President Cheney and his hard-line lawyers, I said.

"Explain to me who this fella Libby is. I never heard of him, and I thought I knew Dick Cheney."

He also took a fleeting shot at Bush's "signing statements," those curious documents that Bush attaches to legislation he signs, stating that, in effect, he doesn't have to pay any attention to the law he's just enacted because he has the authority under the Constitution to do something else.

"That's pretty casual," he complained.

By now he was tiring of business, and abruptly changed the subject: "Let me tell you what my routine is.

"I used to be an early get-up guy. I think you knew that. I now sleep until 8:15. I get up, [until recently] usually take a swim. I have breakfast, orange juice or one orange, prune juice, a piece of toast, and maybe three or four kernels of those biscuits—shredded wheat. Then my staff has the papers up in front of me. I read the *Denver Post* or the *L.A. Times,* depending where I am—I'm an avid newspaper reader—and then I read the *Denver* [he meant *Washington*] *Post, New York Times,* the *Grand Rapids Press,*" his hometown paper.

"I consume newspapers, and I catch criticism from my dear wife that I'm an addict as far as newspapers are concerned, but I think that newspapers are my Bible. I have to have the background of newspapers to discuss the world's problems."

His reading regimen was over in time for lunch at 1:30, followed by a new addition to his routine—a two-hour nap.

Unlike Lyndon Johnson, who napped every workday as president, "I never took a nap at the White House or in Congress. But [now] it revives me."

He was down to one corporate board affiliation—his close friend Sandy Weill's Citigroup. His evening routine was similarly scaled down. He almost never went out anymore, he acknowledged.

When he mentioned the public policy school being erected in his name at the University of Michigan, I told him Bush was hoping to raise a half-billion dollars for his library and a "democracy institute" think tank. "Good luck," he said, laughing. Even by Texas standards, that was real money.

"Some of these libraries cost too much, they've gotten pretty extravagant." He didn't like it that some libraries, meaning Bill Clinton's, gloss over the negative.

"I'm proud of my library. It's informative, it's a good source of information for politicians and acamedicians [*sic*]."

I smiled at the appearance of an old malapropism. There were several words he could never pronounce: "guarantee" always came out "*garantee*," "geothermal" was "geothermer," and pointy-headed know-it-alls like Jim Schlesinger were invariably "acamedicians."

He volunteered that he hadn't spoken to Jimmy Carter or Bill Clinton in a while.

"Clinton is like a loose bullet," he said.

But is he a good former president? I asked. "If you agree with his presidency."

As another burst of coughing interrupted his wandering train of thought, Betty Ford emerged at the door of the study.

"You ready, Mother?" he asked.

"Whenever you are."

"Well, let's go have dinner—breakfast," and we adjourned for lunch.

We'd been caucusing in the desert regularly for more than three decades, beginning with that memorable 1974 interview when he was vice president. He'd always been extraordinarily generous to me, and a strong professional relationship had developed. Yet today was a first: he'd asked me to stay for lunch.

As he struggled out of his easy chair, his frailty became even more apparent. It's only a very short distance from his study to the dining room of their one-story ranch home, but Ford couldn't walk without a cane, a nurse at one elbow and Betty at the other.

We sat down in the sun-filled room. I noticed that the sterling silver seemed familiar. King Richard, by Towle, a traditional pattern. Same as my first marriage, I said. Ford winked, as if to reassure me there are indeed second acts in politics and love; Betty Bloomer had been a young divorcée when he'd tumbled hard for his wife of fifty-eight years.

Even before the vichyssoise had been cleared and the poached chicken with grapes arrived, Ford raised what was plainly a huge sore subject: the insistence of his doctors that he avoid his Colorado home because of the mile-high altitude. He loved the mountains, even though his schussing days were long past. Almost seventy years later, he still loved to reminisce about that Vermont ski trip he and his hot-number Manhattan model girlfriend had taken in 1940. He and Betty were both excited about returning to Beaver Creek in June. But nobody else thought it was a smart idea anymore. Even a total loyalist like Dick Cheney would later tell associates, "He has no business being at that altitude."

"The doctor, he always says we can't go, but we go," Ford grumped.

Even this year, with his frail constitution?

Before he could answer, Betty signaled their mutual defiance. "We're going, God willing. We've had a great quantity; now we're interested in quality. At this time of life, you live life one day at a time, and we do as we hope. Not we do as we please, but we do as we hope.

"We're going to give it a try, and if it doesn't work, we'll just come back here and go find a hotel on the coast and stay there."

He asked about my wife and ten-year-old son, whom he'd met on a previous outing to Rancho Mirage. I said Andrew was headed off to sleepaway camp in Maine and that Mom was excited but very nervous. That triggered a Ford flashback to a camping trip with his two oldest sons and his stepfather somewhere near Traverse City, Michigan.

"We were stupid; we didn't make reservations and got up there at eight o'clock at night, tried three or four places and they couldn't take anybody, and somebody finally said, 'We can give you a couple of tents and two bunks.' My father slept with Mike and I slept with Jack. They were about ten and twelve years old. We didn't get much sleep."

By now we were rushing headlong down Memory Lane. I told him I'd been in Omaha for a speech recently and had gone over to see the site of his birthplace. He remembered that he (and I) had visited the place when he was vice president. The house had burned down and the lot was a dilapidated, weed-infested corner. Now there was a floral garden named for Betty, and commemorative plaques to her husband. He was tickled to hear the grounds were scrupulously maintained by the Omaha Young Republicans.

As shoptalk gave way to small talk about friends, families, and fond memories, Ford was still brooding about his doctors.

As the vanilla ice cream and strawberries were served, Ford offered me a familiar substitute.

"Well, we still have butter pecan ice cream around here," he said, grinning, harking back to the days when *Air Force One* never left a tarmac anywhere in the world without an ample supply of his favorite dessert.

"The doctors let you have that?"

"We have it *anyhow,*" he roared, relishing another potshot at his medical Torquemadas.

Toward the end, Ford displayed a sentimentality I'd rarely seen in him. We talked a lot about the *Air Force Two* days, when just seven journalists and a vice president desperate to hold his beloved Republican Party together amid the wreckage of Watergate hurtled around the country in a lumbering twin-engine Convair propjet. My fondest memories in journalism are anchored in those magical, mystical days, I wanted him to know.

"We all thought you knew you were going to be president," I said.

"And you always tried to get me to say something that I shouldn't," he said. "But I never did." At least not often, at least for our tastes.

One burst of nostalgia swiftly led to another. I said my grandparents' home in Houston had burned down, and that I always visited the bedraggled lot whenever I was in town. That triggered his flashback to the place he always considered home.

"When I wake up at night and can't sleep," he recalled, in a voice suddenly very far away, "I remember Grand Rapids."

He also remembered what a bad man his real father was, how he'd beaten his mother and then left the two of them with no money. He recalled the day his father had shown up in Grand Rapids years later, asking for his son Leslie King. I'm not Leslie King, I'm Jerry Ford, he'd replied. "Well, I'm your father," the man said. "Can we talk?"

"Boy, if you don't think it was hard having to go back and tell my mother and stepfather that I'd just had coffee with my real father—that was really hard."

Nevertheless, he knew, "I was a lucky fellow. I was blessed with a magnificent mother and an equally good stepfather. One of the saddest things about the White House [years] was, my mother and stepfather didn't have access. Mother would have loved it. She would have been there, fussing and fuming with the staff, and she would have loved it. She deserved it."

Caught up in the nostalgia, I reminded him of one of my most riveting recollections from the 1976 presidential race. Ford had ended that campaign with a marathon cross-country blitz that carpet-bombed thirteen states in twelve days, including three swings through Pennsylvania. He ended with an election-eve rally in Grand Rapids, voted in the morning, then flew back to Washington to await America's verdict.

At the windswept airport, he paused for a brief ceremony dedicating a mural to his life and career. It was pure hometown boilerplate until he looked at the images of his parents.

"What has ever been done by me in any way whatsoever, it's because of Jerry Ford Senior and Dorothy Ford," he'd said, breaking down.

I turned to Helen Thomas of United Press International, the other *Air Force One* print pooler for the ride back to Andrews Air Force Base.

"It's a metaphor for the election," I guessed. "He's going to lose."

Betty must have sensed that the two sentimental slobs flanking her at the lunch table were close to spinning pathetically out of control. As usual, she rescued the moment. "I remember Grand Rapids, too, Jerry," she said, smiling. "I remember you played football and looked gorgeous on the beach in swim trunks."

"Now, Mother." He grinned, savoring what the grizzled Texas Ranger captain in *Lonesome Dove* calls the sunny slopes of long ago. A trace of color fleetingly returned to his pallid features. "Now, Mother, let's don't go down that road."

As we lingered over coffee, he was wiped out, physically and emotionally. "Well, I'm sorry to have to throw you out, but I need to have my nap." Sadly, he wasn't kidding.

Betty and Carol helped him from his chair. By doctor's orders, he stood there for twenty seconds to regain his equilibrium. Midway to his study, he reached a dining room chair that had obviously been strategically situated for him.

"Let's stop here for a moment," he said, and sat down to rest, leaning on his cane.

I didn't want to see any more of his distress, so I grasped his hand, thanked him for his hospitality, and urged him to take care of himself.

"You, too, Tom," he said.

For the first time in a third of a century, he didn't walk me to the door. There was simply no way. As he mustered his strength just to make it to his bedroom, Betty Ford handled the courtesies.

"Please take care of him," I said.

"We're trying," she replied with a wan, wistful smile.

As I walked to my rental car, I remembered his haunting line: When I wake up at night and can't sleep, I remember Grand Rapids.

The hairs on my arms stood on end, just as they are doing as I write now, as they've done every time I recall that powerful, poignant moment.

It suddenly was apparent why he'd finally invited me to lunch at long last.

In his typically gentle, understated fashion, Jerry Ford was telling me goodbye.

# FIFTEEN

# November 2006

B Y THE FALL OF 2006, Ford was deteriorating rapidly. As they'd vowed at our May lunch, he and Betty had indeed defied the doctors and flown out to Beaver Creek in June. After a couple of weeks, with oxygen canisters helping them cope with the altitude, both of them were tolerating the mountains better than expected. Even his disapproving doctors were surprised at how well he was adapting.

Then, on August 15, Ford checked into the Mayo Clinic in Rochester, Minnesota. A terse statement from his office said he was there for "testing and evaluation." In short order a pacemaker was inserted into his chest to help regulate his heartbeat. A few days later, he had an angioplasty that found major cardiac blockage. Stents were implanted in two of his coronary arteries to help with the blood flow to his weakened heart. He wasn't strong enough to tolerate what he really needed: a valve replacement.

The conventional wisdom suggested he'd had a reaction to the altitude, as some of his pals and doctors had feared might happen. That

wasn't the case at all. What was true is that Ford had seen some cardiologists from Mayo at Beaver Creek who had briefed him on some new
medical advancements that might improve his quality of life. He was
faltering, and knew it; anything that might prolong his life was worth
exploring. So he had decided to fly to Mayo for an assessment.

Shortly before the Fords were to leave for Minnesota, Betty Ford experienced serious leg pain. With daughter Susan accompanying her,
the Secret Service drove her to Denver. It was a blood clot, and she
needed surgery right away. But she wasn't letting her husband go to
Minnesota without her, so the doctors reluctantly agreed to postpone
the surgery until she got to Mayo.

Her vascular surgery was never publicly acknowledged by Mayo or
the family. In April 2007, she checked into the Eisenhower Medical
Center near her home. The family confirmed that she'd had surgery;
they didn't disclose that it had taken six hours to remove two more clots.

Two weeks after arriving at Mayo, the former president was dis-
charged and flew home—but to Rancho Mirage, not back to his
beloved Beaver Creek aerie, where he'd always waited out the fierce
desert summers.

The surgery ravaged what little stamina he had left. Even keeping
to the indoors to ward off the heat's dangerous effects, he was essentially
an invalid as he recuperated.

He was extraordinarily weak by then, having trouble walking or
even conversing for more than a few sentences at a time. He needed
round-the-clock nursing help. He still read his papers religiously, took
a few phone calls, and watched television, but he couldn't walk more
than a few steps without resting, and even that required help.

As word trickled out that he was failing, old friends would call and
ask to mail in a photograph or artifact for what they must have sensed
was surely a final autograph. They were told that he just isn't signing
autographs anymore. Oh, he'll do it for *me,* they would say. But he
wouldn't, because he couldn't. The simplest of tasks had become too
much of an ordeal.

Still, Ford told aides and old pals he was determined to make one final commute home. On October 13, he was penciled in to attend the dedication ceremonies at the Gerald R. Ford School of Public Policy. Frail as he was, it was so important to him to return to his alma mater one last time that he had assured me in May he'd break his ban on the airplane flights that wore him out to be there.

"After football practice I'd walk to my job waiting tables," he reflected. "I'd pass by this run-down vacant lot with weeds and broken glass. Never did I imagine that seventy years later, that lot would be the home of the Gerald R. Ford School of Public Policy."

Even as he weakened, Ford kept thinking about the Ann Arbor festivities. One old friend told him that if you walked to the very top row of Michigan Stadium, the massive "Big House" where Ford had played in the thirties, you could see the Ford School. He was excited, almost giddy, by the news, and gleefully repeated the story to well-wishers.

In May, in fact, one of his closest friends flatly predicted to me, "One way or another, he will stay alive for the Ford Center dedication in the fall."

Ford hadn't put it that way in May, but his determination to be there was unswerving. "I'm going out there," he doggedly insisted. "That's the only flying I'll do [anymore]. The university said they would build us a building if we raised $11 million or $12 million, and we did it."

The week of the dedication, he was still making plans to fly east. But two days before the festivities, an e-mail arrived from Penny Circle.

"So sorry to tell you—we aren't going to AA. He can't make the trip. I am heartbroken for him and disappointed for everyone." The reality went unspoken: only a man who was dying would have no-showed something so dear to his ailing heart.

That grim news made me resolve to see him again. In conversations with his aides, I'd mentioned weeks before that I'd be in Palm Springs in November for an oral history interview and hoped to see Ford. The "body language" was iffy to negative. There are good days and bad days, we'll just have to see, was the message. It was pretty apparent I was being discouraged from pressing for time. I made it clear I wasn't interested in another interview; we all understood there was no way he could have handled a real conversation. Still, I was being waved off for even a simple drop-by.

On the morning of November 14, though, Penny said he was feeling okay and that I should come over around 11:30 so she and I could talk first.

"Prepare yourself," she warned me. "He's not what he was." She asked me to keep our visit to five minutes.

As we walked over to the house a couple of minutes past noon, I asked if it was true the Colorado home was on the market. I wanted to eyeball the place again because several of our most memorable encounters had been there.

"Let's talk about that after you see him," she said.

Before he uttered a word, I finally understood why some of Ronald Reagan's closest friends had refused to visit him at the end.

The president was in his sunlit study, the same room where I'd interviewed him in May and where he had shown such spunk. Instead of using the same big easy chair, however, he was propped up in a hospital bed near the sliding door, facing the television.

Pale and painfully feeble, he had on precisely the same casual clothes he'd worn at our last meeting in May. Unable to summon the strength to bring his right arm across his body, he reached up with his left hand and weakly grasped my outstretched right. A celebrated political faux pas tactlessly emerged from my one-liner history bank; when he'd met a judge with a crippled right hand, Richard Nixon had once exclaimed, A lefty, just like Bob Dole.

I'd steeled myself for his frailty, but hadn't expected to find him bedridden; I hope I was able to conceal my shock as I asked him how he was doing.

"You've slimmed down," he answered. That was a relief; at least he knows who I am, I thought to myself.

The conversation was strained because he could barely speak. I asked him what he thought about the midterm elections, but he couldn't answer for several seconds.

"Terrible," he finally said. I mentally kicked myself; it was a cruel mistake to have tried any substantive topics with him.

The day I arrived in Palm Springs, Ford had become the longest-living former president, surpassing Ronald Reagan. His office had released a touching statement:

"The length of one's days matters less than the love of one's family and friends. I thank God for the gift of every sunrise and, even more, for all the years He has blessed me with Betty and the children, with our extended family and the friends of a lifetime."

Seeing him forty-eight hours later, I knew he couldn't have written those words, much less spoken them, although I learned much later that he'd read them beforehand and approved their release.

There was likewise no way he could have signed the piece of memorabilia I'd brought along, so I didn't even try. But I did pull it out of an envelope to show him, hoping he'd get a lift from the memory.

It was the program from a meeting of the Association of American Editorial Cartoonists at Boston's famous Parker House Hotel on May 25, 1974. He was the featured speaker, and one of the cartoonists had drawn a caricature of Ford in his Michigan football uniform. He was resolute, hands on hips, girding for gridiron combat. Instead of his old number 48, the jersey carried number 76, a premature metaphor for the bruising primary battle he would later wage with Reagan.

Ford took the oversized orange program in both hands and studied it intently for a few seconds.

"I used to play football," was all he said.

Suddenly, Betty Ford walked in unannounced to say hello. She was almost as frail as he was, far more so than at our lunch in May; the strain of keeping him alive had plainly taken an enormous toll on her already-fragile constitution.

Betty and Jerry never spoke in that interlude, but the moment he saw her, his eyes lit up. If only for an instant, he was back at the

Michigan beaches with Betty Bloomer, gorgeous in his swim trunks and crazy in love.

Four minutes after I'd been ushered in, it was time to go.

Neither of us could handle much more.

I tried a lighter note: "Phil Jones asked me to tell you that you'd better behave yourself, and he's going to be watching to make sure you do."

Jones was one of that tiny Band of Brothers from *Air Force Two,* now retired from CBS News. He'd always been one of Ford's favorites, notwithstanding his habit of annoying the hell out of Ford with barbed questions he'd rather not answer. In April 1975, Ford had broken into a full gallop on a California tarmac to avoid answering a Jones query about Vietnam going down the drain.

A big grin spread across Ford's face. "Oh, that Phil." He smiled.

"You've lost some weight," he said again.

As I took his hand for the last time, Ford had one final request.

"Come back again," he said in a voice barely above a whisper.

Ever positive, to the very end.

"You bet I will, Mr. President. Please take care of yourself."

As we walked back to her office, Penny delivered a jolt of her own. The Beaver Creek home wasn't up for sale yet, but would be soon. She said she'd arrange for me to walk through. "But it's a shell," she warned. "It's been totally cleaned out."

That meant the Fords would never see their favorite retirement hideaway again. He was too sick, and she wasn't going without him.

Later, I learned his aides had tried to dissuade him from seeing me because they didn't want me to remember him that way. Maybe Reagan's friends had been right to stay away at the end, I thought, preferring to remember him in his heyday, when he was larger than life.

But I told Penny, with more of an edge than I intended, that I'd remember Jerry Ford many ways, and none would be the sickly, hanging-on remnant of happier days gone by I'd just seen. I'd remember the day we hit an air pocket descending into Palm Springs late one night and a reporter's gin-and-tonic arced from its glass, over a seat and right onto

Ford's head, triggering a nervous giggle. I'd remember that April day in 1974 when he grabbed my tie and politely ordered me to forget something he shouldn't have blurted out. I'd remember the evening in 1997 when he (with Betty on an extension line) called my wife before her cancer operation.

And I'd remember a sweltering August afternoon in the East Room when the grace and quiet resolve of "Big Red," as old friends called him because of his reddish-blond hair, steadied a fractured nation.

In distress I called Melanie, described what I'd just observed, and told her if she ever saw anything like that with me she had my permission to pull the plug immediately.

As I drove back to my hotel, out of nowhere the haunting lyrics of the country-western classic I once heard Buddy Holly perform popped into my head.

"The sun is out, the sky is blue, there's not a cloud to spoil the view, but it's raining, raining in my heart."

From the moment I'd seen him, I knew the next time I visited Sand Dune Road, he'd be gone.

FOUR DAYS AFTER our painful farewell, Ford watched his beloved Michigan Wolverines blow an undefeated football season by losing to Ohio State. He was a certified Big Blue fanatic, dutifully watching all their games on DirecTV and occasionally shooing away aides demonstrating the poor judgment of interrupting him.

His gridiron days were so central to his persona that he'd inserted the Michigan band into his funeral plan. When he arrived in Grand Rapids for the final time, the band would serenade him with the stirring strains of "The Victors," the storied Wolverine fight song.

In his ninety-fourth year, that moment was near at hand.

In early December, Dick Cheney telephoned with the welcome news that Congress had approved legislation naming the CVN-78, the Navy's next nuclear aircraft carrier, the USS *Gerald R. Ford.*

"He was a happy guy," Cheney told a longtime acquaintance.

But just as I'd experienced in November, Ford was having trouble speaking more than a few words at a time. When Cheney called, Steve

Ford, his youngest son, was on an extension line to help deal with the extended gaps in the conversation between the former president and his star pupil.

Mel Laird, one of his closest political friends and a former congressman and secretary of defense, called him to say goodbye, but Ford literally couldn't talk.

Inevitably, death-watch rumors surfaced. Desert TV stations reported his condition had deteriorated dramatically.

The family suspected that the Fords' minister, the Reverend Robert Certain of St. Margaret's Episcopal, was the source. Certain had been asked in writing to stop talking about family matters, but kept talking.

Reluctantly, just before the Christmas holidays, I joined the throng of reporters struggling to find a polite way of asking if it was time to begin sprucing up their obit packages.

"It's not good; you saw him," Penny Circle told me in late December, the strain creeping into her voice. "But nothing has changed since you were here. I'm going to L.A. for Christmas, and you should go home to Texas."

An old Ford friend was blunter: "He's going to die soon, but only God knows when."

The Ford family Christmas card presented another sobering omen. Like millions of Americans, the Fords used their annual holiday greeting as a photographic tableau of the ever-expanding clan. Usually the Fords were photographed in ski gear surrounded by their children and grandchildren. In 1994, they opted for a photo of halftime festivities at his alma mater when the University of Michigan retired his football number 48.

For the first time in decades, there was no photo with the 2006 card. It was just a plain-vanilla note with a timeless wish: "May this 2006 Christmas bring more wisdom to the way we look at the world and more love to the way we live in it!"

His signature at the bottom was another giveaway: the red "Jerry Ford" was bright and bold, far different from his actual signature in the last months.

By the time the card arrived in my mailbox on December 23, he was in extremis. One by one, his vital organs began to fail. "Everything was shutting down," one of his closest friends would later recall. The congestive heart failure had so weakened his immune system that the guy who had run reporters half his age into the ground in the *Air Force Two* days couldn't fight off yet another infection.

On December 26, at 6:45 P.M., Leslie Lynch King Jr., known more familiarly as Gerald Rudolph Ford Jr., died in his sleep. There are some who were very close to him who will always believe that in one monumental final act of kindness to his family, he somehow willed himself not to die on Christmas.

Betty and their three sons were at his side; Susan had been there for days, but had just returned to Albuquerque to be with her family.

He passed away in the study of his home, in the same hospital bed where we'd said our farewells on November 14. The cause of death was recorded as arteriosclerotic cerebrovascular disease.

Belatedly, his funeral educated a new generation of Americans, millions of them unborn when he'd left office, to his three decades of government service.

"Finally there's some understanding of all the good things that guy did," said Brent Scowcroft, his national security adviser, shortly after the services.

There was a therapeutic aspect to his send-off as well. In the middle of a wrenching and polarizing war, the national psyche sorely needed an uplifting occasion. In death, Ford once again had helped his country, if only for a moment.

"The country needed something to pull it together again," Steve Ford told me at the Pentagon naming ceremony for his father's aircraft carrier eleven days after the funeral.

For all the eulogies, the valedictory of the Ford years may have been pronounced by Henry Kissinger at the 1981 dedication of the

Ford Library on the Ann Arbor campus of the University of Michigan: "The consolation you have, Mr. President, is that most of the constructive things that have happened since have been based on policies you originated."

Like John F. Kennedy, he wasn't president long enough to create an indelible record of accomplishment. He lacked Ronald Reagan's flair and communications skills, and Bill Clinton's political dexterity.

He assembled a strong cabinet and senior White House staff, but was too tolerant of their infighting and, like most presidents, had trouble cleaning out deadwood. "There are times when I really wish he could kick some ass," one of his closest White House aides admitted to me one day in exasperation.

Yet his 896 days as president were momentous, especially for the normalcy he restored to the office and the process of governance.

"People look on him as having managed an interim presidency," a former senior aide said a decade after the 1976 election, "but he's still basically well liked and respected."

In part that was because of who replaced him. Jimmy Carter presided over a presidency perceived as a failure by many Americans. Inevitably, Ford's reputation was enhanced, just as the elder George Bush has benefited retroactively from the unpopularity of his son and his policies.

He was an ordinary guy in the noblest sense of the term, a steady, solid Michigander whose old-fashioned virtues were the perfect antidote for a nation desperate for stability and civility.

Utterly uncomplicated, lacking in artifice or pretense, he toasted his own English muffins and scooped his golden retriever's poop from the South Lawn. He didn't like opera or ballet and didn't care who knew it. He never developed a taste for fancy food, preferring steak and butter pecan ice cream to any other menu combination. He always counted becoming the first Eagle Scout president one of his proudest moments.

At his first press conference he was asked if he planned to issue ethical guidelines to avoid another Watergate. He crisply replied, "The code of ethics will be the example I set." Coming from Ford, an icon of personal probity, that required no follow-up.

Ford may have well have presided over the last genuinely civilized presidency. After him, the process became dog-eat-dog; there always had to be a loser. He wasn't like that, and would have hated the corrosiveness and hyperpartisanship of today's Washington environment.

In that vein, there was something else he did that I never appreciated at the time but certainly salute today. Unlike most of today's political practitioners, he had an old-fashioned sense of public accountability. On every trip he took as vice president—thirty-five weeks, forty-one states—he scheduled at least one press conference, where he was routinely hammered about his support for Nixon, Watergate, the tapes, impeachment, and the like.

Even though it complicated the political tightrope he was trying to negotiate, Ford never stopped meeting the press, and he did it with good cheer and civility. He thought it was part of his responsibility as an elected leader. His stand-up performance at a very difficult historical juncture is a lesson worth remembering, especially in today's control-freak political environment.

"Amidst the worst constitutional crisis since World War II, thank God for Jerry Ford," Dick Cheney told me in 2002. "He was there when the country needed him. He served superbly under extraordinary circumstances."

A year later, at a ninetieth birthday celebration at the White House, President Bush lauded the 38th president as "a fine gentleman and a faithful public servant" who had brought America safely through one of her darkest periods.

"Many presidents have stayed longer," Bush noted, "but few have left the White House with greater respect from the American people, and none ever did more to restore the dignity and credibility of the office of president than Jerry Ford."

Heading into the twilight, Ford was serene about his place in history. Not many others may have noticed, but he always took great satisfaction in the fact that it was he, not the disgraced Richard Nixon who desperately wanted the honor for himself, who presided over the nation's Bicentennial observances.

(In typically peripatetic Ford fashion, he scheduled so many events in four days of celebration that they spilled over past the Fourth of July, ending with a swearing-in of new citizens at Thomas Jefferson's Monticello home on July 5, 1976.)

"He'll go down in history as a good man and a good president," an old friend once said, "and that suits him just fine."

All of us in this crazy business of journalism retain instances that stick in our brains, moments that really weren't newsworthy or happened past deadline, so they never made it into print or onto the air, but are memorable nevertheless because they offer an unexpected window into the character and humanity of a public life.

For me, one of those iconic insights occurred just four days after Gerald Ford became president, as he was fiddling with the speech he would give to a joint session of Congress in less than two hours.

Suddenly, Ford looked up from his text and a postprandial martini.

"Howard, have you had dinner?" he asked Commander Howard Kerr, the naval aide who had delivered the final speech draft to Ford's modest home in the Virginia suburbs.

When Kerr said he hadn't eaten, the new president led the officer into the kitchen and plucked the remains of the new First Lady's tuna noodle casserole from the oven. Ford spooned out the entrée onto a plate and put it on the kitchen table. "Have some dinner," he told Kerr. "I'm going to go work on the speech."

A similar human moment happened at 5:53 P.M. on the afternoon of February 28, 1976. President Ford was barnstorming Florida during that bitter primary contest against Ronald Reagan. Toward the end of a typical marathon Ford day—16 events, 13 cities—he got caught in a sudden downpour at the Royal Park Shopping Center in Boca Raton. In no time, he was drenched. When he started to speak, his hair was slicked back, his suit totally wrinkled. The leader of the free world was an absolute mess. And he knew it.

"We've had a little rain, and I should apologize for my appearance," he began his remarks. "But there's an old saying: 'Aristocracy is of the soul, not of the cloth.' So I don't look very good, but I think I'm a darned good president."

I suspect history may well decide someday that Ford's legacy can be summarized by the title of his memoirs, *A Time to Heal.* But I'm not an oracle, or a pundit, I'm just a reporter. So the historians can sort out the darned-good-president part of it.

As for the rest, to borrow one of his favorite phrases from the *Air Force Two* days, I can say, without any hesitation, reservation, or equivocation, he was a darned good person.

As Billy Joel sings, these are the times to remember, for they will not last forever.

I was reminded of that bittersweet truth on a return visit to Sand Dune Road in May of 2007. The process of shutting down Ford's office had begun, but his study remained eerily intact. A lifetime of memorabilia still dotted the paneled walls. A photograph of his public policy school at Ann Arbor was in the middle of his desk, as if he'd just picked it up and proudly shown it off to a visitor. The chair where I'd sat for our interviews, to the left of his blue leather highback executive chair with the presidential seal, occupied its customary place. Reflexively, I sat there again.

Precisely the same as always—almost.

Afterward, I drove over to the old International House Hotel, the site of our epic Easter 1974 interview. After several incarnations, it was being converted to an upscale Holiday Inn. A chain-link fence kept the curious away from the construction. The barrier couldn't keep me from luxuriating in those sunny slopes of long ago, as an old Texas Ranger captain liked to describe them.

En route to my hotel, I passed a large billboard that jerked me back to reality:

GERALD "OUR" FORD, 1913–2006

It had been a long, fateful, exhilarating journey. Those of us fortunate enough to have been along for part of the ride cherish the experience, and savor our memories.

For that, and for many other personal kindnesses, large and small, the traditional salutation ending presidential press conferences seems only fitting:

Thank you, Mr. President.

## ACKNOWLEDGMENTS

THIS UNDERTAKING has been marinating for more than three decades, but I wasn't certain there was enough material for a book until my off-the-record interviews with Gerald Ford had progressed for several years. Not until our January 1999 conversation, where he talked provocatively about President Bill Clinton, was I finally sure.

Over the years, many colleagues and friends have encouraged me to write this book. Chief among them are the peerless Peter Goldman, my longtime *Newsweek* colleague, linchpin of the magazine's quadrennial special election issues and the most graceful political writer on the planet; David Beckwith, a former competitor who has, alas, abandoned journalism for politics; Owen Ullmann, *USA Today*'s deputy managing editor for news; Patrick Butler, a vice president of the *Washington Post* and onetime Ford speechwriter; and *Weekly Standard* executive editor Fred Barnes, who flew on some of those momentous *Air Force Two* flights in 1974.

No project of this magnitude can succeed without the forbearance of employers. I've benefited by the strong endorsement of Mort Zuckerman, the *Daily News*'s chairman and publisher. Editor-in-chief Martin Dunn's enthusiasm and understanding were particularly welcome, and much appreciated. I'm also grateful to chief executive officer Marc Kramer and editorial administration wizard Ed Fay for cheerfully arranging a brief leave of absence for me so I could finish the writing.

The paper's Washington bureau proved yet again that a boss is only as good as his troops. Ken Bazinet, Regan Conley, Mike McAuliff, James Meek, and Rich Sisk seamlessly took up the slack of my divided attentions without complaint and with their usual professionalism.

I'd be remiss without noting the educators who helped along the way: Ernestine Farr, my high school journalism teacher; the late David Bowers, my journalism adviser at Texas A&M University; and the incomparable Mel Elfin, bureau chief and mentor for most of my twenty-five years at *Newsweek*. In writing this book I tried to remain ever-faithful to Mel's persistent reporting mantra: "choicest color, quotes and anecdotes."

For seventeen years, my wife, Melanie, has fumed while devotedly salvaging fifteen thousand pages of my *Newsweek* files, written between 1968 and 1993, from periodic basement floodings. Finally, there's an answer: I couldn't have done this book without them. They were a Niagara of critical information, including many long-forgotten events and interviews with Ford and his inner circle.

Most of the book's content is the product of proprietary interviews with Ford and other original reporting; however, some material was first published in *Newsweek* between 1974 and 1985. In these cases I've endeavored to credit the magazine fully; any omission is unintentional. An abbreviated version of Chapter 14, which recounts my last interview with Ford, appeared in the *Daily News* two days after his death.

Three comrades-in-arms from the *Air Force Two* era were essential in reconstructing those heady and historic months. My dear friend Phil Jones of CBS News, who has been after me to write this book since the days when he drove Ford nuts with his always fair but to-the-bone questions, searched his memory and his own voluminous files to help fill critical knowledge gaps, especially in Chapters 2 and 3. Howard Kerr, Vice President Ford's naval aide and an eyewitness to much history, did the same—as did Ron Nessen, who covered Ford for NBC News and became his White House press secretary.

More accomplished authors were generous with their wise advice, notably Ford biographer James Cannon; presidential scholar and Ford intimate Richard Norton Smith; and former Bush 41 speechwriter Curt Smith, an authority on baseball's golden throats. I'm also indebted to historian Douglas Brinkley for steering me to a remarkable collection of letters to Ford from presidents and other prominent individuals.

One of the more enjoyable footnotes to this book was tracking the afterlife of Slingshot Airlines, Ford's pocket-size *Air Force Two* that figures prominently in Chapter 2. Captain Herb McConnell of the U.S. Air Force lent invaluable help with my search, as did Mark Bunner of the IFL Group in Waterford, Michigan, and Wendy Draper of Kelowna Flightcraft in Kelowna, British Columbia. They helped document the plane's commercial incarnations after leaving government service. Don Holloway, curator of the Ford Museum in Grand Rapids, tracked down in record time a plaque that provided the plane's tail number, aiding the detective work considerably.

Vice President Cheney, whom I've covered since we both had hair in the Ford administration, was generous with his time and his recollections of the Ford years and beyond. I suspect he'll be less than thrilled with some of Ford's musings in Chapter 12, but make no mistake: to his final breath, Jerry Ford loved Dick Cheney.

Ken Hafeli and Stacy Davis of the Ford Library at Ann Arbor provided invaluable research assistance, backstopping my feeble archives with a trove of documents and photographs. Joe Barnes of Rice University, a colleague from the Baker book, also provided yeoman assistance in helping me plumb 142 boxes of files at the James A. Baker Institute, in Houston.

ACKNOWLEDGMENTS

Within the extended Ford family, his two retirement chiefs of staff, Bob Barrett and Penny Circle, have been saving me from myself since 1974. Bob stepped down after six years but has remained close to both Fords; Penny has been with them for more than a quarter-century. Their loyalty to and affection for the Fords, and their friendship to me, are irreplaceable. The same goes for Marty Allen, chairman emeritus of the Gerald R. Ford Foundation. Judi Risk of the Ford staff has also gone out of her way to be helpful over the years.

I was fortunate in previously having worked with the experts at G. P. Putnam's Sons on former secretary of state Jim Baker's diplomatic memoirs. That prior relationship diminished the need for much translation between author and publisher. To describe publisher and editor-in-chief Neil Nyren and publicity director Marilyn Ducksworth as consummate professionals grossly understates their talents. The same is true for president Ivan Held, whose instant enthusiasm for this project was infectious. Agent Gail Ross navigated the complex and mysterious landscape of publishing for me.

As I interviewed Ford in his retirement years, the love of his life was never far away. In my mind's eye I fondly recall Betty Ford unexpectedly popping in on us to tease, ask for news from Washington, and keep her husband squared away. Watching their still-madly-in-love byplay was a privilege, and an inspiration. She's one gallant lady.

Melanie Cooper was a political researcher at *Newsweek* long before our marriage. She has continued to improve my copy ever since, and is a wellspring of encouragement. The same is true for our son, Andrew, whose excitement over the book touched me like nothing else. As any writer will attest, more than anyone they've borne the brunt of this project, graciously tolerating my essential disappearance for several months. They'd already been enduring my absence at anniversaries and birthdays for years, and deserve better.

# INDEX